New Wine & New Wineskins

Deacons Today

ANTHONY GOOLEY

COVENTRY
PRESS

Published in Australia by
Coventry Press
33 Scoresby Road
Bayswater Vic. 3153
Australia

ISBN 9780648566151

Copyright © Anthony Gooley 2019

All rights reserved. Other than for the purposes and subject to the conditions prescribed under the *Copyright Act*, no part of this publication may be reproduced, stored in a retrieval system, or transmitted in any form or by any means, electronic, mechanical, photocopying, recording or otherwise, without the prior permission of the publisher.

Scripture quotations re from *The New Jerusalem Bible*, copyright© 1985 by Darton, Longman & Todd, Ltd. and Doubleday, a division of Random House, Inc. Reprinted by Permission.

Cataloguing-in-Publication entry is available from the National Library of Australia http:/catalogue.nla.gov.au/.

Cover Design by Ian James - www.jgd.com.au
Text design by Megan Low, Film Shot Graphics - www.fsg.com.au

Printed in Australia

Contents

Table of Abbreviations 6

Introduction 9

1. New Wine: The Intentions of the Council 33
2. Foundations on Sand: The Dominant Paradigm 73
3. Foundations on Rock: A New Paradigm 123
4. Heralds of the Gospel: New Mission and New Evangelisation 169
5. Setting the course: Coordinates for Formation 209
6. Our Sister Phoebe: Women Deacons 251
7. New Wineskins: Reception of the Council 301

Dedication

For John Neil Collins

A great Australian Biblical scholar.
With gratitude for your scholarship and friendship.
If there were a Nobel Prize for Biblical research
it would be yours.

TABLE OF ABBREVIATIONS

AC	Apostolic Constitutions
Acts	Acts of the Apostles
BDAG	Bauer–Danker–Arndt–Gingrich (BDAG); A Greek–English Lexicon of the New Testament and Other Early Christian Literature
CA	Catholic Action
CC	Congregation for Clergy
CCC	Catechism of the Catholic Church
CDF	Congregation for the Doctrine of the Faith
CDWS	Congregation for Divine Worship and the Discipline of the Sacraments
CIC	Codex Iuris Canonici (Code of Can Law for the Latin Church)
CST	Catholic Social Teaching
EG	Evangelii Gaudium
FT	First Testament (Old Testament)
GIRM	General Instruction on the Roman Missal
GNB	Good News Bible
GS	Gaudium et spes
ITC	International Theological Commission
JB	Jerusalem Bible
LG	Lumen gentium
LXX	The Septuagint of Greek version of the FT
NAB	New American Bible
NMI	Novo Millennio Ineunte

Table of Abbreviations

NRSV	New Revised Standard Version
PCILT	Pontifical Council for the Interpretation of Legislative Texts
RCIA	Rite of Christian Initiation of Adults
RSV	Revised Standard Version
SC	Sacrosanctum concilium
SDO	Sacrum Diaconatus Ordinem
ST	Second Testament (New Testament)
UISG	International Union of Superiors General (women)

Introduction

And no one puts new wine into old wineskins; if he does, the wine will burst the skins, and the wine is lost, and so are the skins; but new wine is for fresh skins

Mark 2:22

It is the contention of this book that the permanent ministry of deacon as envisaged by the Second Vatican Council is a new wine. I believe that we are trying to pour this new wine into old wineskins. The whole possibility, the hope and gift of the Holy Spirit, which is the permanent ministry of deacon, is being lost because the skins have burst. If we want to see this ministry flourish for the good of the Church and the proclamation of the Gospel as the Council intended, we need to pour this wine into new wineskins. I want to outline for you why I believe this is so and also to suggest some ways in which we might pour the new wine into the new wineskins.

I should comment on my intended audience for this book, so that you know what to expect from it. I have in mind four primary audiences: lay and ordained pastoral ministers, deacons in the Catholic Church, those who are responsible for the initial and ongoing formation of deacons and the bishop with whom deacons are meant to be close collaborators. I am hoping that the general reader with an interest in the ministry of the Church and theology will also pick up this book.

I am a theologian but I am not primarily writing for theologians and this means that I will attempt to explain most technical theological terms and assume no prior knowledge of theology in general or the theology of ministry. My tone will be less aimed at my fellow academics and directed more toward the kind of language that a Christian with some basic theological and Biblical knowledge will comprehend. Perhaps this means I will lack some of the precision the academy may demand but I think journal articles are where we speak to each other in our special language. That is the place for very deep and very precise discourse. Having said this, I do not want you to have the impression that I plan to be imprecise or non-scholarly in my approach; it is more about the language register that I will use.

Like the reader, I have a context and context can and does influence the way we think and write. I am a Roman Catholic deacon from a diocese in Australia. I am a theologian who has worked in a variety of academic contexts from major universities to small graduate theological institutes. I have been in pastoral ministry in a diocese as an advocate for inclusion of people with disabilities and I have been involved in adult faith formation in non-academic settings for decades and I have some limited parish ministry. I am married, with children, mortgage, loans and bills and, until very recently, a dog owner as well. I am a white Australian, coming from a predominantly Irish Catholic background, growing up in

Introduction

a working-class family in a regional town and graduating to the middle class as a result of an opportunity to have free university education that otherwise I would not likely to have had. (A tradition we no longer have in my country, where all students now pay a co-payment for university education and the federal government pays the rest.)

Like most Australians of my generation (born 1961), I grew up with little awareness of the indigenous people on whose land I lived. As a child, I had even camped in a national park named after them, the Bundjalung People of Northern NSW. I would have been in my early twenties before I even knew this fact. Nor was I very aware of a continuing history of exclusion and displacement of the indigenous people of my country and processes that remained active government policy up until the late 1970s and, in some States, the 1980s. I mention this because I think we need to break what one of our historians calls "the Great Australian Silence".[1] I am a post Vatican II Catholic in the sense that I have no direct experience of any other way of being Catholic except what I know from after the Council which was held in four sessions during 1962-1965.

Perhaps one of the most significant things about me and the book you are about to read is that I encountered the work of John N. Collins and his major work; *Diakonia: Reinterpreting the Ancient Sources*, as well as other journal articles and books written by him. I and many other scholars from various parts of the world, writing in a variety of languages and

---

1 In 1968, W.E.H. Stanner delivered a lecture, The Great Australian Silence in which he argued there was a 'cult of forgetfulness practised on a national scale' concerning many areas of Indigenous and non-Indigenous history in Australia, such as invasion and massacres.

contexts, owe John enormous gratitude for his groundbreaking research. His work has shattered the old paradigm of diaconate and ministry. His work set me and these other scholars on this journey to develop a solid foundation for a theology of diaconate.

Like me, John is an Australian. He is a Biblical scholar. John N. Collins began his doctoral work in the 1970s and had no interest in deacons or any knowledge of this permanent ministry newly restored to the Church. For his doctoral thesis, he was making a study of one tiny but significant sentence in the Second Testament (ST).[2] John examined Mark 10:45. In that sentence are some words from the Greek *diacon*

---

2   By Second Testament, I mean to refer to what is commonly called the New Testament. In recent years a number of Biblical scholars and some theologians have suggested that the terms Old and New Testaments are problematic because old and new can suggest the new has superseded the old or is better. Some scholars opt for the terms Hebrew Scriptures and Christian Scriptures. I find such terms problematic. Hebrew Scriptures does not satisfy me because there are two basic versions of the First Testament, one is found in Hebrew and the other in Greek. The Greek version is called the Septuagint, commonly abbreviated as LXX. Catholic and Orthodox Churches follow the Septuagint list of books and Protestants follow the Hebrew version, which is why Catholics and Orthodox have more books in their Bible than Protestants. When we read the Second Testament, the majority of all reference to the First Testament are from the LXX and not the Hebrew version. This makes sense, as the Gospel spread among Greek speaking Jews and Gentiles and this was the version they used in their synagogues. I find the term 'Christian Scriptures' completely at odds with the Christian tradition. One of our first heresies, promoted by the presbyter Marcion, was that the First Testament was not in fact Christian Scripture. Orthodox Christian faith (I don't mean the Orthodox Churches) has always asserted that the books of both testaments are Christian scriptures. So, I am sticking with FT and ST.

Introduction

word group.[3] The ST was written in a language called *koine* or common Greek. The *diacon* words are translated in Mark 10:45 as serve and served. These *diacon* words provide our basic words for ministry and one of them, *diaconos* (deacon) has come into our language as a loan word from Greek. His primary interest was Christology.

John asked a very simple and important fundamental question; what did these *diacon* words mean to the people who wrote them? How did people contemporary with Mark use these words and comprehend them? Another way to ask the same question is: what is the semantic profile of the *diacon* group of words? No one before John had asked these fundamental questions about their meaning. That did not prevent people from writing about their semantic profile in the Greek lexicons of the ST. We shall see that the development of the semantic profile without the scholarly research on the fundamental question of usage in the ancient word proved to be fatal for the development of at least three fields in theology during the twentieth century. The three fields of; ecclesiology, theology of ministry and a theology of diaconate are directly influenced by this fatal flaw. To some extent Christology too suffers in its own way. In this book, we will focus mostly on the diaconate. So, let us briefly

---

3   A brief word about spelling of Greek words in English. Sometimes there is not an equivalent letter or sometimes two letters in English can do the same job as a Greek letter. Therefore, sometimes alternate English spellings of Greek words exist. In a number of sources, you will encounter *diacon* and others *diakon*, where translators choose either c or k for the Greek letter kappa (κ), which looks like an English k.

survey the restoration of the ministry of deacon in the Latin Catholic Church.[4]

A partial restoration begins

On the Feast of St Ephraim of Syria, a deacon and Doctor of the Church, 18 June 1967, Paul VI issued *Sacrum Diaconatus Ordinem: General Norms for the Restoration of the Permanent Diaconate in the Latin Church* (SDO hereafter).[5] In doing so, he provided the canonical means to restore a ministry that had been largely absent – although not entirely – from the Latin Catholic Church since around the tenth century. The Second Vatican Council had called for the restoration of the ministry in continuity with the decision made at the Council of Trent more than four and a half centuries before. SDO was

---

4 Terminology is always a difficult issue in referring to the Catholic Church. In ecumenical dialogue, the Roman Catholic Church indicates all 22 autonomous churches that comprise the Catholic Church. Most people are familiar with the numerically biggest Catholic Church which is the Latin Church, also called the Roman Church. This church follows the liturgical, spiritual and legal tradition of the Church of Rome, where the Bishop of Rome resides and who is known also as the pope. There are many other Churches within the communion of Churches that is the Catholic Church. There is the Ukrainian Greek Catholic Church, the Maronite Church, the Melkite Church, Chaldean Church and many others. These have their own liturgical rites, spiritual traditions and legal code as well as their own head or patriarch. These Churches are called Catholic because they are in full communion with the Bishop of Rome. For all but the Maronite Catholics, they have an Orthodox counterpart that shares the same traditions but is not in full communion with the Bishop of Rome. To make matters even more confusing, a Catholic Church is found in an autonomous diocese or local Church and the universal Church exists in and from such local Churches, as a communion of communions.

5 *Sacrum Diaconatus Ordinem*. http://w2.vatican.va/content/paul-vi/en/motu_proprio/documents/hf_p-vi_motu-proprio_19670618_sacrum-diaconatus.html

not destined to bring about a full restoration of this ministry because Paul VI only provided a means by which national or regional episcopal conferences could petition Rome to allow them to restore the threefold Order within their territories. Even then, no diocesan bishop (or equivalent in canon law) was required to restore the three-fold Order in his jurisdiction. As a consequence, many episcopal conferences have never made the request and many dioceses (local Churches) have not restored the full three-fold Order. Perhaps Paul VI should have more accurately styled his *motu proprio*; general norms for the partial and somewhat idiosyncratic restoration of the permanent diaconate in the Latin Church.

John XXIII made an extremely important decision for the preparation of the Second Vatican Council (1962-65) about how the topics for the Council were to be determined.[6] Initially, the Preparatory Committee for the Second Vatican Ecumenical Council had planned to draw up a survey and ask bishops, heads of clerical religious institutes and pontifical university theology faculties to respond. One of the obvious limitations with surveys is that questions may be drawn up in such a way that those who prepare it have their concerns addressed and do not learn what is truly on the minds of respondents. Surveys can be a little like laying train tracks that guide the discussion in a predetermined course. Instead John XXIII decided to write to this same intended audience with a simple question: what should the Council consider in its deliberations? In this way, the concerns, issues and

---

6   Alberigo, G.; Komonchak, J. (1996) *History of Vatican II: Volume One-Announcing and preparing for the Vatican Council II: Toward a New Era in Catholicism*. Orbis Books: New York. p. 109

projects of the world episcopate and sometimes the local churches could be expressed freely.

It was the task of the Preparatory Commission to sort through all of the responses that were received and to tabulate the results in some meaningful way. In some cases, a single bishop would write back with his ideas without any consultation with the local church, some bishops consulted with their clergy and some even organised meetings for clergy to help prepare a response. More significantly, in my view, was the small number who consulted with the local church, including clergy and laity.[7] The fact that some bishops spoke with their local church indicates they already had some concept that they were indeed head of and part of the local church and not merely administrators of a canonical jurisdiction. To put this theologically, they had a sense of the ecclesiology of communion (*communio* in Latin and *koinonia* in Greek) and their place as vicars of Christ as the head of the body which is the local Church. This ecclesiology will feature prominently in the Council and post conciliar developments and is extremely significant for understanding the theology of Holy Orders that emerges from the Council.

Once all of the results had been tabulated from the responses three items stood out far and above the rest of all topics suggested for the Council.[8] The first topic was a theology of the episcopate. This topic was on the agenda for Vatican I

---

7   Alberigo, (1996) *History of Vatican II*; Chapter II provides an overview of the preparatory phase.
8   Alberigo (1996); 108 and Ditewig, W (2007) *The Emerging Diaconate: Servant Leaders in a Servant Church*. Paulist Press: Mahwah, N.J. pp. 94-119. He provides an excellent summary of developments at the Council on the deacon debate.

(1870) but that Council had to be abandoned because of the Franco-Prussian War and the actions of the Kingdom of Italy to take Rome from the Papal States. Significant questions existed about the episcopate. Was it a sacrament? What were its effects if it was a sacrament? Were bishops vicars of Christ in their own right or were they dependent on the pope? How was a bishop different from a priest? What is the nature of the relationship between the bishops collectively and the pope? There were other questions about episcopate that the Council would consider.

The second ranked item of significant interest for the episcopate was greater use of the vernacular languages in the liturgy. Many bishops, especially from the poor South, from Africa and Asia, spoke about the impediment of Latin in evangelisation and formation of the people through liturgy. Many bishops reminded us that use of the vernacular was the norm for the Church a long period of history; even the choice for Latin in the Mass at the time was because it was the vernacular or common language of the people when people had ceased speaking Greek. The Council of Trent did not mandate Latin in the liturgy but made a much more modest assertion. The Council only insisted that those who said that Mass celebrated in Latin was not valid were wrong.[9] After the Council of Trent some Catholic dioceses, especially in German speaking lands, did – for a time opt – for the vernacular as a way of countering Lutheran objections.[10] Both the issue concerning the theology of the episcopate and greater use

---

9   Gooley, A (2014) *Bite Size Vatican II: A very brief introduction to the Council and its four constitutions.* St Pauls Publications: Strathfield, NSW. pp. 131-143
10   Gooley, (2014) p. 132

of vernacular languages had been fermenting in church circles during most of the twentieth century and especially during the decades immediately preceding the Second Vatican Council.

The third highest priority seemed to be something quite new. The third most significant topic to emerge from the consultation was the restoration of the permanent ministry of deacon. In the period of World War II (1939-45) and following, there was a growing discussion about the possibility of restoring the permanent ministry of deacon in the Latin Catholic Church. Most of this discussion occurred in Germany and amongst presbyters (priests) incarcerated in the so-called Priest Block of the Dachau concentration camp which had been established by the Nazi regime. It is significant for our later discussion that the first discussion begins amongst German speakers because they would have been familiar with the German neologism *Diaconie*, which denotes Christian social service or loving concern for the poor. This word had come into popular use in the late nineteenth and early twentieth century. The neologism *Diaconie* had evolved from the revived "diaconate", or deacon house movement, among the German Evangelical Churches (Lutherans) in the nineteenth century. We will look at this deacon house movement later but for now we simply need to note that it was a Christian ministry started by Pastor Theodore Fliedner and his wife Friederike for the care of the poor in the newly industrialising cities of Germany. They called the women who worked in this ministry deaconesses and the men deacons.

Introduction

A number of books and articles were written by Catholic scholars and others interested in the restored ministry of diaconate during the 1940-1950s. Among these are included *The Case for Permanent Deacons* by Johannes Hofinger and *Diakonat, Stefe oder Amt (Diaconate Rank or Office)* by Otto Pies.[11] These books took up a largely functionalist understanding of ministry. That is ministry was largely the product of the necessity of social organisation of the Church; and ministers could be more or less defined by what functions they performed or roles they occupied within the social structure of the church. The authors focused on what deacons could do. They were also influenced by the German Lutheran experience of a "diaconate" which was primarily about care of the poor, the sick and those on the margins. During the twentieth century, *Diaconie* would expand into a major State funded social welfare enterprise employing a million or more people in Germany to provide this work.

Not all involved in *Diaconie* were members of the deacon houses but were ordinary men and women trained in a professional setting at Diakonic Institutes, which are found throughout Germany and the Nordic countries. These institutes are like colleges or universities that train women and men in the fields of social work and nursing and related disciplines. They are not unlike Catholic teachers' colleges that were once found in countries like Australia. These colleges were primarily founded to train Religious Sisters and Brothers and then admitted others to their programs.

---

11 Hofinger, J (1959) The Case for the Permanent Diaconate. *Catholic Mind.* 57; p116 and Pies, O (1960) Diakonat; Stufe oder Amt. *Theologie Glaube* 50; pp. 10-28

Deacons and deaconesses in the Lutheran system are a little like Roman Catholic Religious, so the analogy is quite a close one.

Discussion about the possibility of restoring the permanent ministry of deacons also occurred at the meeting of Catholic Action (CA) in Rome 1947. Catholics in the English-speaking world are less familiar, perhaps, with CA as it was not as strong a movement among them as it was amongst continental Europeans, especially in France, the Netherlands, Belgium, Italy and Germany. CA looked at ways and means of Catholics directly engaging in social and political questions of their day within the framework of Catholic Social Teaching (CST). The movement aimed to inject the perspective of the Gospel into these situations in recognition of a rapidly secularising Europe and marginalisation of Catholic and other Christian voices. CA attempted to provide a robust intellectual defence of this engagement as a counter to growing Marxist and also nihilist trends amongst intellectuals and on university campuses. Some within this movement saw the potential for a permanent ministry of deacon which would bring the presence of the Church's ministry and ministers within the sphere of ordinary life of families and culture.

There had been a worker priest movement in France and some other places in Europe where priests attempted to combine pastoral work with being a worker in secular employment alongside of and among the laity. This experiment was not viewed favourably by some bishops and by Rome and so the experiment came to an abrupt end. Others wanted to explore this possibility again in the form of diaconal ministry. Pius XII was so impressed with the

Introduction

suggestions about the possibilities of diaconal ministry at the 1947 CA conference that he even considered restoring the ministry by his own initiative but was dissuaded from this course of action.

Karl Rahner and other theologians had regular contact with the groups discussing the possibility of the diaconate referred to as 'deacon circles'.[12] There were some prominent German laymen among them such as Hannes Kramer who promoted this discussion. Some of these had approached their bishops about the possibility of ordination. Rahner attempted to develop a theological foundation with which he could promote the restoration of this ministry among bishops.

As a German theologian, Rahner was deeply influenced by *Diaconie* and the model of diaconate as it had developed in the deacon house movement among Lutherans. He was strongly aligned with the servant model of the Lutherans and the idea that Acts 6 is the foundation of the diaconate as a ministry with a primary character of humble service for the poor and marginalised. He was aware of other traditions within Catholicism but he draws mostly on the servant paradigm as it has developed within German consciousness.

Vatican II makes some steps

The Council took up the question of the diaconate. We will explore this in more detail in the next chapter. For now, we will just note a few things. We need to recall that restoration was the number three ranked issue for the world-wide episcopate. All other issues falling away into such small

---

12 Keating, J. (ed.) (2006) *The Deacon Reader*. Paulist Press: Mahwah, NJ. pp. 32-33.

numbers, there was a fairly even spread on these topics. In considering the restoration of the diaconate, the Council did not appeal to Acts 6. This is significant. The Council did consider why it was that the Council of Trent had considered a restoration. This too is significant. The Council describe the diaconate in fairly vague terms and not with the precision it could have given. We shall why these last two elements are significant for understanding the motivation of the Council. When the vote came for the restoration, there was overwhelming and early support, with little debate, the vote *for* was 1,903 and the vote *against* was 242.[13] The will was there and the Spirit was moving strongly among the bishops on this issue.

The only real sticking point in the debate was about who should be admitted to this ministry. It was the question about admitting both married and celibate men to this ministry that caused the greatest struggle. Some of the Latin bishops saw it as a weakening of the clerical discipline of choosing presbyters only from among celibate men in the West. Some argued that if deacons could be chosen from among both groups then some men who otherwise might enter the presbyterate would not; or that this move would eventually lead to accepting married and celibate men for the presbyterate, which is the Eastern Catholic practice. Some Eastern prelates like Maximos Saigh, Patriarch of the Melkite Catholic Church, urged his Latin brothers to do just that, and open both ministries to celibate and married men. In this way, both vocations would shine more brightly he argued. In the end the bishops voted 1,598 (629 opposed) to permit both

---

13   Ditewig (2007) *The Emerging Diaconate*, pp. 110-119

married and celibate men to the Order of Deacon. This is why it is incorrect to call the permanent diaconate the "married diaconate" as some do. There are both celibate and married deacons in the Latin Church. On this point, it is worth recalling that Eastern Canon law and Western canon law align. Married men may be ordained but ordained men may not marry. Celibate deacons like presbyters make a promise of celibacy to the Church and a widowed or divorced deacon or presbyter may not normally re-marry.

Post Conciliar developments

After the Council, the diaconate began to be restored in a number of dioceses in Germany and then the USA, almost as soon as *Sacrum Diaconatus Ordinem* was published. Almost half of the worlds Latin Catholic deacons are to be found in the USA. Large numbers of deacons exist is Europe with France, Germany and Italy having the largest numbers after the USA.[14] Initially, there were no guidelines for deacon formation. The duration, quality and scope of diaconal formation varied quite widely from diocese to diocese and from region to region. In some places the ministry of deacon

---

14 The Pontifical Yearbook 2017 and the "Annuarium Statisticum Ecclesiae" 2015, 06.04.2017 states in its summary that the population of permanent deacons shows a significant evolutionary trend: an increase in 2015 of 14.4% compared to five years previously, from 39,564 to 45,255 units. The number of deacons is improving on every continent at a significant pace. In Oceania, where they do not yet reach 1% of the total, they have increased by 13.8%, amounting to 395. The figure is also improving in areas where their presence is quantitatively significant. In America and Europe, where about 98% of the total population of deacons is found, they have increased in the relevant period by 16.2 and 10.5 per cent respectively.

was restricted almost entirely to liturgy. In other places, the deacon was restricted almost entirely to charitable services: establishment of soup kitchens, visiting prisoners and other corporal works of mercy.

Gradually, there emerged in Catholic circles a theology of diaconate following the lines established by the Lutheran Churches in Germany in the nineteenth century. This theology chose as a foundation Acts 6:1-7 and developed a theology of service, charity and humble care and concern for others based on a reading of this text that depended on textual additions to carry that argument. Soon, two other texts began to feature in discussions about deacons – John 13:1-19 and Philippians 2:5-11. The lure of jugs and towels as a deacon motif was too strong to resist when it was wedded to the servant mythology derived from a particular reading of Acts 6.

In one sense, the reception of the ministry of deacon after Vatican II had no clear rationale or pattern. It had no coherent theological framework, except the one borrowed more or less unreflectively from the Lutheran tradition. The theology of ministry in general was also moving in this direction with a long line of argument that Christians had specially sought out these *diacon* words for ministry because they appealed to the Christian sense of lowly and humble service in imitation of Jesus who was said to servant *par excellence*. The servant leader Christology and theology of ministry depended heavily upon a particular reading and grammatical structuring of Mark 10:45. The entire theology of ministry and even ecclesiology in the twentieth century is influenced by this tradition and all of it built on false foundations. No one, until

John N. Collins bothered to ask if Christians had actually co-opted these words as their words for ministry because they suggested humble or lowly service. No one had asked what the word group meant to them. All were relying on the same semantic profile asserted without any evidence or research as to the actual meaning of the words in this group. At least, until John N. Collins published his work in 1990.[15]

Explorations in this book

We are still at that point where the ministry of deacon, that gift of the Holy Spirit restored at Vatican II, has not been fully received into the life of the Church. In each of the chapters of this book, we will explore what diaconate is or could be and how we might go about fostering a reception of the Council. In chapter one of this book, we will look at what it was that motivated the Second Vatican Council to restore the permanent ministry of deacon and what the intentions of the Council were in doing this. This is the new wine of which I spoke above. It is essential to orient ourselves in this way if we are to evaluate the successful fulfilment of these motives and intentions. We will explore in more depth the antecedents of this restoration and see what theological currents set up a particular kind of diaconate that may be at odds with the Council and also at odds with deeper foundations in Tradition and Scripture.

We have a very helpful source to use for this exploration. During the 1990s, the International Theological Commission (ITC) devoted some time to consideration of intentions and

---

15   John N. Collins (1990) *Diakonia: Reinterpreting the Ancient Sources*. Oxford University Press: Oxford, UK.

motives of the Council regarding deacons and published the results in a document called; *From the Diakonia of Christ to the Diakonia of the Apostles*.[16] The title of the document immediately highlights that the *diacon* words, including *diaconos* or deacon, are not directly correlated with deacons as we understand the ministry today. They have a broader meaning that we will consider later. Jesus is a *diaconos* or at least exercises a *diakoneo* or ministry on behalf of someone (Mark 10:45) and Paul defends his claim to be considered and apostle based on his being a *diaconos* (1 Corinthians 3), so we need to make sure we hear these terms in the broad meaning before we immediately associate them with deacons.

Chapter two will explore a trio of the Scriptural texts on which many attempt to create a foundation for the ministry of deacon. Some of these are the most cherished texts for deacons when they think about their ministry: Acts 61-7, John 13:1-15 and Philippians 2:5-11. We will see that these texts, in fact, have nothing to say about the ministry of deacon and that if Acts 6 does have something to say about them, it is not what most purport it to say. The interpretation of these texts and their applications to deacons is preconditioned by what I call the servant myth. This myth operates as the dominant paradigm through which a theology of diaconate developed. It is also like a genetic mutation passed on from one generation to the next and replicating a defect. We will explore why these texts and their interpretation through the servant paradigm is like a house built on sand.

---

16 International Theological Commission (2003) *From diakonia of Christ to the Diakonia of the Apostles: Historico-Theological Research Document.* Catholic Truth Society: London, UK.

Chapter three looks at foundations that can be solid as a rock if we work from the semantic profile developed by John N. Collins. We will look at what his work reveals and how it shatters the dominant paradigm or servant myth, and also how his work contains possibilities for building on something stronger. We will also see how the ecclesiology of communion and the definition of episcopal ordination as a sacrament, combined with Collins' work provide a new way to move forward and build a strong theological foundation for Holy Orders and the Order of Deacon. Reforms to the *cursus honorum* introduced by Paul VI, whereby a man ascended grades to achieve the highest level of Holy Orders, which was priesthood, will be explored. We will look at why this reform has not been successful. A new model of Holy Orders emerges from Vatican II and will prove more fruitful for the life of the church when it is fully received.

Chapter four will explore the potential of the diaconate for new evangelisation and for creative responses to many new pastoral challenges today. We will see how Collins' work and the new lines of possibility in the theology of Holy Orders open up the ministry of deacons to a much wider scope – a scope that can also include care for the poor and those on the margins, if that is where the gifts of deacons take them. The point is that charitable work and social concern are not the defining characteristics of this ministry. We will revisit Acts 6 and see in it a paradigm for the new evangelisation and the creativity in the Holy Spirit for the Church to shape her ministries. We will need to touch on a few issues concerning canon law and also the *Directory for the Ministry and Life of Deacons* issued by the Congregation for Clergy.[17]

The *Directory* offers many possibilities for the ministry placement of deacons which avoid a narrow focus on social work or deacons as substitutes for presbyters where they are scarce. The full expression of the ministry of pastoral work, word and liturgy needs to be opened up and implemented in the life of every local church (diocese) and every parish community. Frequently, deacons are appointed to parishes to do the work an assistant presbyter might do or a transitional deacon, and sometimes his ministry is restricted to a narrow liturgical range because that is all that he is allowed to do. None of these approaches reflect the motives or intentions of the Council and they represent a view of deacon that is in many ways pre-Conciliar and an echo of the mono-presbyterate.

Discernment of diaconal vocations and some question relevant for the initial formation of deacons will be taken up in chapter five. The joint introduction to the *Norms for Formation and Directory for the Ministry and Life of Deacons* issued by the Congregations for Clergy and Education, introduce two very important considerations to the formation program. First, they note that the absence of the permanent ministry of deacon from the life of the Church for such a long time does not means that there are no points of reference for a theology of diaconate that can provide a foundation for formation. We will explore what some of these points of reference might be.

---

17   Congregation for Clergy (1998) *Directory for the Ministry and Life of Permanent Deacons*. St Pauls Publications: Strathfield. NSW.

Secondly, they link the need for a properly grounded theology to the orientation of formation and the ends which are to be attained in that formation. I will argue in this chapter that because we have the wrong theology – either a servant/charitable theology – or we still try to fit deacons into the transitional model, we cannot find the correct orientation in formation and therefore cannot arrive at the proper ends of formation. Some specific problems and questions regarding the formation of deacons are also addressed. What kind of theological formation is required? What pastoral formation? What spiritual and human? How will it be provided, especially when many of the candidates for formation are mature men with families and secular employment and may not be close to places of theological education and central places where they may gather for the other elements of formation? This chapter may be of particular interest to those responsible for the formation of deacons.

Pope Francis is not the first pope under whom some consideration of the possibility of ordaining women as deacons has occurred. During the pontificate of John Paul II, the ITC commenced a study of the question. In chapter six, we will look at the question of ordaining women as deacons. It is an important question and one that could not, I believe, have even been considered at the Second Vatican Council. They struggled enough with the question of celibacy for deacons. Consideration of women as deacons would have seemed something entirely foreign in the 1960s. Since that time, the women's movement has highlighted the missing voice of women in the Church and also opened up fresh interest in the sources concerning this question.

There are some very fruitful lines of enquiry available for us to consider this question and I suggest that the line on which Bishop Francis of Rome has set this exploration is not in fact a fruitful one. I am very happy to be proved wrong in my assessment but the comments the Pope has made about his commission in May of 2019 seem to indicate that I am correct in my assessment. I will argue that there are very good grounds for confidence that ordaining women as deacons has roots in the Tradition and should not only be considered but implemented. At the same time, I will argue that we need to be realistic and not imagine that ordaining women as deacons will be the beginning of some extraordinarily long transitional diaconate toward presbyteral ordination as happened in parts of the Anglican Communion. John Paul II, Benedict XVI and Francis have each reiterated the teaching that the Church has no authority to ordain women as presbyters and that such a teaching is to be regarded by all Catholics as definitive. We will have to touch on that topic as well. I know this last sentence may disappoint some women readers and others but we need to explore this together none the less.

In our final chapter, we will look at new wineskins in which to pour the new wine of the permanent ministry of deacon. Chapter seven will examine reception of the ministry of deacon as part of the reception of the Second Vatican Council. For this reception to take place we require that the ecclesiology and spirituality of communion take root in the Church. It is essential for understanding the relationship of the ordained to the laity and to understand who we are when we gather as Church. Communion and mission belong together as one. Without deep communion in Christ, mission simply degenerates into activity or loving concern that anyone can do. Any one at all – an atheist, a Jew or a Hindu – can show loving care and concern for another. What is it then that makes Christian loving concern different, if indeed it does? We need to cultivate the right perspective if we are to pour the new wine of diaconate into new wineskins. Some things we will have to let go and others we will have to take up. I believe the challenge is worth taking up for the good of the Church and the world.

We will cover some territory together in this book. I hope that you will read and ponder and engage in your own deep reflections. I hope it is the kind of book that you can come back to at different times and learn new things from it. I hope that you enjoy the journey with me and seek wisdom along the way. If there is some feeling of disorientation as you read, listen to that and ponder on it. What feelings are evoked? What thoughts begin to form? How does it touch your heart? Are you consoled by what you read or are you disturbed and discomforted? I am hoping that this book starts an internal conversation for you and then I hope you externalise it and share some of what is in your heart and mind with others.

At the end, I hope you will have some sense, like me, that we have a task ahead of us. That task is to make sure that we pour the new wine of the ministry of deacons into new wineskins so that the skins will not burst and the good wine can be shared with all for the good of all. We want the diaconate to thrive because it is a gift the Holy Spirit, restored to the Church through the voice of the Second Vatican Council.

New Wine: The Intentions of the Council

Some historical evolutions

Since ancient times, there has never been a Catholic Church without deacons. The ministry of an office holder called a deacon – one who had an active role in the ministerial structure of the Church – is evident from the second century of the Christian era. Before that time, we have hints of the presence of a person called a deacon with a ministry role in the early Church. Before that, we have people referred to by the title deacon and others referred to as deacons in the Second (New) Testament. Catholics have maintained the ministry of deacon right up until the present day. Since the twelfth century, the majority of deacons, though not all, have been men on their way (transitional) to be ordained as *presbyter*s who are also called priests.[1] The Second Vatican

---

1 I will normally refer to what Catholics commonly call priests or pastors (in some countries) as *presbyters*. This is the word Vatican II recovered for that ministry. In *koine* Greek it means elder. *Presbyter* was used for many centuries before the various priest words were attached

Council (1962-65) was not adding a new ministry to the Church in its decision to establish the permanent ministry of deacon but was restoring its permanent form alongside of the transitional one that already existed.

There have been times when the Catholic Church did not have ministers called *presbyters* even while there were some who were referred to as *presbyters*. Even into the third century, Catholic churches had men called *presbyters* who were not ministers as such.[2] The *koine* Greek word *presbyter* means elder. Synagogues had a council of elders and it seemed that this practice survived for some centuries into the Christian era among some Christian communities. The *presbyters* functioned as a council of elders to advise the leadership of the synagogue and later in some Churches the name would be given to the bishop's advisors.

Initially, they did not have a ministerial function, like the deacon and *episcopos* (bishop). Later in history, as the Church experienced rapid expansion, the *presbyters* would be given ministerial tasks by their bishops. Eventually they, like the bishop, would be referred to as priests and this would have reflected the fact that the *presbyters* now shared in the presidency of the Eucharist for smaller communities, when

---

to them. We will see why this language is important as the book develops. In reality there is no such thing as a "transitional" deacon because the sacrament of orders imparts character and if a man did not proceed to *presbyteral* ordination he remains a deacon. If he were automatically laicised because he did not proceed to *presbyteral* ordination this would seriously undermine Catholic doctrine of sacraments and the sacrament of order in particular.

2   Bart Koet study on Ignatius of Antioch and his "deacons" and Apostolic Constitutions. A paper presented at Diakonia Symposium, University of East Finland, 2017. Unpublished.

the bishop was not present. In Greek, the word for priest is *hiereus* and in Latin *sacerdos*. The term priest was used because they would preside at the Eucharist which was understood to be a participation in the once and for all sacrifice of Christ and priests in the Jewish and pagan world presided over sacrifices. At some point in history, the word priest would be applied to presbyters. The word priest came into modern English through Old German, then into Saxon and then into our modern language, at which point the words presbyter and priest fused in Catholic terminology.

In the period before the twofold ministry of deacon and bishop was developing, there were many other kinds of ministers with different titles and functions within the community but we are focusing only on these two. The *presbyters* would later join deacon and bishop as the third part of what Catholics today understand as the sacred ministry or the threefold Holy Orders. By the time we reach the ninth century, only a few of the other ministries outside of these three survive and even then, some of these are eventually absorbed into the *presbyterate*, along with what had been a separate and distinct ministry of deacon. By the tenth century, the *presbyterate* – almost always now called the priesthood – would eclipse the episcopate and the episcopate too would be absorbed into this priesthood. The pinnacle of the sacrament of orders would become the priesthood and a bishop was regarded from the tenth century until 1965 as a priest with additional juridical powers. This is why it was possible and logical for bishops – prior to the reforms of Vatican II – to refer to what we know as *presbyters* and themselves as "we priests".

Bishops were at that time just a variation in the species of "priest" or *sacerdos*.

I only mention this information about deacons and *presbyters* because we need to be aware that the ministry of the Church took some time to develop and that initial situations, even up until the twelfth century, could be quite fluid and different from what we know today. We will in another chapter touch on how the pattern of ministry developed into what is called the course of honours (*cursus honorum*) by which a man would ascend up through the ranks during his priestly formation until he attained the top rank which was simply called priesthood.[3] We shall see, later, that it took some time for the ranks to form a stable pattern. It was, for example, normal prior to the ninth century for bishops to be chosen from among deacons and not *presbyters* (priests). It was common for them to be directly ordained a bishop without a *presbyteral* ordination in between. Even after the tenth century when it was supposed to happen, according to canon law, that a deacon had to be ordained a *presbyter* before he could be ordained bishop, this pattern was not always followed. Pope Hadrian V (1276) was a deacon when elected Bishop of Rome and he died after only weeks in office as Pope and before he received *presbyteral* or episcopal ordination.

---

3   We will look at the *cursus honorum* later. For those interested in learning about its development should consult John St. H. Gibaut; (2000) *The Cursus Honorum: A Study of the Origin and Evolution of Sequential Ordination*. Peter Lang; New York.

The permanent ministry

The decision by the Second Vatican Council to restore or re-establish the permanent ministry of deacon in the Latin Catholic Church was in part a fulfilment of the decision of the Council of Trent to restore this permanent form of ministry many centuries before.[4] It was, however, more than an exercise in historical retrieval. The Second Vatican Council had its own reasons and motivations too. We need to understand what these reasons and motives were so that we can begin to orient ourselves to the topic we are exploring. Once we begin to understand these, it will become clear why I argue that the diaconate today is a new wine and, therefore, why new wineskins are required.

We are fortunate that a study completed by the International Theological Commission (ITC) and published in 2003 provides us with some insights into the reasons and motivations of the Council. The primary purpose of the ITC document was to explore the possibility of admitting women to the diaconate.[5] Conducting this exploration has done us a great service in helping to understand what it was that the Council wished to be restored or re-established. The implications of understanding these motives and

---

4   Refer to LG29 and Joint introduction
5   Pope Francis instituted a commission to study the question too but restricted it only to questions that had largely already been covered and the central question was about their functions were and some historical elements. Their report has not been revealed as of my writing but I expect little progress because they were asking the wrong question. See Chapter 6. The parameters were too narrow and the conclusion from that question seemed forgone. I may yet be surprised.

intentions is significant for receiving the ministry of deacon in the Church and also for the question of ordaining women to this ministry.

I should note my reservations about the ITC document. There are two primary reservations that I have, for what is otherwise a useful document. First, in developing its theology of the diaconate and its treatment of Biblical and Patristic sources, the ITC relies upon a semantic profile of the *diacon* group of words that was outdated at the time ITC was completing its study (1990s). The *diacon* group of words give us the words, deacon and diaconate and also, via a longer process, the word ministry and ministerial. This development we will explore later and it has immense significance. The ITC relied on a non-scholarly semantic profile of the word group that clustered around concepts such as; "service toward another", "charitable or loving concern" and which carried connotations of "lowly or humble service". This profile was replaced in the major Greek ST Lexicons by the profile published in 1990 by John N. Collins. We will touch on that profile in the next chapter.

The second reservation is that the majority of sources and the principal authors of the ITC document rely upon German scholarship in which this outdated semantic profile is found. To compound this problem, the German neologism *diaconie*, which means Christian social service, reinforced the faulty semantic profile and influences the ITC document through the contribution of German scholars. *Diaconie* entered the German language through the mis-identification of the *diacon* words with words for charity, humble service and care and concern for another. We will touch on the history of this term in subsequent chapters. The reservations mean that we must reject or treat with extreme caution much of what the document says about the theology of diaconate.[6] For our present purpose in this chapter, we will not be relying too much on the treatment of the *diacon* words and so these reservations will be less significant in this chapter, although they cannot be avoided altogether.

Some objections

Before we look at the ITC document and the intentions and motivations of the Council, I want to draw our attention to some objections that are made to the restoration or re-establishment of the permanent ministry of deacon. I want to do this now before we look at the intentions and motivations of the Council so as to bring them into relief for you against what the Council has to say. Some readers may already be familiar with these objections and the way in which these have been expressed. I am going to describe them here but not respond to the objections. I am not going to provide counter arguments directly for these because my hope is that readers will be able to do some of this as we study together the ITC document. Subsequent chapters will also help you formulate some of the counter arguments to the objections.

We should also note these objections are not raised about the transitional diaconate. Most Catholics find the transitional diaconate unobjectionable because (if they think of it at all) they think of it as a kind of apprenticeship year

---

6   John N. Collins (2016) *Gateway to Renewal: Reclaiming Ministries for Women and Men*. Morning star Publications: Northcote; Vic. A Litany of Errors in the ITC Document. pp. 103-118.

for the priesthood. Catholic *presbyters* and laity often only consider the so-called transitional diaconate as the final period of waiting before a man is to be "ordained". Both *presbyters* and laity forgetting that a deacon is ordained. I suspect they mean "real ordination" or *presbyteral* ordination. That kind of language betrays a pre-Vatican II outlook or lack of reception of the teaching of the Council.

A number of objections to the permanent ministry concern the functions of a deacon. Some object that a *presbyter* can do all that a deacon can do. This leads them to ask: so why do we need a ministry of deacon at all? In fact, a *presbyter* can do even more. He can anoint the sick, hear confession and grant absolution and, most importantly, he can preside at the Eucharist. A deacon cannot do any of these. A related objection is that a deacon is taking away from the *presbyter* some of his functions or is, perhaps, in milder forms of this objection, duplicating them. Deacons proclaim the Gospel, preach, baptise, witness marriages (in the Latin Church only), preside at the rite of Christian burial, and administer sacramentals, invite the exchange of peace, announce the dismissal at the end of Mass and preside at the rite of Viaticum and prayers in nearness of death (the last rites of the Church).[7] All of these things are currently

---

7   Latin Catholics are sometimes confused about "the last rites of the Church". The reforms of the liturgy after Vatican II restored anointing of the sick as just that, anointing of the sick, and separated this anointing from the last rites of the Church, which are given to someone approach and preparing for death. Prior to the reforms it was called extreme unction, a final anointing that constituted the last rites. The last rites today are Holy Communion, given as *Viaticum* (literally food for the journey) and prayers in nearness of death. Deacons and *presbyters* are ordinary ministers of these last rites. But only a *presbyter* can include an absolution of sin within the rite of *viaticum*.

done by *presbyters*.

I have heard it said from *presbyters* that deacons clutter the sanctuary and are not needed in the liturgy. Once, after assisting at Mass with a *presbyter* who was visiting our parish, he remarked to me; "Deacons don't do much in the liturgy, do they?" His assumption being that the deacon only proclaimed the Gospel, proclaimed the Prayer of the Faithful, prepared the chalice, assisted with the elevation, invited the exchange of peace, assisted with distribution of communion, cleansed the sacred vessels, reserved the Blessed Sacrament and dismissed the people. That is, he was thinking that only things a deacon does in the liturgy of the Mass could be described by those parts he performed. By this same reasoning the lay person who read the first reading did very little and the ones who took up the collection even less.

Readers may recognise the problem of this functionalist understanding of what the *presbyter*, deacon and people are doing at Mass. His question exposes his lack of grasp of the theology of the nature of liturgy and harks back to the pre-Vatican times when the *presbyter* said Mass and the people came to hear it. He seems not to grasp that Christ prays the liturgy in, through, and with his whole Body, in head and member united in one voice and body.[8] This was from a

---

In the Eastern Catholic and Orthodox Churches, a marriage must be solemnised by a *presbyter* for its validity because he is the minister of the sacrament and so a deacon may not celebrate this sacrament. In the Latin Church, a *presbyter* or deacon is the Church's witness to marriage and the baptised bride and groom are the ministers of the sacrament. So a Latin deacon can preside at a Latin Catholic wedding.

8 *Sacrosanctum Concilium*#7 and General Instruction on the Roman Missal: With Application for Australia. St Paul's Publications: Homebush. # 5 hereafter referred to as GIRM.

presbyter ordained in the late 1980s. This is another variation on the objection concerning the functions of deacons.

A second point of objection also related to functions – or what is it that deacons do – comes from the point of view of the laity. Three of the great graces and recoveries of the Second Vatican Council were the recognition of the baptismal vocation of all God's people, the equal call to holiness in all states of life and the recovery of the concept of the common priesthood of all baptised Christians. All of these recoveries take place within the framework of a theology and ecclesiology of communion (Greek; *koinonia* and Latin *communio*). We need to keep communion/*koinonia* in mind because it is significant for a number of the developments we will be considering. We will look at the ecclesiology and spirituality of communion a bit more closely later.

The Council affirmed that baptism is the basis for mission, holiness and the liturgical action of the whole Church, but not ministry. Prior to the Council, the prevailing theological understanding that dominated Catholic approaches to spirituality and spiritual formation was that priesthood and Religious Life (monks, nuns, Sisters and Brothers, some clerics) marked a higher calling to the way of perfection than the life of the laity. It seemed that holiness itself was hierarchical and that the vast majority of the Church, the laity, had to be content with a lesser way or a lesser share in holiness. The call of all the baptised to the same holiness and the belief that all could attain to that same holiness, regardless if one were a priest, Religious or lay person, found throughout the documents of Vatican II, is a clarion call to participate in the one mission of Christ.⁹ The Council attempted to restore some lay ministries in the liturgy to the laity, that of lector and acolyte. We will see in later chapters why this would only be a partially successful restoration and one that still requires further development before it is fully restored and received into the life of the Church.

Following the Council, two developments occurred more or less spontaneously and which were not foreseen by the Council itself. The first is that many Religious women (sisters) moved out of the traditional field of mission of their Religious Institute, such as education or nursing, and into parochial ministries and roles within dioceses which had been largely part of *presbyteral* ministry and some moved to fields which were new ministries altogether. This movement was partly driven by a new sense of identification of Religious with the laity. Technically, only the ordained are clergy and so all Religious not ordained are laity. Clerical Religious Institutes are those in which the majority of members are clerics such as the Jesuits or Redemptorists.

The second development was among lay women and men who were not vowed members of religious communities. These were also moving into parochial ministries: as pastoral assistants, sacramental coordinators, liturgy coordinators and directors of religious education programs in parishes and also some diocesan settings. Accompanying both of these developments was an increase in enrolment of these same Religious and other lay people in formal theological programs of studies in seminaries, theological colleges and universities.

---

9   Chapter five of *Lumen gentium* outlines the universal call to holiness but this theme weaves its way through the whole Council.

Often, they were studying alongside of men being formed for the *presbyterate*.

The Council did not foresee these developments. The Council seemed to expect that the universal call to holiness and a reinvigorated sense of mission among the laity would be translated into women and men taking seriously their obligation to live the Gospel and inject the spirit of the Gospel into family and work life, and within the institutions of society. The teaching on the laity assumed that they would act as a kind of leaven in society at large as a mission of the Church to the world. Perhaps this remains an unfilled hope of the Council waiting for full reception.

Against the backdrop of these two spontaneous developments, the permanent ministry of deacon was being re-established in a number of dioceses throughout the world. A burgeoning lay ministry movement was rapidly developing throughout the 1970s and 80s at the very same time that the permanent ministry of deacon was also flourishing. Most of this lay ministry was *ad intra*, that is concerned with the internal life of the Church rather than ministry within and to the world, *ad extra*. With very little catechetical and theological formation about what this diaconate was, it was perhaps understandable that some would consider it to be a rival to the lay ministries that were evolving. In fact, it was not uncommon to hear the phrase, "lay deacon" or "married deacons" used to refer to permanent deacons. The term had no official status and seemed to have developed as a way of distinguishing transitional deacons on their way to *presbyteral* ordination from the permanent ones. The language of lay deacon has not entirely disappeared.

A few examples may illustrate how this language and the confusion that it reveals still operates. In the first example, a deacon was being inducted into one of these ancient orders of knights and dames who continue to do good works and support the mission of the Church in various ways. In this particular order of knights and dames, distinctions are made between clerical and lay members. These distinctions are reflected in aspects of their insignia and also where they sit in liturgical gatherings. The newly inducted deacon took his place among the clerical members of the order. One of the knights, who was a *presbyter* with a senior role in his diocese (Vicar General), said to the deacon; "Michael, you have to sit over there", while pointing to the lay knights and dames. The deacon replied, "but I am a deacon". To which the *presbyter* said, "Yes, I know, you should be over there." This banter went back and forth to the amusement of many, until another *presbyter* who was a Judicial Vicar said to the Vicar General; "Michael is sitting in the correct place. He is a cleric. You became a cleric when you were ordained a deacon too." The Vicar General left the deacon where he was but remained with a confused expression on his face.

A second example concerns instructions for deacons about how to dress. The first example concerns liturgical dress when they are leading a vigil service before a funeral. This instruction I discovered was included in a number of diocesan guidelines for deacons in the USA. They are instructed to vest in a suit and tie, "in keeping with their status". Although "status" is not defined in this section of the guidelines, one is able to work out that as a suit and tie are normal secular dress, and the dress of a lay man in the

USA, the status means as a lay person. If the writers of these guidelines, which contain this instruction, had consulted the Rite of Christian Burial and the part pertaining to vesture, they would have discovered that *presbyters* and deacons are advised to wear an alb and stole at a Vigil and at the Rite of Christian Burial which is not celebrated with Mass. Both deacon and *presbyter* may wear a cope as well.

I suspect the same confusion exists about the clerical status of deacons when it comes to non-liturgical clerical dress. In the past few years, I have attended international gatherings of deacons. It is apparent that different countries and different dioceses have a variety of approaches to clerical dress for deacons.[10] Some deacons wear black suits and Roman collars, some have obvious clerical insignia like a cross on their lapel and some wear no identification. Some wear clerical dress only in some limited situations where the need seems greater to identify as a minister. Canon law only says that permanent deacons are not obliged to wear clerical dress unless their bishop so obliges them.[11] Therefore they can wear clerical dress if they wish or feel they need to in any situation. There is nothing in canon law about deacons or *presbyters* asking permission of their bishop to wear clerical dress. It

---

10   I have my own reservations about clerical dress generally. I know it has a witness value and can also assist the laity by identifying a minister for them but I also believe deeper reflection is required not only with regard to deacons but all clergy. I have a short article about deacons and clerical dress on the website of the National Association of Deacons (Australia) if you are wanting a few more thoughts. http://www.ausdeacons.org.au/downloads/content/1742.pdf

11   There is no canon that says a deacon may not wear clerical dress or that he may be prevented from doing so. Can 288 states he is not obligated to wear it unless his bishop determines that he is obliged. There is nothing in the canon about asking permission either.

is, however, very common, particularly in the USA, to find in diocesan guidelines a stipulation that either deacons are not permitted to wear clerical dress or must seek the permission of their bishop to do so. I suspect that these requirements are part of the same confusion about the status of the deacon as a cleric.

The final example concerns forms of address. In some counties, even just in some dioceses in some countries, the official term of address for a deacon is, "Rev. Mr". This term is an anachronism derived from English language usage that had begun to wane in the nineteenth century. It survived in some Catholic dioceses as a way of referring to transitional deacons up until Vatican II. Originally, the term simply referred to any minister of the Christian religion: Protestant Pastor, Catholic Bishop or *presbyters* or Orthodox clergy. Its revival in some dioceses for permanent deacons creates "brand confusion" to use a term from marketing.[12] It suggests that the permanent deacon is not quite a cleric but not quite a lay person. A confusion which is still found in some dioceses that list clergy in one section of their diocesan directory – in which a list of all transitional deacons, *presbyters* and bishops may be found – and in a separate listing they have permanent deacons. They seem not to know that deacons are clergy.

To conclude our look at objections, I will share a few vignettes to illustrate the strength of the resistance to the re-established ministry of permanent deacon. I am only doing so to illustrate some of the confusions and questions that this

---

12 For those who would like a guide to how to refer to deacons, see my article Terms of Address at https://ausdeacons.org.au/generalTopics/Terms%20of%20Address%20for%20Deacons.pdf

ministry provokes and to contrast it with our explorations of the intentions of the Council. The details of dioceses or countries is not actually relevant to the stories. I have found from personal conversations with deacons from a number of countries that many of these stories may be found repeated in many places. We need to remember that there are lots of positive experiences deacons and dioceses have had with this ministry but I am only dealing with objections here for the purpose of contrast. Objections do not tell the whole story.

A deacon shared the experience he had at a celebration of Mass which he found quite powerful. Deacon Albert was member of the commission for ecumenism in his diocese. Every two years, there was a State conference for each of the Catholic commissions of ecumenism in each diocese in that State to come together to exchange ideas and projects. One year, the bishop of the diocese that was hosting the conference invited the delegates to his house for Mass and dinner. Mass was to be held in his private chapel which would normally only accommodate a dozen people and there were almost twenty present. He invited Albert to assist him at Mass and invited the four *presbyters* present to concelebrate but advised they would have to sit in the front row because of a lack of space. None of the *presbyters* chose to concelebrate. When it came time to distribute communion, the bishop asked that people remain where they were and that he and deacon Albert would come to them. One *presbyter* who was very outspoken in his anti-deacon views was in the congregation. He received the host from the bishop but when Deacon Albert offered the cup, he folded his arms and looked away. After Mass, the bishop commented to Albert about the behaviour of the *presbyter* and expressed his shock that the *presbyter's* well-known dislike for deacons extended to turning his back on the Precious Blood of Jesus.

Roberto is a deacon who has qualifications in theology and social work. He had worked in a government agency providing community support services. Before his ordination, he was a minister of communion bringing Holy Communion to parishioners in hospitals and nursing homes. A few years after ordination, a position became available on the pastoral care team of a Catholic hospital which was operated by an institute of women Religious. He applied for the position but was not successful. Some weeks after, he was met by a person who introduced himself after Mass and who told Roberto that he had been on the selection panel for the pastoral care position. He said that his conscience was disturbed by the process that was implemented. He and one other member of the selection panel put Roberto on the top of the list. He said he was the one with the best qualifications and relevant experience. He claimed none of the other applicants came close. The third member of the panel was a Religious Sister of the Institute that operated the hospital. She made it clear that the Institute would not consider a deacon for any position in the hospital no matter how well qualified and experienced. Some deacons report that they conceal their diaconal identity if they are applying for positions in Catholic organisations so as to avoid the risk of discrimination.

In some cases, even the thought of having deacons in a diocese is considered problematic or is discouraged. Recently, I was sent a link to a story in Ireland about opposition to the reintroduction of the permanent ministry of deacon in a diocese there. The *presbyters* protested so strongly that the bishop closed the program even before it got started and he also apologised to his diocese for even having thought about reintroducing this ministry.[13] A number of deacons have shared with me that in their diocese the vocations team are allowed to promote vocations to the *presbyterate*, Religious life, married life and single life but not the diaconate. On vocations Sunday, prayers are offered for an increase in vocations for all of these except the diaconate. In spite of this, these same dioceses often receive enquiries about the diaconate. It seems that prayers are being offered to God for a variety of vocations, but when God replies with sending diaconal ones, some don't want to receive what is sent. The diaconate is the fastest growing Order in the Church, even outstripping the growth of some religious orders.

One final vignette. A number of years ago, I was invited to give some public lectures about the diaconate and lead a clergy conference day on this theme in a diocese that was celebrating the tenth anniversary of the reintroduction of the diaconate. During the question time, I was asked by a *presbyter* about when a bishop is unable to appoint a *presbyter* to lead a parish because of a shortage.[14] He wanted to know if the bishop is free to appoint either a deacon or a lay person.

I gave my usual answer with my usual caveats. The first caveat is that there must be a genuine need and that no

---

13 Irish bishop bows to pressure, says he will postpone introduction of permanent deacons September 17, 2014 by deacon Greg Kandra, The Deacon's Bench. https://www.patheos.com/blogs/deaconsbench/2014/09/irish-bishop-bows-to-pressure-says-he-will-postpone-introduction-of-permanent-deacons/
14 Can 517§2

presbyter at all is available to appoint. The second is that as soon as a *presbyter* becomes available, the bishop is bound to appoint one and to replace the lay person or deacon he may have appointed. Then I stated what canon law says and how this is interpreted in two documents, one of which is adopted by the pope, using the technical expression, *in forma specifica*. This expression means that the pope is adopting the interpretation as definitive. I outlined the good theological foundations for my caveats and also for what canon law says. I stated quite clearly and correctly that if a deacon is available, the bishop is bound to appoint him and not a lay person. The bishop of the diocese was present for this answer and I had the documents with me to hold up for the group.

Several months later, I received an email from the *presbyter* who had asked the question. He informed me that the bishop had that exact situation occur and called for expressions of interest from deacons and lay people and appointed a lay woman. Not even the requirements of canon law and an interpretation of the relevant canon adopted by the pope, or sacramental ordination and theology of Holy Orders, was sufficient to appoint the deacon who should have been appointed. More significantly, the appointment of a lay person above a deacon is a repudiation of the Catholic faith regarding sacraments and the sacrament of Holy Orders in particular. This should be of some concern to us because the bishop is the chief teacher of the Catholic faith in his diocese.

The motives and intentions of the Council

We are able to examine now the motives and intentions of the Second Vatican Council in restoring the permanent ministry of deacon. In reading this section, you may want to begin comparing and contrasting some of the objections above with what follows.

Our starting point is to examine the language that the Council uses when it considers the permanent ministry of deacon. We can see in the table that three Latin terms are used to refer to the reestablishment of the permanent ministry of deacon. These three terms cluster around a similar semantic range in English which share similar connotations: restoring, renewing, re-establishing and reactivating. That is, they concern something which already exists and which is not a novelty being introduced. The ministry of deacon already exists – it is simply being given some new life in a new context. The first two pairs of terms suggest making something new from what has previously existed. What is to be re-established and reactivated has always been present but now it requires a new life for the present time. Renewal suggests not the old wine of either the transitional diaconate on the way to *presbyteral* ordination nor the old wine of a particular historical expression of the diaconate. What the Council meant by its decision to restore this permanent ministry of deacon will become a little clearer shortly.

TEXT	LATIN
Lumen gentium 29a	restitutio
Ad gentes 16f	restauratio
Orientalium Ecclesiarum	instauratio

All three connote the idea of restoring, renewing, re-establishing and re-activating. ITC 2003 p53

The Council and the Joint Introduction to the Basic Norms for the Formation of Permanent Deacons and Directory for the Ministry and Life of Permanent Deacons both refer to the decision of the Council of Trent as an element contributing to the decision to re-establish the permanent ministry of deacons.[15] In the Joint Declaration, we read, "The permanent Diaconate, restored by the Second Vatican Council, in complete continuity with ancient Tradition and the specific decision of the Council of Trent, has flourished in these last decades in many parts of the Church — with promising results, especially for the urgent missionary work of new evangelisation".

There are three elements we need to note here. First, we see that the permanent ministry of deacon is part of the ancient Tradition of the Church. For those not familiar with this language, tradition using a capitalised "T" means the faith of the Church which has been handed on since ancient times or the Apostolic faith. Tradition here does not mean a custom or a practice but is a reference to the faith of the Catholic Church. The Catholic faith about the nature of Holy Orders is that "the divinely instituted ecclesiastical ministry is exercised in different orders by those who right from ancient times are called bishops, priests and deacons."[16]

Secondly, we see that the Council of Trent (1545-1563) had decided long before Vatican II to re-establish the permanent ministry of deacon. However, that Council did not see its decision come to fruition. I am glad that it did not do so because the diaconate as understood at that time was

---

15 Congregation for Catholic Education and Congregation for Clergy issued the joint introduction which form part of their documents of the respective Congregations; *Norms for the Formation of Permanent Deacons* and *Directory for the Ministry and Life of Permanent Deacons*, in 1998.

16 LG 28a

essentially a liturgical role. There may have been a danger that it would not have been fully restored with respect to the ministry of the word and pastoral ministry if it had been restored at the time of Trent.

The third element to note is that the Joint Declaration links the restored permanent ministry of deacon with the new evangelisation. We will look at this more closely later but for now we should note that this indicates the Second Vatican Council had something new in mind for the diaconate and was responding to new needs and pastoral situations for the Church of today.

We need to look very briefly at why Trent had decided to restore the ministry of deacon. The ITC document addresses this topic briefly.[17] I have distilled into a simple table the complexities of the arguments down to three points of dispute between the Reformers and those who wanted to affirm the Catholic faith. Not all of the various Reformers argued for the same things or in the same way and they frequently radically opposed each other on various points of doctrine and church life.[18] They did agree that ministry and ministers in the Church were necessary for the good ordering of the Church and the proclamation of the word and sacraments.

---

17 ITC (2003) *From the Diakonia of Christ*; p39-42
18 I will not include the Anglican communion here because they represent a very different solution to the questions raised by Reformers and this has layers of subtlety beyond the scope of this book. They maintained a threefold order but denied its sacramentality and they redefined the concept of *presbyter* so that it aligned more with the Reformed concept of pastor and not that of the Catholic sacerdotal or priestly concept. They did this while still calling the minister a priest.

REFORMERS	CATHOLIC
Deny divinely instituted ministry	Affirm divinely instituted ministry
Reduce ministry to either one single ministry of the Word (and Sacrament) or include one of oversight (episcope)	Affirm the threefold nature of Orders-deacon, presbyter and bishop
Deny sacramental nature of Order- assert necessity	Affirm sacramental and affirm essential

They agreed that not all Christians were ministers or had a ministry (*diaconia*) and they agreed that only some were called and delegated or commissioned to minister and preside over a community. They understood that ministry was not founded on the sacrament of baptism but on a specific calling and commissioning. All of this they shared in common with the Catholic Tradition. The point of departure was that the Catholics held to the Tradition that the threefold order of bishop, *presbyter* and deacon was divinely instituted and part of the essential nature of the Church. The Reformers believed that ministers were only necessary because the Church was a society and societies need structure but they were not of the essence or divinely instituted aspect of the Church's life. They did not believe that the recovery of the concept of priesthood of all the people meant that all were ministers – both Luther and Calvin condemn those who say the opposite, as those who wish to destroy the Church.[19]

---

19   John N. Collins (1992) *Are all Christians Ministers?* E.J Dwyer: Sydney. pp. 17-26

It seems almost a logical progression that if ministry derives from the social organisation of the Church that the Church would have some freedom in establishing the form that such a ministry would take. The Reformers, therefore, denied the necessity of the threefold order. They either argued for a single ministry of word and sacrament in which a minister presided over a local congregation, which was now designated a church and some argued that there could also be a ministry of oversight (*episcope*) and kept a twofold ministry. Generally, they called the minister of word and sacrament a pastor or perhaps a minister of the word and those who maintained an office of oversight called that minister a bishop. Most Lutheran communities maintained a twofold order. Calvin had an office of deacon in his Church structure but these were not ordained ministers. His deacons were analogous to a parish finance council in present Catholic terms. They were responsible for the finances of the church and the maintenance of the church property. In some churches of the Reformed tradition, that remains the nature of the office of deacon.

In contrast to the Reformers, the Council of Trent affirmed the Catholic Tradition and faith of the Church that the threefold order was essential for the life of the Church. At the time of the Council, the Catholic Church in fact had no permanent sign that affirmed its own faith in the threefold order. There were permanent *presbyters* and permanent bishops but no permanent deacons. Even at a Mass that required a deacon, another *presbyter* would simply dress as a deacon and take the deacon parts or not bother to even dress as one and take his parts vested as a *presbyter*.[20] Canon law required an interval of a year between diaconal and *presbyteral* ordination but this was frequently ignored and very short intervals, sometimes only of days were observed. It was clear to the Catholic and the Reform side that the Catholic Church could not credibly argue that these three orders were divinely instituted and of the essence of the Church if they never really had an effective sign of one of these orders, the deacon.

Finally, we should consider the significant rift regarding the sacramental nature of Holy Orders. Catholics believe Holy Orders is a sacrament established by Christ. At Trent, they affirmed this aspect of Catholic faith even though they knew of the historical evolution of the sacrament. They believed that Christ established seven sacraments and that each sacrament has an outward sign which points to the sacramental grace. In this way, Christ provides grace through the sacraments for the building up of the Church. Therefore, the ordination of deacons contains a sacramental grace for the life of the Church and contains specific grace not available in this way through other sacraments.

Two sacraments are designated sacraments which impart character – baptism and Holy Orders. That means these sacraments may be conferred once only as they "mark"

---

20   As recently as 2015, I witnessed a presbyter vested as a presbyter in a Cathedral Church when the Archbishop was presider, process in with the Book of Gospels, like a deacon, proclaim the Gospel, mix the water and wine like a deacon, elevate the chalice as a deacon, invite the sharing of peace and dismiss the people, just as a deacon would. He also concelebrated as a *sacerdos* would. The same Archbishop had written a journal article a couple of years before on the theme of, "Say the Black and Do the Red" but this liturgy was brown. A mixture of black and red.

or conformed the recipient to Christ in a specific and one-off way. That is, each brings about an ontological change. A baptised person is no longer like any other person on the planet: she or he is now part of the Body of Christ and therefore part of each person who is baptised into that same body (Romans 12:5, 1 Corinthians 12:12-14). The Reformers accepted only two sacraments as established by Christ; baptism and Eucharist.[21] Anglicans also only affirm two sacraments but in some forms of Anglicanism (Episcopal churches) allow some practices like the sacraments such as confession.[22]

It was in response to these three areas of dispute that the Council of Trent recognised the necessity of restoring the permanent ministry of deacon. Sometimes, the Council of Trent is presented as a council against the Reformers. Certainly, the Council was trying to respond to the crisis in the Church and the schism that was unfolding because of the rupture that had occurred with those who would become known as Protestants. Trent was not only reactionary – as perhaps the Catholic Counter-Reformation period may be characterised – but Trent made some genuine attempts to listen to and respond to questions raised by reformers. Protestants were invited to the Council and some Catholic

---

21 Again, returning to the Anglican or Episcopal Church, their Thirty-Nine Articles only accepts two sacraments and the other five as like sacraments. Anglicans of a more evangelical or low Church nature emphasise the two and those or a more catholic nature tend to emphasise the two plus five model.

22 Article 25 of the 39 Articles accepts only two sacraments. https://www.churchofengland.org/prayer-and-worship/worship-texts-and-resources/book-common-prayer/articles-religion

theologians and bishops understood the objections of reformers and tried to address them.

Even in matters of the language of the liturgy, Trent adopts a very narrow position, only saying that those who say that the Mass celebrated in Latin is invalid are wrong. The Council itself allowed for celebration of the liturgy in vernacular languages provided that it was not tied to the invalidity of Mass in Latin.[23] The Council acknowledged that the reformers were correct that Catholics could not credibly claim that they believed all that they believed about these three points in dispute so long as they did not have a permanent ministry of deacon alongside of the permanent ministries of *presbyter* and bishop. In response, the Council of Trent decided to restore the permanent ministry of deacon in the sixteenth century. It never came to fruition because the canons and other legislation to enable this to become a reality never eventuated.

This brief background for the Council of Trent explains why the decision at Vatican II to restore the permanent ministry of deacon is in continuity with Trent. Now that we have that context, we may focus more directly on Vatican II.

---

23 A little excursus could be introduced here. Trent did not create a Tridentine Liturgy, it merely asked for some uniformity in practice, while allowing for legitimate diversity, which resulted in the Mass of Pius V. This mix remained in force until the reform of the liturgy in 1969. Secondly, it did not mandate Latin. Those attached to the liturgy of Pius V, sometimes and incorrectly called the Tridentine Mass, or less accurately, the Traditional Latin Mass, who insist this is a Latin language liturgy are mistaken. It can be celebrated in the vernacular and with the people's part said by the people and not the deacon. The Traditional Latin Mass is that of GIRM 2010 (Benedict XVI) in its ordinary form and in its extraordinary form is the Mass of John XXIII formerly that of Pius V.

Although a variety of arguments for restoring the permanent ministry of deacon was present at the Council, the ITC brings our attention to the central point that; "a motive of faith, namely the recognition of the gift of the Holy Spirit in the complex reality of Holy Orders, furnished the ultimate justification for the Council's decision to re-establish the diaconate".[24] Vatican II wanted to affirm what Catholics believe about the sacrament of Holy Orders and it is this sacramental and theological perspective through which the restoration should be viewed and the objections evaluated. The Council wished to affirm the Catholic faith which acknowledges a threefold order and to once again allow the reality to be expressed by having all three permanent ministries restored. The Council also restored the ministry of bishop and attempted a restoration of the *presbyterate*, even preferring the term *presbyter* to priest to describe the ministers in this Order. We will examine these restorations in subsequent chapters.

Three motives for the restoration of the permanent ministry of deacon are identified by the ITC.[25] These are summarised in the table. We have already seen that that the first motivation is the primary one and that it is a theological motive. Therefore, if we want to evaluate the reception and rejection of the diaconate, we must first do

First Motivation (theological)	Motive of faith and the threefold order
Second Motivation (pastoral)	Pastoral care of communities and new evangelisation
Third Motivation (theological and pastoral)	Open the grace of diaconal ministry to the Church

---

24   ITC; p. 57
25   ITC; pp. 57-59

so on theological grounds. We can ask, for example, if any arguments for the rejection of the ministry are in fact opposed to, challenge or in any way deny the Catholic faith about the sacramental and divinely instituted ministry. In essence, all that Trent affirmed about the sacrament of Holy Orders, Vatican II affirms.

We must consider the diaconate as we do the other two orders. The diaconate is willed by Christ for the Church and as a gift of the Holy Spirit so that the Church may be built up in grace for holiness and mission.[26] It is a participation in the apostolic ministry by which the *communio* of the Church is continuously formed.[27] Each specific calling of a man as a deacon, as the rite of ordination itself makes clear, is a reception by the local Church (diocese) of the gift of a minister. An ordained minister makes Christ present in a way that is permanent, sacramental and which has been discerned by the Church. It is Christ who provides this gift for the Church by the power and presence of the Holy Spirit.[28]

The laying on of hands, in the rite of ordination of a bishop, *presbyter* or deacon, is always done in silence to indicate that ordination is a consecration and work of the Holy Spirit, in which the Church is merely receiving and not creating.[29] The prayer which follows is an *epiclesis* or calling down of the Holy Spirit that signifies the specific graces for the Church that flows through the one who is ordained and to the Church.

---

26 CCC §§1538, 1551, 1581
27 CCC §§1536, 1570
28 CCC §§1572, 1584
29 I recommend readers explore the Rite of Ordination and the excellent commentary on the rites by Susan Woods; *Sacramental Orders*. Liturgical Press: Collegeville, Minn. 2000.

In a very real sense, the grace of ordination does not stop or rest on the one ordained, as some special elevation of an individual Christian, but flows through and is for, the communion of the Church.[30] That is, the primary object of the grace of ordination is ecclesial. No one can confer grace on himself and so Christ raises up ministers through whom he can minister the word and sacrament to build up the holy people. The diaconate is a participation in the mystery of sacramental grace in which Christ makes himself present in the midst of his Church by word and sacrament and like the other two orders is necessary for its life.

At this point, the reader may wish to return to the section above where we considered some objections and ask to what extent such objections are consisted with an affirmation of Catholic faith in the sacrament of Holy Orders and the sacramental economy in general. Readers may also want to substitute bishop or *presbyter* into the objections above because the Church believes the same about all three orders. Readers may also wish to consider if the objections rely primarily on political and sociological arguments rather than theological and sacramental foundations.

The second motivation is pastoral. The two pastoral issues noted are care of communities in the absence of a *presbyter* and the new evangelisation. We will look at pastoral care of communities first. If a bishop is truly unable to appoint a *presbyter* to the pastoral leadership of a parish or a remote Christian community, he may appoint a deacon if a deacon is available.[31] If a deacon is available, he may not appoint a

---

30   CCC §§1584, 1585
31   CIC Can 517§2

lay woman or man because of what Catholics believe about the sacrament of Holy Orders.[32] Catholics believe Christ has called this man and consecrated him in the Holy Spirit for the ministry of the word and sacrament to build up the communion of the Church and that is the prime reason for the preference for an ordained person in this situation.

Parish leadership is not the normal or usual or intended ministerial appointment for deacons. Several bishops during the debate at Vatican II on the restoration of the diaconate made what should be an obvious point: deacons can never be substitutes for *presbyters*. A parish is a eucharistic community and microcosm of the diocese over which the bishop presides at every Eucharist, though obviously not in person. A bishop presides at the Eucharist because he is a bishop and a *presbyter* presides because there is a bishop.[33] As soon as a *presbyter* becomes available, he must be appointed to the parish and

---

[32] The code itself makes this clear by placing deacon first in the list. The *Directory for the Ministry and Life of Permanent Deacons*, as in the case of the *Directory on the Ministry and Life of Priests*, has, together with its hortative character, juridically binding force where its norms "recall disciplinary norms of the Code of Canon Law" or "determine with regard to the manner of applying universal laws of the Church, explicate their doctrinal basis and inculcate or solicit their faithful observance".(1) In these specific cases, it is to be regarded as a formal, general, executory Decree (cf. canon 32). Directory §41 states; "Where permanent deacons participate in the pastoral care of parishes which do not, because of a shortage, have the immediate benefit of a parish priest, they always have precedence over the non-ordained faithful." The document adopted *in forma specifica* by Pope John Paul II *Ecclesiae De Mysterio* states; Art 4 §1, "the preference which this canon gives to deacons cannot be overlooked." See also Anthony Gooley (2017) Preference for the Ordained in Pastoral and Liturgical Leadership. *The Canonist*. Vol 8/1; 110-12

[33] I develop this concept in the subsequent work on Ministry and Holy Orders.

replace any deacon or lay person who had been appointed under canon 517§2. Charity and justice would suggest that a bishop should appoint the lay person or deacon to another suitable ministry. Because this is always the exception and hopefully rare type of appointment, it should never be a main consideration for the restoration of or ministerial appointment of deacons.

New evangelisation is not a term that can be found in the documents of Vatican II. It is a term coined and much promoted by Pope John Paul II and subsequently developed by his successors Benedict XVI and Francis. Francis' encyclical, *Joy of the Gospel,* is devoted to amplification of this theme.[34] Antecedents for the term may be found in Paul VI's letter, *Evangelisation in the Modern World* and scattered throughout the documents of Vatican II. The Council had noted the de-Christianisation and secularisation of countries where Christianity traditionally had strong roots and it raised questions about the effectiveness of the evangelising efforts of the Church. It attempted to shift the Church from a posture of maintenance of the people we have in the parish, to one of mission and outreach to those who had drifted from the Church and to those who were yet to hear the Gospel. John Paul II coined the term new evangelisation and amplified what he meant by it. New evangelisation was to address new situations of evangelisation with new ardour, new vigour and with new initiatives and in new contexts.[35] Pope Francis

---

34 Pope Francis (2013) *Gaudium Evangelii: The Joy of the Gospel.* Apostolic Exhortation. Libreria Vaticana Editrice: Vatican City.
35 John Paul II The Task of the Latin American Bishop. *Origins* 12 (March 24, 1983), p. 661

spells out the urgency of discerning new pastoral strategies with forceful clarity in his letter *Joy of the Gospel*.

At the Council, many of the bishops saw that the ministry of deacon could be a way of doing something new and inserting the Gospel into new situations. Because deacons may continue in secular work and because most are married men with families, they are able to be present in the world in ways that *presbyters* in the Latin Church are often not able to achieve. Deacons are also able to be appointed to full time ecclesial ministries and remunerated in the same way as *presbyters* and transitional deacons.[36] The primary focus of diaconal ministry is not care of a parish but care for specific communities or activities within a diocese or within a parish. Some of these ministries could be outreach and evangelisation and care of; families, couples preparing for marriage, youth, particular migrant communities, Catholic school communities, universities and industrial chaplaincies, and a host of other possibilities.[37]

One of the insights of the Council was that ministry could be freed and made more radical and operate in new ways once it was understood that ministry was not only to be limited to *presbyteral* ministry and leadership of a parish. An entirely new way of bringing the presence of the Church's ministers into new contexts and using new methods is possible. *Presbyteral* and parochial ministry is no longer the only pattern of ordained ministry as it was immediately prior to Vatican II and the restoration of the permanent ministry of deacon.

---

36 Directory 16-20
37 Directory 26-42 outlines just a few of the many possibilities.

The ITC make this observation about the decision of the Council; "Indirectly, Vatican II was also to initiate a clarification of the identity of the priest, who did not have to fulfil all the tasks necessary to the life of the Church. In consequence, the Church would be able to experience the riches of different degrees of Holy Orders. At the same time, Vatican II enabled the Church to go beyond a narrowly *sacerdotal* understanding of the ordained minister."[38] The terms *presbyter* and priest (*sacerdos*) had fused in Catholic theological language in practice if not in terms of etymology, so that priest was synonymous with *presbyter* and therefore the second term was redundant, and all that they did was identified as priestly. Remember that priesthood had also absorbed the ministry of bishop and all lay ministries as well as those of deacon. The theology of the time identified the most significant power of Holy Orders as the power to consecrate the Eucharist. Becoming a bishop, therefore, did not add a sacramental power, according to this theology. They did not consider that the priest exercised his priestly role along with all of the baptised. It seemed natural to think that priest and *presbyter* were synonymous. The presence of permanent deacons makes obvious that not all of the sacred ministry is *sacerdotal* because a deacon is not a *sacerdos*. There is more to being a *presbyter* than being a priest, in other words. More on all of this later.

---

38   ITC; p. 58

The principle not form

Finally, we must examine a most significant observation about the intentions of the Council made in the ITC document as it pertains to my argument that the permanent diaconate is a new wine requiring new wineskins. The ITC suggests that the Second Vatican Council intended to implement the principle and not any particular historical form of the diaconate.[39] The ITC observes: "Vatican II showed some hesitation in its description of the permanent diaconate which it was restoring. In the more doctrinal perspective of *Lumen gentium*, it tended to place the emphasis on the liturgical image of the deacon and his ministry of sanctification. In the missionary perspective of *Ad gentes*, the focus shifted towards the administrative, charitable aspect of the figure of the deacon, and his ministry of government." The ITC continues: "It is however interesting to note that nowhere did the Council claim that the form of the permanent diaconate which it was proposing was a restoration of a previous form". That is: Laurence of Rome, Francis of Assisi, Ephraim of Syria or a Nicholas Ferrar and countless others might give us some idea of how deacons have exercised their ministry in the past but we may not want to copy their ministry as the model diaconal ministry.[40] Vatican II was not indulging in reviving or retrieving any particular form which the diaconate may have taken in the past.

---

39   ITC, p. 62. All of the following quotes are from this same page and paragraph.
40   Owen Cummings; *Deacons and the Church*, Paulist Press, New York, 2004. He devotes chapter 5 of his work to explore the life and ministry of this diverse group of deacons.

The ITC makes a crucial distinction; "What it re-established was *the principle of the permanent exercise of the diaconate,* and not one particular form which the diaconate had taken in the past..." The distinction is between principle and form. The principle takes us to the sacramental and ecclesial mystery and constitution of the Church and the role of the permanent deacon in witnessing to the permanent and divinely instituted nature of a threefold order. The ITC argues that "the Council seemed open to the kind of form it [diaconate] might take in the future, in function of pastoral needs and ecclesial practice, but always in fidelity to Tradition". If we accept that it is the principle and not any particular form, we can see than we must reject some of the objections. The objections do not reflect what Catholics believe about the sacrament of Holy Orders.

Principle also leads us to a rejection of the transitional diaconate and a focus on parochial ministry as it lived by *presbyters* as our models. Transitional diaconate cannot be the model because it is in effect an apprentice for *presbyterate* and not focused on diaconate at all. Its focus is parochial ministry and acquiring the skills and insights in preparation for eventual leadership of a parish community. That is, transitional diaconate is not the focus of formation of permanent deacons. Nor can we make the servant, lowly service, or charity the model or principle around which to develop our theological reflection. That path is no longer viable since the work of John N. Collins on the semantic profile of the *diacon* words.

The ITC suggests that "the apparent indecision and hesitancy of the Council" about specifying the form "might serve as an invitation to the Church to continue working to discern the type of ministry appropriate to the diaconate through ecclesial practice, canonical legislation, and theological reflection". In other words, having been inspired by the Holy Spirit who guides and animates a Council to restore the principle of the permanent diaconate, the Council is open to the continuing work of the Holy Spirit to complete the project. When we look at the objections to the ministry, it seems many are not keen for the Holy Spirit to continue to guide and inspire the Church in allowing the form to take shape. At the moment, I suggest ecclesial practice reveals, at worst, a hardness of heart to receive this aspect of the Council; and, at best, a fumbling attempt to implement a diaconate that really has the *presbyterate* and *presbyteral* type ministry in mind.

The revised code of canon law is clearly a work in progress when it comes to deacons. It will need to evolve to take account of the form that is yet to fully emerge. There has been some theological reflection but, as I argue in this book, for the most part that theological reflection is hampered by the acceptance of a false semantic profile of the *diacon* words and so it has not been as fruitful as it could be. If that theology is to be faithful to the Tradition, it must take seriously the sacramental and ecclesial dimensions of Holy Orders as the foundations for further development. It must also look honestly and deeply at the Tradition as it concerns women and the diaconate. If the principle and not form is to be restored, how are we to incorporate the ministry of women deacons from the past? We will take this up in another chapter.

What we are looking for is a diaconate for today. "The almost total disappearance of the permanent diaconate from the Church of the West for more than a millennium has certainly made it more difficult to understand the profound reality of this ministry. However, it cannot be said for that reason that the theology of the diaconate has no authoritative points of reference, completely at the mercy of theological opinion."[41] The norms list some of these reference points as: an ecclesiology of *koinonia*/communion, the sacrament of ordination, the gifts of the Spirit received at ordination, the rite of ordination, the theology of sacraments of character and the powers conferred. We have touched on some of these sources above and will return to some of them later. The one essential reference point must be the recovery of the meaning of *diakonia* and *diakonos* from the Scriptures and the early documents of the Church. In order to do this churches, deacons and others interested in ministry must go through the work of John N. Collins. Collins is the first study of the *diakon* group of words and his work represents a paradigm shift in our understanding of *diakonia*. His research was later confirmed by the work of Anni Hentschel who approached the word group independently of Collins and for a different purpose.[42] Once the task is undertaken, *diakonia* can be fully appreciated and the gift of this ministry and it potential in the Church can be more easily fulfilled.

---

41 *Norms*, §3
42 We will touch on Dr Hentschel's work in the next chapter.

Conclusion

The creative possibilities for diaconal ministry are opened for the Church by following the Council in its distinction between principle and form. I argue that the Council, in choosing this path, recognised that what was to be restored was a new wine requiring new wineskins. The wineskins are the form that the diaconate may take in order to meet the needs of new times and to respond to the needs in new and fresh ways. We have seen that making of the new wineskins has been hampered by a raft of objections and, dare I say it, objectional practices that marginalise and demonise deacons. In the light of a sacramental theology, we need to challenge these objections and practices because they erode Catholic faith in the sacraments and frequently display a lack of charity that erodes communion in the Church. We must frankly admit that these objections to the diaconate are also a rejection of the grace which Christ offers the Church. The making of new wineskins has also been hampered by trying to fit the diaconate into the old wineskins of the transitional diaconate and *presbyteral* ministry focused on leadership of a parish. I think we can agree that the task of making new wineskins for this new wine remains ahead of us.

One of the other tasks that lie ahead of us is letting go of a cherished model. When we move away from restrictive notions of the deacon as being primarily defined by service, as the minister of charity, or social justice, which is at present the dominant paradigm, other creative possibilities emerge. This is not to say that an individual deacon may in fact be called to primarily focus on charity and justice. Deacons are primarily those who proclaim the Gospel, in the name of their bishop, to the assembled community and those dispersed. Like the bishop, whom they serve, they have a *diakonia* to build up the community of faith and reach out to dispersed Christians and to those who have yet to hear the Gospel.

Restricting our understanding of deacons as principally servants of charity and justice not only reveals a disregard for the Scriptural witness but leads to sterile debates about the identity of deacons and closes our eyes to new possibilities for the new evangelisation to which deacons are called to contribute. When we look to the Scriptures and the early tradition of the Church, we see those who are described as *diakonos*/deacons engage in a vast array of activities. Only some of their activities would include what we call charity or justice. We need to let go of the servant myth in order to receive fruitfully the gift of the Spirit which is the ministry of deacons. It is to this task that we turn our attention in the next chapter.

FOUNDATIONS ON SAND: THE DOMINANT PARADIGM

Readers will be familiar with Jesus' parable about a house built on foundations of sand (Matthew 7:26). Such houses are likely to be destroyed and swept away when rain and floods come. The dominant paradigm of the theology of ministry – as it has developed in the twentieth and twenty-first centuries both in Roman Catholic and Protestant theological traditions – is a theology built on foundations on sand. This is especially true of the theology of ministry as it has developed for the ministry of deacons. In this chapter, we will explore the foundations for the house that is the "theology of diaconate". Our attention will be directed more fully toward the diaconate in this volume. We will explore why the foundations, which are the dominant theological paradigm, may be considered as unstable sand and therefore make the house vulnerable to destruction by a flood. We shall see that in fact the flood has arrived and the house has collapsed. I suggest that some theologians and ministers in the Church live in the house that has collapsed around them but live in a state of denial. Perhaps the denial is more a case of disbelief and disorientation rather than blindness to their situation.

The Nobel Prize for medicine and physiology in 2005 was presented to two Australians, Robin Warren and Barry Marshall, who made a discovery that turned conventional medical wisdom on its head. Through a process of careful observation and experimentation, they were able to demonstrate that stomach ulcers were the result of inflammation causes by a bacterium (*Helicobacter pylori*) and as a result treatment would require only a short course of antibiotics. All that had previously been believed and taught in medical schools and written in textbooks about the causes and treatment of stomach ulcers has had to be abandoned. What Warren and Marshall achieved was the equivalent of a Copernican revolution in medical science and human physiology. They shattered the dominant paradigm. We may consider the previous foundations for stomach ulcer causes and treatment as being built on sand and we were ignorant of this until the research washed away those foundations. That house collapsed and was rebuilt with new foundations. The key lesson here is that because the new research was accepted, a better and stronger house could be constructed.

Significant paradigm shifts like this require deeper reflection within the communities in which they occur. Adjustments have to be made to new ways of thinking and speaking about phenomena of which we had been previously so certain and which are now presented in a new light. A process of reception and assimilation follows such dramatic paradigm shifts.¹ In the case of scholarly discoveries, the information will be disseminated through journals, conferences and education programs which will have to be adjusted to take account of the new discovery. For Warren and Marshall, the ready acceptance by the medical community may have been hastened through having been named winners of a prestigious international prize that is the Nobel.

A discovery of no less magnitude, at least in the world of Biblical studies and theology, has been made by John N. Collins, also an Australian, in regard to the *diacon* group of words in the Second Testament and extra-Biblical sources. His work represents a paradigm shift in our understanding of ministry in general and the diaconate in particular. The *diacon* group of words supply our ministry type words in the Second Testament and, of course, one of those words, *diaconos*, has found its way into English and most other languages as a Greek loan word which names a type of Christian minister, a deacon. Collins' discovery is on the same scale as the Warren and Marshall's discovery in terms of how it has fundamentally overturned the accepted wisdom.

The significance of this discovery was described in terms of a paradigm shift and as "challenging a dogma of New Testament scholarship" by Jerome Murphy O'Connor in his review of Collins' major work on this word group.² In

---

1 I am drawing on the concepts of paradigm and paradigm shift as developed in the work of Thomas Kuhn (2012) *The Structure of Scientific Revolutions*. Fourth edition. University of Chicago Press: Chicago
2 Jerome Murphy O'Connor review John N. Collins *Diakonia* (1990), in *Revue Biblique* 102/1 (1995),151-153

his study *Diaconia: Reinterpreting the Ancient Sources*, Collins has shattered the accepted and conventional wisdom that emerged around the meaning of *diacon* words since the nineteenth century and along with it the accepted paradigm for the theology of ministry that has prevailed throughout the twentieth century and into our own.[3]

The dominant paradigm about the theology of *diacon*ate is that it is primarily a ministry of lowly service, social work and charitable activity. It is bound closely to the caritative (charity) words or the words for love and loving service in most commentary on this ministry. Most of the theology concerning the ministry of deacons and their spirituality has focused on service to others and in some sense of charitable service or care and concern for the poor and marginalised as the distinguishing or primary characteristic of diaconal ministry. One scholar interpreting diaconate through this lens asks; "Can we see in the institution of the Seven in Acts chapter six, the institution of the first directors of Catholic health care?"[4] Deacons are presented in many texts and journals on diaconate as being something like ordained social workers.[5] The service lens is so dominant that modern translators of the Bible, at least since the 1940s, have had to make their own interpolations and scribal additions into

---

[3] John Collins; *Diaconia: Reinterpreting the Ancient Sources*. OUP, London 1990. The work will be referred to as *Diaconia*.

[4] Phyllis Zagano (2004) *Called to Serve: A Spirituality for Deacons*. Ligouri Press: Ligouri, pp. 38-43

[5] William Ditewig (2015) *The Deacon's Ministry of Charity and Justice*. Liturgical Press: Collegeville. James Keating (2015) *The Heart of the Diaconate: Communion with the Servant Mysteries of Christ*. Paulist Press: New York. Stephanie Dietrich et al (2014) *Diakonia as Christian Social Service*. Wipf and Stock: Eugene

the texts of Scripture to make the text of Scripture align with the dominant servant paradigm and the major theological dictionaries in which such an interpretation had been imbedded until *Diaconia* was published in 1990.

Dominant images and interpretations can have profound effects on how we hear and read a text. To illustrate with three examples gathered from my own experience in facilitation of adult faith education classes, we can see how received wisdom can distort what we read. In adult education classes, I have had participants shocked to discover; that there is no apple in the text of the Fall in Genesis, that Matthew's Gospel does not say there were three magi just more than one and that there is no horse from which Paul could fall in his conversion story in Acts. All of these simple assumptions, although of little significance, get in the way of reading even before any exegesis takes place. It is not surprising then to find that Biblical translators, commentators and others, relying on a prior understanding of what a deacon is, have to find ways of squaring the text of the Bible with the received interpretation.

This prior understanding, which forms the dominant paradigm, has developed from two main sources. First, the lived experience of the ministry of deacons especially in the Lutheran and Reformed churches model which found its way into the Catholic interpretation of the ministry. The second source which is the major theological dictionaries of the Second Testament in which the semantic profile of the *diacon* words had previously been described by such concepts as servant of the poor, lowly service and charity.⁶

Since the 1940s, translators of the Bible have made their scribal additions to the text of Acts 6:1-7. To the nature of the complaint the Greeks make about the source of the neglect of their widows in 6:1, translators insert either of these words "of food" or "of funds" and to Acts 6:2 where the Apostles propose a solution so that they can remain devoted to prayer and preaching, say they are "not to wait *on* tables", translators insert the preposition "on" before the word tables. It is important for us to note at this point that not a single Greek manuscript of Acts 6:1-7 contains any of these words – 'food', 'funds', or 'on', and that no translation of this text contains these words prior to the 1940s. While these interpolations or scribal additions are seemingly small, they represent an attempt on the part of translators to keep the meaning of the text of Acts 6 within the accepted meaning of diaconate that had come from the two sources mentioned above.

I am not suggesting any fault or blame in this. I only want to make the observation that it is the accepted dominant paradigm that guides the translation process and forces the scribal additions. If the paradigm were to shift, then the scribal additions would not be necessary to make the text align with the dictionaries and the practice of diaconal ministry as one predominantly characterised by charitable

---

6 We find in texts such as Wilhelm Brandt (1931) *Dienst und Dienen im Nuen Testament,* a typical definition of diaconia on page 71: diaconia- "a plain helping activity, a service rendered to the neighbour, not a service as rendered to a master whom one serves... not service in relation to obedience but in relation to the neighbour." This is a complete inversion of the actual meaning of *diaconia*.

service or lowly service or concern for social justice and such related concepts.

Nor is it surprising that theological reflection on the diaconate, also based on the service paradigm, arrives at a kind of social work model. This theology is based on the translation of Acts developed in such a way as to align dictionary and practice with the text. The circular and ultimately false reasoning of the service paradigm continues to feed a theology of the ministry of deacon and a flourishing servant spirituality of the diaconate that simply cannot be sustained. This will become clear as we trace the history of this development. We need to note here that this same false paradigm influences the theology of ministry generally, and some trends in ecclesiology which speak incorrectly of a diaconal church and our interpretation of key Christological texts such as Mark 10:45. Discussion of these last three is beyond the scope of the present work.

The texts of Acts 6 will be considered in some detail later but we need to make note of a few points about it before we move on. First, we must note that it has featured significantly in the development of the theology of the ministry of deacons. Many authors developing a theology or spirituality of diaconate considered Acts 6 as a foundational text for the ministry and indeed as the text which purports to give an account of the establishment of this ministry. We owe this idea to Eusebius' *Ecclesiastical History* and the attribution to Irenaeus of Lyon, who in the second century provided this interpretation of the text.[7] We also need to note that this

---

7   Eusebius, *The Church History*, (Book 2.1.1.) transl. Paul L. Maier (Grand Rapids: Kregel Publications, 1999), 57

interpretation lacks significant supporting evidence because the key word, *diaconos*, is missing. *Diaconos* is the noun form of the *diacon* word group, from which we derive our Greek loan word deacon. We need to note also that the Second Vatican Council does not appeal to Acts 6 in its consideration of the restoration of the ministry of deacon largely because of the ambiguity of the meaning of the text and the absence of the key word *diaconos*.[8] Finally we need to note that those who do depend on this text for their theology or spirituality of the ministry of deacon do so in the post 1940s translations with its scribal additions.

Diaconia: reinterpreting the ancient sources

John N. Collins did not commence his work on the semantic profile of the *diacon* group of words in the 1970s because he had an interest in the theology of ministry or an interest in deacons. His focus for his doctoral dissertation was a Christological text – Mark 10:45. He was interested in the meaning of the *diacon* words in the text, which are rendered into English as 'serve' and 'served': "For the Son of man himself came not to be served (*diaconairthenai*), but to serve (*diaconairsai*), and to give his life as a ransom for many."[9] What was the meaning of the service the Son of Man was to accomplish and who was he serving in its accomplishment? These were the questions that he wanted to explore. In order to answer these exegetical questions, he asked a more fundamental question: how did Greek speakers understand

---

8   ITC para. 40
9   Mark 10:45 from *New Jerusalem* Bible. Darton Longman & Todd. London. 1985

these *diacon* words in the period prior to, contemporary with and after the composition of the Gospel text under consideration? His study surveyed multiple sources from poetry, drama, legal texts, Biblical texts, other religious texts, descriptions of banquets and many other contexts in which the *diacon* words were used. What he wanted to achieve was a semantic profile of this group of words.

He was the first scholar to undertake the systematic development of a semantic profile of these words. That he is the first, is extremely significant because a semantic profile was already in use, especially the influential BDAG (Bauer–Danker–Arndt–Gingrich); which covered a range of meaning familiar to many who know the theology of diaconate as it stands today:

> diacon- words presented diaconia as "the symbol of all loving care for others" and "a mark of true discipleship of Jesus." As applied to Jesus at Mark 10:45, "to serve" is "much more than a comprehensive term for any loving assistance rendered to the neighbour"; rather, it expresses the notion of "full and perfect sacrifice, as the offering of life which is the very essence of service, of being for others, whether in life or in death."[10]

The existing semantic profile influenced the translators of the Bible in the 1940s to make their scribal additions and

---

10 Refer to Bauer–Danker–Arndt–Gingrich (BDAG); A Greek–English Lexicon of the New Testament and Other Early Christian Literature. University of Chicago Press: Chicago. See editions prior to 2000 and after.

this profile influenced the development of the theology of ministry and of the diaconate. The dominant semantic profile, prior to Collins, was not based on research or any study of the semantic scope that could be derived from Greek usage in a careful study of sources. The profile was produced by observation of what deacons in the German Lutheran (Evangelical) Church were doing in the nineteenth century and following. That the semantic profile prior to Collins was lacking scholarly research foundations is of extreme significance for the present discussion. Before we look at the semantic profile developed by Collins, we need to see how the foundations of the dominant theological paradigm of servant, service, concern for the poor and similar, developed and found its way into influential documents such as BDAG.

The profile is deeply imbedded in Protestant theology of diaconate and the social organisation of charitable works conducted by these communities. The work is simply referred to as *diakonic* or the *diakonic* mission of the Church. It also gives rise to such terms as the diaconal Church, meaning a serving or servant church. The same words find expression in some Catholic theology too. The International Diaconate Centre's 2017 conference was about "healing in a Diaconal Church". The entire edifice of this Protestant program of charitable works and institutions which support them is built on this profile and this profile is not built on the Scriptural foundations its promoters claim. Anni Hentschel arrives at this conclusion in her own work on the *diacon* profile;

> In the 19th century the concept of *"Diakonie"* was introduced as the foundation for the offices of deaconesses and deacons. This concept

owes much less to biblical terminology, however, than people thought. Judged from the perspective of biblical sciences, a number of errors of interpretation occurred. Some of these, we must say, were "productive" mistakes in that they contributed in practice to a strengthening of love of neighbour. Nevertheless, the idea that *Diakonie* should develop in its practitioners a special kind of humble service and self-denial is far from what the biblical text means.[11]

Since the nineteenth century revival of the diaconate in the Protestant Churches, notably the Lutheran Church in Germany, the myth of deacon as servant has developed as the dominant received wisdom. The myth has no foundation in the Biblical evidence. Collin's work shatters the myth and a new paradigm has to take hold. Jerome Murphy O'Connor, a pre-eminent Scripture scholar, correctly assessed the impact of Collins' discovery when he wrote, "This work will mean a major revision of the accepted dogmas of Biblical interpretation". Unlike the immediate reception of the work of Warren and Marshall, the paradigm shift has only partially occurred since Collins published his findings in 1990. Unless

---

11 "Diakonie in der Bibel" in Klaus-Dieter K. Kottnik and Eberhard Hauschildt, eds, *Diakoniefibel: Grundwissen für alle, die mit Diakonie zu tun haben* (Gütersloh: CMZ Gütersloher Verlag, 2008), 17-20, citing p. 20; see also her "Gibt es einen sozial-karitativ ausgerichteten Diakonat in den früchristlichen Gemeinden? ["In the early church did a diaconate exist that was characterised by charitable service?"], Pastoral theologue 97 no. 9 (2008): 290-306, in which her response is a definitive negative.

churches, theologians and those interested in the diaconate begin to engage with Collins' work, no real progress can be made in our understanding of the diaconate and reinterpreting it for the life of the Church today. This chapter will attempt to give a brief history of the development of the servant myth, then briefly examine Collin's main findings and conclude with some initial considerations for the reinterpretation of the diaconate.

Development of the myth

It is frequently argued that the distinctive or primary character of deacons is that they are servants called to the charitable and social justice ministry of the Church. The belief that service is distinctive of deacons is the servant myth. It is based on a false reading of Acts 6 and it has consequences for the way in which the Church receives the ministry of deacons. Breaking down this myth is the first step in restoring an authentic diaconate in the life of the Church.

Diaconate as a permanent order in the Roman Catholic Church almost completely ceased around the 11th century although there were exceptions right up until the 19th century. One may recall St Francis was a deacon, Pope Hadrian V was a deacon (who never got around to being ordained bishop) and the last Cardinal Deacons who were actually deacons and not bishops (which is the current practice) were; Teodolfo Mertel, a layman, who was named cardinal by Pope Pius IX in 1858 and received ordination to the diaconate later in the same year, and Giacomo Antonelli, who died in 1876 as Pius IX's Cardinal Secretary of State, who remained a deacon when named cardinal in 1847.

Diaconate survives as a transitional order prior to ordination as a *presbyter* (mostly referred to as priests), and usually for a period of twelve months, during which time the about to be ordained *presbyter* gains some pastoral experience. It survives in dioceses where there is no permanent ministry of deacon as well as in those in which that permanent ministry exists. The emphasis in this transitional period is not on diaconal ministry *per se* but training and preparation for *presbyteral* ministry, more narrowly described as the priesthood.

Canonically and sacramentally, the so-called transitional deacon is in fact a member of the order of deacons. If he did not proceed to *presbyteral* ordination, he would remain a deacon with all of the rights and obligations of diaconal ministry and bound to celibacy. His diocese would be obliged under canon law to afford him his rights to sustentation which includes his remuneration and care for him as it would any *presbyter*.

These are the same rights for permanent deacons, as there is only one order of deacon. (CIC Chap 3 *The Rights and Obligations of Clerics* and can 288 for derogations.) This transitional deacon could apply for laicisation after ordination if he wanted to, but such laicisation should not be presumed automatic, if we are to honour our doctrine about the nature of Holy Orders. The so-called transitional deacon is ordained as a deacon because of the persistence of the *cursus honorum* or course of honours through which a man ascended to the "higher orders". We will look at the *cursus honorum* in some detail later.

Catholics understand that such "transitional deacons" are sacramentally deacons but the sociological and psychological reality is quite different from this. This is acutely evident whenever there are transitional deacons present at the Chrism Mass in a diocese that has permanent deacons. The transitional deacon will normally spend all of his time chatting with the *presbyters* when all the clergy are vesting for the liturgy. When the master of ceremonies calls for the clergy to line up in processional order, he will finally join the deacons but with some look of embarrassment at having to do so. Immediately after the liturgy, he will re-join his *presbyteral* colleagues. Even though both the transitional and permanent deacons are clerics with all the same rights and obligations (apart from the specific derogations provided in the law, Can 288), only the rights of the transitional deacon will be honoured and he will receive financial support from his parish and diocese in accordance with the universal and local law, during his time of pastoral placement.

One *presbyter* confided to me that he spent his entire diaconal placement year wearing his stole over the right and not left shoulder and not even the *presbyter* of the parish commented, if he noticed. All Catholics know, as does the transitional deacon, that this man is an apprentice *presbyter* and his diaconal ordination is merely the final step before his 'real' ordination. Most *presbyters* and bishops will remember for their anniversary of ordination the date of their *presbyteral* ordination and not their diaconal one. So, although it may be canonically true that all *presbyters* and bishops were once deacons, the psychological and sociological reality is far from that, and I will challenge later the idea that such a transitional order is actually the same thing as the permanent ministry of deacon.

In Christian communities that developed after the Reformation, the diaconal ministry largely disappeared from the time of the Reformation until it made a reappearance as a non-ordained or lay ministry in the Lutheran Church in Germany during the 19th century. Calvin had a place for a person called a deacon in his church structure but this was not an ordained ministry and was and still is largely confined to collecting the money from the congregation to support the work of the church and the maintenance of the church buildings in those communities, such as the Presbyterians, which follow in Calvin's tradition.

The motivation for the re-introduction of deacons to Lutheran Churches was not primarily theological but pastoral. It was a special project of Lutheran Pastor Theodore Fliedner and his wife Frederike. The Lutheran communities which introduced deacons did not do so as an ordained ministry but as a kind of outreach worker specialising in the corporal works of mercy in order to meet the needs of the poor, the sick, abandoned children and prisoners. Sometimes communities of men and women deacons were formed and supported by local congregations to undertake this social work and live in a Deacon or Deaconess House. These communities of women and men deacons are similar in many ways to Roman Catholic apostolic Religious Institutes such as the Sisters of Mercy or Sisters of Charity for women and the Marist Brothers or Christian Brothers for men. Like their Roman Catholic counterparts, the Lutheran deacon house members shared a common house, property and prayer and most wore a distinctive religious dress like a habit and, like Sisters and Brothers, were not ordained.

The Fliedner's chose the word deacon/deaconess to describe these non-ordained women and men based on their own reading of Acts 6. They saw reflected in this text a decision of the Church to meet the needs of the widows who were being overlooked in the daily distribution of food or funds and based their own movement on this interpretation. They made no effort to ground their understanding of the story in exegesis of the text, or to enquire what the *diacon* words might have meant within the life of the first Christian communities. Nor were they deterred by the fact that the word *diaconos* (deacon) does not appear in the text. Instead, they relied in the claim by Irenaeus that the Seven were deacons.

So embedded did this 19th century understanding of diaconate – as service to the poor and acts of charity or social concern – become in the German speaking world that eventually it would give rise to the German neologism, *diaconie*. *Diaconie* denotes Christian social service or expressions and acts of social concern and indicates the social work or social justice mission of the Church. A similar progression occurred in other European languages and begins to form the dominant paradigm for diaconal ministry in the Nordic diaconal experience and spreads throughout various Protestant communities such as the Uniting Church and Methodist Church. The mis-identification of these words infects the theology of ministry as it develops in the twentieth century and the ecclesiology that depends on this dominant paradigm.

Up till now, I have used the image of a house built on sand but I want to introduce another metaphor briefly. The mis-identification of the *diacon* word group with the various words for charity and social service may be considered like a genetic mutation. When a mutation occurs in a gene the mutation is passed on to all subsequent generations. The "*diacon* gene" experienced a mutation during the nineteenth century and following. The defective gene was passed on to its offspring – the restored diaconate in the Lutheran and subsequently other churches, and through the theology of ministry as it developed in Protestant and Catholic sources during the twentieth century.

The mutation was passed on through the theological dictionaries of the Second Testament and the mutation passed into ecclesiology via the creation of the language of a '*diaconal* church' which finds its first expression in the 1960s. Finally, the mutation is passed on to the restored diaconate in the Roman Catholic tradition. For the Catholics, the expression of the mutation has not been as strong as it is in the Protestant tradition, but is still present. Perhaps protection against the mutation may be found in some other dominant "genes" which are carried in sacramental theology and the theology of holy orders in the Catholic Church. To extend the metaphor further, what is required now is gene therapy, to see if we can repair the defect and produce healthy offspring once again. We can begin some of the attempt to correct the faulty gene by going back to some of the most cherished Scriptural texts which provide some of the foundations for the servant myth and try to correct the genetic mutations as we find them there.

What happens in Acts 6.1-7?

Is Acts 6 the starting point for the ministry of deacons? This problem constitutes a question in its own right. If that text is taken as paradigmatic for the ministry of deacon, how should we interpret the text?[12] What therefore can we say from this text that constitutes the essential element of the ministry of deacons? We need to keep in mind that the Second Vatican Council did not appeal to this text in its decision to restore the permanent ministry of deacon and that the noun for deacon does not occur in the text. Since Acts 6 is so deeply implicated in the development of the servant myth, we need to examine the text closely.

Frequently, readers assume that the Seven were called to meet the material needs of the Greek widows who were neglected at the daily ministry or ministrations. Therefore, the service they were called to perform is some form of charitable service. This understanding of what is happening, it is argued, establishes the authentic and distinctive character of deacons. This is the beginning of the deacon as "servant myth". This myth is a belief that the distinctive and defining characteristic of a deacon and diaconal ministry is service, usually in the form of charity, especially to the poor and those on the margins of Church and society. It is a myth that continues to distort our understanding of the diaconate and hampers the full reception of the fruits of this restored ministry. Curiously, it never seems to touch the transitional diaconate, which is accepted without question or indeed

---

12 Keep in mind that some people do regard the text as the foundation of the diaconate. Vatican II does not make that judgement and does not appeal to the text.

much reflection, at least in the Roman Catholic tradition. If service is the distinctive quality of the diaconate, what does this say about the service dimension of the other ordained ministries and the mission life of the Church?

Diaconia is a word Roman Catholics use to describe the ministry of the bishop and it is the only instance of such use without any sense that the word is restricted to social justice or charity (*Lumen gentium* 24). Surely all ministers are called to imitate Christ the servant and a similar attitude should pervade the whole church. I do not argue that deacons cannot have or will not have a charitable or service role, only that it is not the distinctive character of their ministry. The myth does not have its genesis in Acts but is shaped by revival of the diaconate in nineteenth century German Lutheran church, reinforced by translators' choices which shape our understanding of Acts and Catholic reflections on diaconate in post war Germany in the 1940s and 50s. I intend to explore the origins of the myth and suggest why it is not a sound basis for a theology and praxis of the diaconate. The most recent documents of the Roman Catholic tradition on diaconate contain layers of tradition but it is possible to perceive an outline of diaconate that is balanced and avoids the servant myth as a foundation.

Making sense of Acts

In the rendering of Acts 6.1-7 into English (or any other language) translators take some liberties with the Greek text and, like the scribes of ancient times, made their adjustments to the text to make sense of it.[13] The choices translators make have influenced the way we hear and make meaning of this text. In verse one, the cause for the complaint of the Greek speaking Christians, is variously given as a neglect of the widows in the daily distribution *of food* (NRSV), *of funds* (GNB) and *of food* (JB).[14] The RSV is happy to leave the neglect simply at an unspecified daily distribution or ministrations.

The Greek manuscript tradition does not provide any instances of the preposition *of* or the terms *food* and *funds* and in this the RSV reflects the original Greek text. The Greek text does indicate what is being missed in the daily distribution and this can be inferred from the whole context of Acts 6:1-7 and broadly within the use of *diaconia* in the text of Acts as a whole and we shall come to that shortly. It would hardly seem likely that either food or funds could be intended because Acts 5 deals with what happens to disciples who try to neglect others in the distribution of the material goods of the community.[15] Could the Christian community have failed to learn from such a shocking lesson so that in the next verse they are again holding back from what is to be shared?

In 6:2, the apostles complain about not wanting to neglect the word and wait *on* tables (NRSV), neglect the

---

[13] John N. Collins; *Deacons and the Church: Making Connections Between Old and New*. Gracewing, Leomister, 2002, pp. 47-58 The same problem may be found in most translations of this text in most languages since the 1940s.

[14] NRSV is the *New Revised Standard Version Bible: Catholic Edition*. Thomas Nelson, 1990, GNB is the *Good News Bible*, American Bible Society 1976, JB is the *Jerusalem Bible*, Darton, Longman and Todd, 1966. RSV is *Revised Standard Version* 1946.

[15] If the reader is not convinced read Acts 5 before reading on in this book.

preaching and *manage finances* (GNB), neglect the word *to give out food* (JB) and to give up preaching to serve tables (RSV). Again, it is the RSV which resists the temptation to add anything to the text and it does not insert a preposition "on" which is not found in the Greek manuscripts between the words serve and tables nor does the RSV add references to finances or food.

In 6:4, all translators are certain about prayer and with dealing with the word we are most interested in – *diaconia*, which is translated in the way it is most normally used in Acts and the letters of Paul. *Diaconia* is translated here as ministry and in the context of the whole sentence, and Acts in general, as a ministry of the word (*diaconia tou logou*). We should note that the qualifications for the Greek speakers to be selected for this task are that they are to be "full of the Holy Spirit and wisdom" (Acts 6:3). They are not selected because of their ability in mathematics, logistics or other skills which may prove useful if the question was one of a fair and adequate share of food or funds. Wisdom and the presence of the Holy Spirit would be very useful for those primarily tasked with a ministry of proclaiming the Gospel.

If we take the Greek text as it is reproduced in the RSV, we are able to construct a better picture of what is really happening in Acts 6.1-7. The Greek speaking Christians are complaining that their widows are being neglected in the daily *diaconia*. In Acts, *the diaconia* is the proclamation of the Gospel or the ministry of the Word.[16] They are neglected for

---

16 John N. Collins; *Deacons and the Church*, p. 52. I add the emphasis here to indicate that the unifying meaning of *diaconia* in Acts is the ministry of proclaiming the gospel and is used throughout of the work of the apostles, Paul and the other ministers of the Gospel. As

two reasons: the Aramaic speaking Apostles predominantly concentrate their proclamation in the Temple; and the widows, who cannot comprehend the language and for social reasons are mostly restricted to the home, are overlooked in this daily *diaconia*. That the primary problem is a linguistic one is underscored by the word the author of Acts uses for Greeks. He had available to him at least two words for Greeks and one of these identified people who are ethnically Greek while the other denotes speakers of Greek or those whose primary language is Greek. It is the latter term which is employed here.[17] The solution proposed by the Apostles and agreed to by the whole Church is to appoint seven from among the Greek speaking community to do that daily *diaconia* in the homes of the Greek speaking widows or as the expression in the Greek has it, to minister (*diaconein*) tables (*trapezeis*).[18]

Both the Apostles and the Seven had been entrusted with the same *diaconia* which is to minister or proclaim the word. In the prayer and laying on of hands, a share of the apostolic ministry is handed on to the Seven by the

---

cited in John N. Collins, The problem with values carried by diakonia / "Diakonie" in recent church documents.

17   Luke Timothy Johnson (1992) *Sacra Pagina: The Acts of the Apostles*. Liturgical Press: Collegeville. Pp. 104-113.

18   John N. Collins; *Diaconia: reinterpreting the ancient sources*. Oxford University Press, Oxford, 1990. Collins' ground breaking study of the whole family of *diacon-* words in the Bible and extra-biblical sources indicates that service and charity are simply not part of the field of meaning of the word *diaconia* and that the phrase 'minister tables' had a particular resonance with the Greek speaking community as a sacred duty by which one was delegated to perform a ministry of significance and was not confused in Greek usage with the ordinary meaning of servers of food and drink. This distinction is found in the texts of the early Greek Fathers e.g. Ignatius, Trallians, 2.3.

Apostles. To underscore this interpretation, we see that Stephen immediately commences to proclaim the Gospel to the point of giving witness with his life (Acts 6-7.50) and Philip commences his *diaconia* of the word in proclaiming the Gospel, catechising the Ethiopian and baptising (Acts 8) and the only other mention of Philip in Acts (21:8) simply calls him "Philip the evangelist (proclaimer of the Gospel), one of the Seven". The laying on of hands becomes the concrete sign that the ministry entrusted to the apostles is to be entrusted to the Seven.

The thing we do not see the Seven do is charitable works or distributing food or funds to the widows; in fact, we do not see anyone in the New Testament with the title of *diaconos* engaged in a specifically charitable service activity. To point us in the right direction for interpreting the text of Acts 6 the author concludes that "the Word of God continued to spread and the number of disciples increased" (Acts 6:7). If the author had wanted to really say something about food and funds for the widows, he would have indicated the successful outcome with a conclusion telling us something like: and now every one of the Greek widows received her fair share of the funds/food, and he may have been tempted to say they all lived happily in the community ever after. This short exposition of the text should give us some clues as we address the servant myth.

In this text, the Seven are never given the title of *diaconos* but they are called to the ministry of the word (*diaconia tou logou*) and so perhaps the author of Acts had no need of the noun because it is implied in their being appointed to this ministry. We also need to keep in mind that at this very early stage of the life of the Church formal titles of office were not present as we came to understand them in later centuries. Whether or not the Seven were the first deacons, as history calls them, is debateable. The one word that Luke does not use of them is *diaconos* the noun from which we get our word deacon.

Proclaiming the word, leading communities, representing communities and taking messages between communities and other forms of ministry are associated with those who are called *diaconos* in the New Testament. Also associated with those called *diaconos* is the clear delegation and imposition of a mandate for such ministry by the leaders of the community or in Paul's case by the Lord himself (1 Corinthians 3:5, Ephesians 3:7, Romans 15:5, 2 Corinthians 8:19-20). The laying on of hands, which occurs in this text, is a traditional motif symbolising the handing on of a mandate, a practice which will be preserved in the ritual tradition of the Church for ordination and some other rites. Therefore, it is reasonable to infer that the Seven may have been referred to as deacons in the early Church and that later sources reflect that understanding.[19]

How did *diaconia* become service?

We do not have space here to review the many references to deacons in the first nine centuries of the Church, and in particular the first four centuries when so much of the structure of ministries in the early Church was taking shape. A few brief references, taken from the Fathers and used again

---

19   Collins, in the works cited, would conclude that the Seven were not deacons. See his Deacons and the Church p49

in the recent Roman Catholic documents, are testament to an earlier tradition, before *diaconia* was defined as service and deacons as a kind of ordained social worker/charity worker. Three references will suffice to indicate the flavour of this early tradition. Ignatius to the Magnesians, "deacons are entrusted with the ministry/*diaconia* of Christ" and to the Trallians, "deacons are not waiters (*diaconoi*) providing food and drink but executives (*huperatai*) of the Church of God" and finally to the Philadelphians, "take care to use only one Eucharist... there is one bishop in union with the *presbyters* and the deacon."

The earliest witnesses of the tradition reflect the common Greek usage as we shall see when we come to a more complete consideration of Collins. Deacons were not thought of as having a distinctive servant orientation but as part of the broader understanding of the apostolic ministry and leadership of local churches. A recent study from Bart Koet reveals that, in these texts of Ignatius cited above, there is compelling evidence that during the time of Ignatius of Antioch there is still only a dyadic ministry operative in the Church; *episcopos* (bishop) and *diaconos* (deacon).[20] *Presbyters* (*presbyteroi*), he argues, had not yet emerged as part of the active ministry of the Church but functioned as their name suggests, as elders. They seemed to have acted as a council of elders to advise the bishop. Beyond that advisory role they seemed to have no ministerial function and were not associated with priestly (*sacerdotal*) functions. At this period of time, it was the bishop who presided at Eucharist and is

---

20 Bart Koet unpublished paper presented at Diakonia Symposium, University of East Finland, Joensuu. 2017

sometimes known in sources contemporary with Ignatius as priest or high priest *hiereus* or *achehirereus*.

Although it is a broad leap from the early tradition, we need to look to Trent (16th century). By the time the Reformation was underway, the diaconate had become a transitional ministry of limited liturgical functions in the Roman Catholic Church. Luther and others argued that the ministry, as they experienced it, had limited value in the life of the community and saw it more as an appendage to the ministry. The response of the Council of Trent was to insist on the reality and validity of the threefold ministry of deacon, priest (*presbyter*) and bishop as part of the divinely instituted nature of the Church.

Trent called for the restoration of the diaconate as a permanent ministry in the life of the Church. The Council did so in part because it conceded the point made by the Reformers that if diaconate was truly part of the order of the Church then we would have a permanent ministry of deacons alongside that of a permanent ministry of *presbyters* (almost always called priests at this time) and the permanent ministry of bishop. At the time, the episcopate was actually a part of what was effectively a mono-*presbyterate*. This is a topic to which we return later.

Trent's desire to restore the diaconate was not fulfilled until the Second Vatican Council was able to take up the issue again and Paul VI issued *Sacrum Diaconatus Ordinem* in 1967.[21] By 1998, the Congregations for Clergy and for Education issued jointly the *Basic Norms for the Formation of Permanent Deacons* and the *Directory for the Ministry and Life of Permanent*

---

21 Basic Norms and Directory, Introduction §2

Deacons. In these two documents, we find an outline of the teaching of the Roman Catholic Church on diaconate. Although I will come to these in more detail later, what we find in the documents is an interweaving of two traditions: an early tradition that frames diaconate within the broader understanding of the apostolic ministry of the Gospel and a narrower tradition from the 19th century servant myth with a focus on *diaconia* as a synonym for service. Behind these two traditions stand two sources. The first source is the Scriptural foundation which understands *diaconia* a ministry as outlined in the study by Collins. The second source is the revival of the diaconate in the German Lutheran churches in the nineteenth century specifically as a work of charity and social work. It is to this second source that we now turn our attention.

The transmission of a "genetic mutation"

A type of *diacon*ate was revived in the nineteenth century in the Lutheran Church in Germany and gradually this pattern of diaconate was adopted in the Nordic Lutheran and some of the Reformed churches. The Lutheran Pastor, Theodore Fliedner and his wife Frederike established a ministry to care for the homeless and poor who were increasing in number in the industrialised cities. This ministry was not an ordained ministry and was modelled somewhat on the lines of a Roman Catholic religious order as we saw above. The Fliedners took their inspiration from their understanding of Acts 6 as a ministry of charity to the widows who, in their reading of the text, were neglected in the daily distribution of charity and the goods of the community. They called the women in this ministry deaconess and the men deacons. To return to our genetic metaphor, this is the first mutation in the gene of the *diacon* group of words. Without any scholarly warrant or knowledge of the semantic scope of the *diacon* group of words, the Fliedners simply assign this meaning to them.

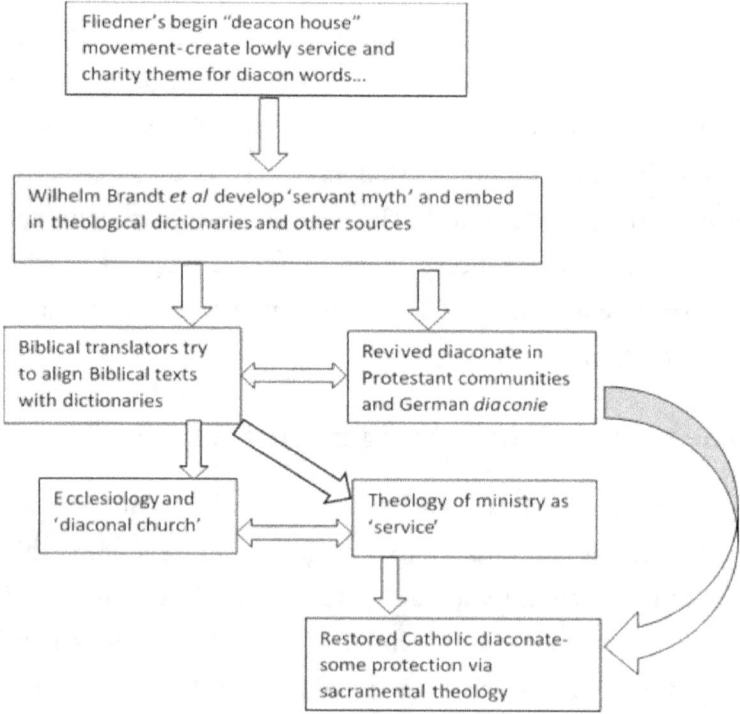

The second step in the development of the mutation is that those who are compiling theological dictionaries of the Second Testament and who will give scholarly credence to the semantic profile now developing, are themselves German Lutherans in contact with this deacon movement commenced by the Fliedners. Wilhelm Brandt who developed along with others a profile of the *diacon* group of words for

Biblical theological dictionaries was a chaplain to the deacon house movement.[22] In reaching for a definition of the *diacon* words, he did not reach back to the Greek usage, as Collins did, but to his experience of the deacon house movement and the charitable work of the deaconess and deacons in their loving concern for the poor and marginalised. Thus, he concluded from his experience of their charitable works, that the *diacon* group of words covered a semantic range that was indicative of charitable service, the social work of the church and perhaps extending to concern for social justice.

These *diacon* words, he argued, were specifically Christian in character as a reaction to a putative difference in leadership styles which characterised the non-Christians of the early New Testament era. He and others argued that Christians had chosen these *diacon* words because of their lowly, self-effacing humble service character as a way of designating what ministry and leadership should mean when it takes on Christian character. This pattern is repeated in all of the major lexicons of the Second Testament developed in the nineteenth and twentieth centuries.

Before we move too much further on this, we need to be reminded that the *diacon* word group are not words only about deacons (*diaconoi*). These *diacon* words are the words that most commonly designate ministry in the Second Testament and which the earliest translators of the Bible from Greek to Latin translated as *ministerium* from which are derived the basic words for ministry in English and most languages apart from German. Jesus is called a *diaconos* and Paul champions his right to be an apostle because he has a *diaconia* and his

---

[22] John N. Collins (2002); *Deacons and the Church*, pp. 5-13

collection for the Church in Jerusalem is described using words from this group too. The word group has significance far beyond deacons and are of significance for all that is written about ministry, some aspects of ecclesiology and, of course, Christology.

The astute reader may have already guessed the third mutation. Translators of the Bible are now influenced by the Greek lexicon on which they depend as a resource to translate passages they encounter in the Second Testament. They translate these in line with the dictionary definitions. They imbue their translations with words in their own language that reflect the lowly service and humble nature of what they believe in contained in the *diacon* words. They even add these words into texts where they do not appear. In at least two significant passages (John 13:1-17 and Philippians 2:4-11), many translators cannot resist translating the word *doulos* (slave) with the word servant. The word slave denotes, in Second Testament times, as it does today, an entirely different world of meaning from that of servant. In the world of the Second Testament, where slaves were prevalent and were powerless non-citizens without even a right to their own life, we can be sure that when the words are used they are used with full awareness of their meaning and would never be substituted by servant words. The idea that the word *doulos* could ever be substituted for *diaconos*, let alone the idea of the persons being interchangeable, is completely out of the question for them as we shall see.

The temptation to make the text align with the received semantic tradition is so powerful that the scribes of the modern era, called translators, find it had to resist adding words into the text of Acts 6:1-7, which many regard as the foundation for the ministry of deacon. We have seen this illustrated above when we examined translations made after the 1940s (JB, NRSV, GNB, NAB) with one made before that time, the RSV. If we go back to sixteenth century into a variety of vernacular languages, the service paradigm is not evident in translations.[23] Like their scribal ancestors, modern translators make their own emendations to the text to correct what they perceive as deficiencies. Since the received tradition tells them that the *diacon* words are about humble service, charity and love for another, they must make the text of Acts 6:1-7 fit that meaning. All that is necessary to make the text fit the paradigm is a few words added here and there to the Greek manuscript. Just small words like "food" or "funds" and even smaller words like the preposition "on" can be just enough to recast the story as one of charitable concern and care for the poor. In this way, the circle is closed, at least as far as the Scriptural sources are concerned.

The fourth and final mutation occurs when the defective gene enters theological discourse about ministry. Most of the initial discourse on ministry, found in the works of German scholars, is steeped in the defective semantic profile. The German discourse on ministry is further complicated by the fact that they did not inherit from Greek via Latin the words in the ministry range. They have only *Deinst*, *deinen* and *Ampt* on which to draw for their discussion, none of which words have roots in ministry or the *diacon* antecedents.[24] The

---

23   Collins (1990) *Diakonia*, pp. 30-35
24   Collins outlines the linguistic roots and problems in the diacon words and words for office and ministry. See *Diakonia Studies: critical Issues in Ministry* (2014) OUP: New York, Chapter 7. A Linguistic

one word they do possess with some linguistic similarity is the twentieth century neologism *diaconie*, which denotes Christian social service, influenced as it is by the semantic profile but not actually being one of the *diacon* words. It only sounds like one. We should note here that influential figures in the theology of ministry in general and of the diaconate in particular – Kasper, Ratzinger and Muller – are all German scholars who do not refer to the *diacon* words but call on *diaconie* instead, with all that the word means for a speaker of German. Ratzinger does this in his letter *Deus Caritas Est*, which is significant for the interpretation of that document.[25]

If further evidence is required of the problem of the mis-identification of the *diacon* words, then Sven Brodd's semantic study needs to be considered. Brodd argues that the identification of *diaconia* with charity (*caritas*) and social service developed into a functionalist understanding of diaconate. He suggests the deacon is defined not from an ecclesiological foundation, based on the Church as *koinonia*, situating ordination within this ecclesial context, but is defined inductively from the sum of the functions performed.[26] Throughout the eighteenth century, a functionalist understanding of ministry developed in Protestant theological circles, a development that would eventually flow into Roman Catholic theology. The result

---

muddle contributed to a theological muddle in ministry generally, ecclesiology, Christology and the theology of diaconate specifically

25 Benedict XVI (2006) Encyclical letter: *Deus caritas est*. St Pauls Publications: Strathfield.

26 Sven-Erik Brodd, Caritas and *Diacon*ia as perspectives on the *Diacon*ate, in Borgegard, Fanuelsen, Hall (eds) The *Ministry of the Deacon: Ecclesiological Reflections 2*, Nordic Ecumenical Council, 2000, pp. 42-43

is that in the Lutheran and Reformed traditions the deacon came to be seen as a kind of ordained social worker in those churches which began to ordain deacons.[27] In his study, Brodd concurs with the work of Collins and indicates that *caritas* and *diaconia* essentially belong to two different conceptual circles.[28] We shall see later how the work of a biblical scholar from Germany, Anni Hentschel, provides the final confirmation that this mis-identification is real.

This trend in a functionalist understanding of ministers was exacerbated in the twentieth century as a greater sense of the self as an independent agent began to emerge as psychology and sociology began to develop as disciplines. The development of role theory in psychology and sociology was applied to accounts for ministries in the church in terms of roles and associated functions. Social theories developed from these newly emerging disciplines began to shape discourse about ministries. Elements of these theories were and remain useful but to rely exclusively on them tends to distort the theological and especially sacramental foundations and interpretation of ministry. Added to this sense of autonomous self was a stream of social analysis following Foucault's analysis of social relations as being explained with reference to the exercise of power and power

---

[27] In the Nordic Lutheran Churches, deacons have had to obtain nursing or social work qualifications before being installed or ordained as deacons because charity was the defining feature of the understanding of *diacon*ate. The practice is changing across Northern Europe as more churches engage with the research of the Australian scholar John N. Collins. A *diacon*ate with a clearer scriptural and ecclesiological foundation is developing with a balance of a ministry of word, liturgy and pastoral aspects.

[28] Brodd, *Caritas and Diaconia*, p. 27

differentials between individuals. The relationship between clergy and laity came also to be described in terms of power over others and the power that came with roles in society. This is not to be confused with the Roman Catholic theology about the powers of Holy Orders.

I have already suggested that this servant myth encouraged translators to align other texts with the semantic profile developed in the theological dictionaries and lexicons of the Second Testament. At least one of these texts, John 13, has become a cherished motif of the theology of deacon and a primary symbolic representation of what is argued to be the essential characteristic of diaconal ministry. A second text, Philippians 2:4-11, has attracted attention in recent decades as another potential bearer of deacon motifs. We need to examine both texts because they are being translated and applied to life in the Church and its ministries in ways that reflect the dominant and false semantic paradigm. I argue that the manner in which these texts are being translated and applied to the diaconate is not justified.

John 13 Jugs and towels

Type the words 'deacon, basin, towel' into a search engine and within a few seconds half a million or more sites will respond to the search. Most of these sites will have something to do with the ministry of deacon in one or other Christian Church. Many Churches, not just Catholic ones, have adopted the symbol of the basin and the towel as part of the logo for their deacon ministry office and use these symbols on the covers of publications. There are numerous blog contributions, articles in journals and popular Christian publications, songs and conference papers from deacons and others about the basin, the towel and deacons. One only need survey on the internet for the symbols used by diocesan deacon offices to see that jugs and towels, a reference to John 13 and verses 1-16 in particular, predominate. Covers of books about deacons employ this image too. Most of the sources want to draw out how the basin and the towel are the pre-eminent symbols of a deacon's ministry and most will want to argue that what is revealed is the essence of the deacon's ministry as one of humble service.

It is very common for themes from this chapter of John, which concerns the washing of the feet by Jesus at the Last Supper, to be pressed into service in talks, books and symbols for the diaconate. Even the optional ritual of washing of the feet in Catholic parishes on Holy Thursday evening can take on the tones and orientation of humble service and charitable concern. The hymns that accompany this optional ritual reinforce the servant myth theology.

On Holy Thursday, 2013, Pope Francis enacted this interpretation of the ritual by choosing to wash the feet of juvenile offenders in a youth prison in Rome.[29] What Pope Francis did in the prison was a profoundly moving action and one which in various ways was repeated in Catholic parishes throughout the world. I do not deny that Christians actually have a calling toward loving care and concern of others. They do. What I want to demonstrate is a more limited project that the text of John 13 means much more than service and refers

---

29 Reported on new papers worldwide but also on Zenit News, March 21, 2013 (Zenit.org)

to a very particular kind of love. We should also note the very critical point that none of the *diacon* word group appear in John 13. That is none of our words associated with ministry or the ministry of deacons in particular appear in this text. Nor do any of the Greek words we might translate in some instances as servant.

There is no institution narrative of the Eucharist in the Gospel of John. In the synoptic Gospels (Matthew 26:26-29, Mark: 14:22-25, Luke 22:14-20) and Paul (1 Corinthians 11:23-26), we find an account of the Last Supper in which the words by which Jesus institutes the Eucharist are used, albeit in slightly different versions, each with their own theological emphasis. John does something very different in his narration of the Last Supper. In John's telling of the institution of the Eucharist, Jesus enacts a parable. That enacted parable is the washing of the feet of the disciples. It is through this enacted parable that Jesus communicates the meaning of Eucharist and links this celebration with his dying and his rising.

In applying this text to Christian living, and to the ministry of deacons in particular, those who do so take liberties with the text or at least do not allow the text to speak for itself. What tends to happen is the text is presented as an enacted parable but not of the Eucharist. It is presented as a parable of humble or self-effacing service or charitable love for another. I argue that we do so because we first, and incorrectly, imagine it to be part of the dominant servant paradigm. Preachers at Holy Thursday liturgy, aided and abetted by the choice of hymns and also theologians thinking about ministry and that of deacons in particular, start off on the wrong interpretative track by casting Jesus' action of washing the feet as something that would have been done by servants when guests arrived for a feast. Therefore Jesus, in substituting himself for the servant here, is being humble and self-effacing.

We can be certain that the foot washing that occurs in John 13 is not that foot washing to which preachers are fond of appealing. If we read the text and not read into it, then we notice that Jesus gets up from the table while they were at supper or during the meal (13:4). This is not the washing of dirty or dusty feet that would have occurred as guests arrived at the house and before they had entered beyond the entry point. Such a task would have been done by a slave or possibly a servant before they took their places or they would do it themselves if neither were present.

We can also be certain that such a task would never be performed by one with the title of *diaconos*. Such men had to be freeborn and of good standing and high honour to be called to such a task which would never include menial tasks like foot washing. We shall see this more clearly when we look at Collins' work on *diaconia*. The author of John's Gospel also knows this because he comes from that thought world and culture. This is why he does not include any of the *diacon* words in this text. Furthermore, if John wanted to make Jesus the substitute for this menial task of washing dirty feet as guests arrived, he would have written something like; "... and as the disciples arrived at the house where the supper was to be held, Jesus washed their feet before they entered into the supper room." But he does not write that.

John wants to say something much more profound than offering an exhortation to humble service of one another. The washing of the feet is the Eucharistic institution narrative enacted in a parable. To make sense of it we need to read it first in the context of the whole chapter and the place of this chapter within the Gospel. If we look at the text, the clues are there for us to provide this wider interpretation. The setting is on Passover eve (13:1). Notice the signals that this foot washing has a deeper context which are set out below.

13:1	Knowing that his hour had come
13:1	He loved them to the end
13:2	Knowing he would be handed over
13:3	He had come from God and was going to God
13:4	He rises (*egeiretai*) from the table
13:4	Lays aside (*titheirsin*) his outer garment
13:8	If I do not wash you, you can have no part with me (or be a part of me)
13:12	He had taken up (*elaben*) his garment
13:15	Pattern or paradigm (*hypodeigma*) I have given you
13:15	As (*kathos*) I did, so must you do
13:16	A slave (*doulos*) is not greater than his master
13:16	One who is sent (*apostolos*) is not greater than one who sent him
13:19	I am telling you now before it comes to pass
13:19	So that when it comes to pass you will know I am [he] (*ego eimi*)

We can see from this list that the context of the foot washing is the arrival of Jesus' final hour, when he will reveal the depth of his love, even to the very end, which has not yet fully arrived. It will arrive in the final sign when the Son of Man is lifted up and glorified on the Cross. Glorified is a word used eleven times in John and it is this word which actually provided the context for the Last Supper in 12:22-24. The last meal is the beginning of that time for Jesus to be glorified and for the Father to be glorified in the Cross. It is clear from the synoptic accounts and Paul that Jesus attempts some teaching and explanation for the disciples about the salvific meaning of his death and the link to Eucharist with the paschal mystery. The fact that they deny him, run from him and hide indicates that they did not understand what Jesus was doing in the institution of the Eucharist.

The washing of the feet in John is surrounded by exactly the same themes as are present in the synoptics. That is, we see Jesus reflecting on his impending death. Jesus indicates that he will be handed over by one of his own and even those who profess to stand by him will in fact disown him. He also tells them that now they do not understand but eventually they will. This understanding will not come until after the resurrection. In the midst of exactly the same setting as is found in the synoptics, Jesus does not take the bread and wine to enact the meaning of his dying and rising; instead, he washes their feet to teach the same point. John only uses the word for lays aside (*titheirsin*) and take up (*elaben*) in one other place and that is in the context of him laying aside his life to take it up again.[30] The allusion in John 13 to this laying aside and taking up only reinforces the paschal dimension

---

30   Francis Maloney (1998) *Sacra Pagina: The Gospel of John*. Liturgical Press: Collegeville. pp. 370-379

of this enacted parable and its link to the institution of the Eucharist.

Since the 1940s, translators have preferred to use servant in translating *doulos* instead of slave. No Greek manuscript has any other word but *doulos* here and so the change is not justified on manuscript grounds. Translators may have chosen the servant word because slave seems like such a remote and ancient concept to us. I suspect that the real reason is that translators in the modern era are influenced by the dominant servant paradigm which did not exert such an influence on earlier generations of translators. One step further along this chain, and because we have imagined or heard servant and because the dominant servant paradigm is meant to have something to do with deacons (because of the genetic mutation in the *diacon* words that occurred from the nineteenth century), some are led to associate the story with deacons. It has no such association.

A slave is not greater than their master. In the world in which the Gospel is written, the slave was a non-citizen and had no rights at all, even a right to continue living. A slave had no will of his own but could only do the will of the one who was his master. A slave was dependent on the will of the master and responsible for carrying out that will. What is Jesus saying here about his own relationship to the will of the Father? He says that he is like the slave whose will is identical to that of the master. Certainly, in this Gospel, Jesus doing the will of the Father is a consistent theme. Remember that all this is being said in the context of the final hour and the glorification of the Son and of the Father in the paschal mystery.

One who is sent is not greater than the one who sends him. This is true but we need to look deeper into the meaning this would have communicated to John's audience. One who is sent was not greater than, but he did represent the authority and the person of the one who sent him. This is why in the ancient world, it was considered such a grave offence to kill the messenger. In killing the messenger, who came in the name of and with the authority of the sender, it is the name and the authority of the sender to which the offence is directed. Both the one doing the killing and the one who sent knows what this means. It is unfortunate for the one sent that in this transaction, it is only the honour of the sender that must be avenged. What the disciples will eventually come to see for themselves, after Jesus' death and resurrection, is that he and the Father are one. Jesus, in fact, invokes the sacred name by simply saying *ego eimi*, I am. The resonance of this phrase comes through the Greek Septuagint version of the First Testament where the sacred name YHWH is rendered in Greek, *ego eimi*, I am.

The paradigm (*hypodeigma*) that Jesus sets for his community is to make the Eucharist the pattern of our lives, to make dying with him and rising with him the focus of our being. In this community, all are called to the same radical obedience to the will of God that Jesus is to reveal in the cross. We are to be drawn into the paschal mystery so that our lives take on a radical and new orientation. Jesus is not, therefore, acting out humble charitable service, like washing dirty feet, but enacting the institution of the Eucharist in which we do not take part as passive individuals but with the totality of our living. We are meant to be imitators of him by taking up our cross daily.

In Koine Greek, there are two words that can express "as": one is *hos* and the other *kathos*. The first one invokes a simple comparison; as in the sentence, "Marija had the same shirt as (*hos*) Katrina." All that we mean by this is that it is a coincidence or they went to buy their shirts at the same shop. But to say, "Vijaya has the same eyes as (*kathos*) her mother", means not only to compare but to make a causal attribution. In John 13:15, it is *kathos*. Therefore, we are being urged to follow the pattern just as Jesus has followed the will of God and to imitate him in this great love revealed in the cross and perpetuated in the Eucharist. Pope Francis says our lives should take on the shape of the Eucharist.[31] Perhaps the hymns that should accompany this ritual action of washing of feet on Holy Thursday, which would bring out the meaning more clearly, are ones about the cross and resurrection and

---

31 Pope Francis points to this reality at the end of *Laudato Si'* (paragraph 236): It is in the Eucharist that all that has been created finds its greatest exaltation.... He comes not from above, but from within, he comes that we might find him in this world of ours. In the Eucharist, fullness is already achieved; it is the living centre of the universe, the overflowing core of love and of inexhaustible life. Joined to the incarnate Son, present in the Eucharist, the whole cosmos gives thanks to God.... The Eucharist joins heaven and earth; it embraces and penetrates all creation. The world which came forth from God's hands returns to him in blessed and undivided adoration: in the bread of the Eucharist, "creation is projected towards divinization, towards the holy wedding feast, towards unification with the Creator himself" (quoting Pope Benedict XVI, homily for Corpus Christi, 2006). The person Pope Francis most quotes about Eucharist, about social justice and care of the environment is Benedict XVI and the next most quoted is Romano Guardini, a theologian both popes greatly admire. The Francis sayings on these topics people find most radical and challenging are usually those of Benedict XVI quoted by Francis.

the Eucharist, that is, the Paschal Mystery that we have commenced celebrating in the Triduum.

In this brief study of the text of John 13:1-16, we have seen that the text sheds no light on the meaning of diaconal ministry or how a deacon should minister. The text is a parable in action which elucidates the meaning of Jesus' death in the context of God's saving love. There is an exhortation in this text and it is addressed to all Christians, not specifically to deacons. It is incorrect to see in this text an exhortation to humble service toward one another. In this text, Jesus asks us for something much more profound than making ourselves servants of charity. It is true that in other places in the Gospels Jesus does exhort Christians toward acts of service to those in need, but not in John 13:1-16. In this text, Jesus takes us into the heart of the paschal mystery and discipleship.

Deacons, deacon organisations and diocesan diaconate offices need to let go of the symbol of the basin and the towel. It has been misinterpreted and misappropriated. It is important to jettison such imagery for three main reasons. First, to continue to use this imagery as something applying specifically to deacons weakens the power of the parable in action for all Christians by suggesting that there is something in John 13:1-16 that is uniquely diaconal and by extension clerical. Secondly, to hold onto this text as a story about humble service and charitable works and to use the basin and towel as deacon symbols reinforces an unsupportable semantic position. Symbols like this present *diaconia* and its cognates as synonyms for charity and social service when they are clearly not. Finally, the parable is intended for all Christians for them to ponder the mystery of the death and resurrection of Christ and their own readiness to offer, if required, the supreme witness of faith.

Philippians 2:2-11 Exaltation or emptying?

The last of the trio of texts frequently associated with deacons is Philippians 2:2-11. Once again, we should note the most significant point is that none of the *diacon* words occur in this text, nor do any Greek words for servant. In spite of this lack, a number of authors have tried to build a theology of diaconate on the basis of *kenosis* or self-emptying, a word that appears in this text.[32] One has only to type the words deacon and *kenosis* into any search engine for the internet and many references to appear in seconds. Like the basin and the towel, *kenotic* and *kenosis*, have also found their way into book titles about deacons. Like the text from John 13, none of the servant words appear but the word for slave (*doulon*) does make an appearance and has been, since the 1940s, translated as servant and not slave. The same servant myth that drives the scribal additions to Acts 6 and translation of slave to servant in John 13 is at work here too.

---

32 Ditewig, in an unpublished presentation to the National Association of Deacons of Australia. William Ditewig, *The Emerging Diaconate: Servant Leaders in a Servant Church* (Mahwah, N.J.: Paulist Press), 2007, p. 132; Ditewig in the *Deacon Reader* p. 249; The Emerging *Diacon*ate: Servant Leaders in Servant World, Paul McPartlan; Kenosis the essence of prophetic ministry of the deacon, The Character of the Deacon: Spiritual and Pastoral Foundations edited by James Keating; The Deacon as Icon of Christ: Kenosis, Theosis and Servant-Leadership Deacon William T. Ditewig, Ph.D. Executive Director Secretariat for the *Diacon*ate Secretariat for Evangelization United States Conference of Catholic Bishops

The word upon which this theology of deacons is built in this text is found in 2:7, emptied (*econosen*) himself. *Kenosis* is the root word in emptied and can mean poured out or empty. Those hoping to build a theology of deacon on this text generally focus on three words, econosen (*kenosis*) and servant, which – as we know – does not appear in any Greek manuscript and finally the word translated as humbled (*etapeinosen*) in 2:8. The reason this group of words and thus Philippians 2:5-11 is chosen is not because it has any of the *diacon* or deacon words or any association with deacons but simply because of the servant myth. Mistranslation of the slave word for servant makes a connection for those whose theology is already formed in this way. It is entirely circular and without justification.

The author of Philippians 2 is offering an exhortation to the community which seems, from indications in verses 1-4, to have experienced some problems in community life. People within the community were perhaps puffing themselves up with pride. We need to keep this context in mind as we read the text; the author is addressing a specific problem within the Christian community at Philippi, a Roman settlement in what is now northern Greece. He is not saying anything about any Christian ministers, leaders or office bearers in the community but addressing them all generally. He is not addressing deacons because the word *diaconos* (deacon) does not appear anywhere in the whole letter.

After introducing the problem and suggesting some advice, he encourages them not to think of themselves first but to think of others. Then he quotes a hymn for them. Some translations of the Bible make the hymnic quality of verses

6-11 clearer by gathering the text more or less within the rhythm and metre of the words. See the *Jerusalem Bible* for an example of this practice.[33] A number of scholars, noting the shift in tone and intonation of these verses, identify it as an example of an early Christian hymn, composed sometime less than twenty years after Jesus' death, and probably quite early because the author never has to explain the words he is using or why he suddenly switches from prose to poetry. It must have been a hymn that was known to the Church at Philippi and perhaps sung by them at their gathering in the dawn of the first day of the week (Sunday).

If we take the hymn in its entirety from verse five to eleven, we have to see that it is much more than an exhortation to be humble and self-emptying. If we follow the trajectory that Jesus does in this hymn then the emphasis must not be on the downward movement; he emptied (*kenosis*) himself but on his exaltation in verse 9. The text clearly reads that because Jesus emptied himself, even to the point of dying on a cross, therefore God has exalted him or lifted him up. The turning point or hinge of the text is "therefore".

Hurtado argues that this is one of the earliest pieces of evidence of early Christian devotion to Jesus and of prayer directed to him as to God the Father. Verses 9 to 11 are taken directly from Isaiah 23, a text applied to God the Father in the First Testament and now applied directly to Jesus. It is remarkable that so early in the Jesus movement we know as Christianity, such an exaltation of Jesus should be present as a text within the community. The name (*onoma*) above every

---

[33] Alex Jones (Gen Ed) *Jerusalem Bible* (1966) Darton, Longman and Todd: London.

name is that of the Lord God. All should bend the knee, and every tongue confess in heaven, on the earth and under the earth that Jesus is Lord, just as God the Father is proclaimed Lord in Isaiah 23.

In Philippians 2, the author is addressing the problem of pride and rivalry in the community by exhorting them to follow Jesus' example. Take the path of self-emptying and humble yourself and let God look after the rest. Perhaps by this way the Christian will also be lifted up and exalted. It will certainly make for a better quality of community life if everyone is concerned for the welfare and wellbeing of others rather than focusing on themselves. And, besides, if they focus on themselves, they have a team of one on their side, but if all in the community look after the others person's welfare, then there are many who are looking out for the one and lifting her or him up as needed. It is a case of all boats rising on the incoming tide. We need to recall that this is an exhortation to the community not to deacons.

There can be no justification for applying this text to deacons. Not only are the *diacon* words missing and the slave word mistranslated, it simply has nothing to do with them directly or at least any more than any other Christian. Application of this text to deacons and attempts to use it as a foundation for the theology of their ministry is a very recent phenomenon. Most of this work is from the 1990s until now. I suggest that attempts to build such a theological foundation for the ministry of deacon on *kenosis* reflects an attempt to offer a way of saving the servant myth from the obvious conclusions to be drawn from John N. Collins' work which was published in 1990.

In a sense, it is an attempt at modification and accommodation of the old paradigm (the servant myth) to the new semantic profile, which makes such a myth untenable. Thomas Kuhn outlined such a reaction or manoeuvre to findings and information which challenges existing paradigms in science, in his book on scientific progress, *The Structure of Scientific Revolutions*, of which I shall have more to say in the next chapter.

Conclusion: Shaky foundations

We have explored some of the foundations for the current theology of diaconate or what I am calling the dominant paradigm: the servant myth. We have seen that the foundations are built on a misidentification of the semantic profile of the *diacon* group of words. This group of words give us the word for deacon and our basic words for ministry in most European languages other than German. We noted that the semantic profile initially given to these words came not from scholarly research on their usage in ancient sources but from the experience of a newly founded ministry for the charitable care of the poor and marginalised in industrialising Germany during the 19th century.

From this German Evangelical Lutheran deacon house movement, a new ministry of care and concern spread throughout northern Europe and eventually led to the development of the neologism *Diaconie*, which translates directly as Christian social service. From there we saw how contact with the deacon house movement encouraged the compilers of Greek lexicons simply to borrow this meaning from their experience and impose it on the *diacon* word group.

This genetic mutation in the meaning of the *diacon* words found its way from lexicons to translations as translators attempted to harmonise the text with the dictionaries.

The circle was closed when theologians and others wanting to talk about deacons chose some texts in which these servant words now appeared, even though they are not *diacon* words or were texts where additions had to be made to "correct" the text. A trio of texts have been used or misused, possibly abused, in order to provide some scriptural foundations for a servant myth of the theology of diaconate.

If the foundations – at least the Scriptural ones – seem shaky now, then we need to be prepared for the flood that is about to hit them and wipe them away. We need to turn our attention to the work of John N. Collins and ask what is so significant about his publication *Diaconia: Reinterpreting the Ancient Sources*. This is the research which is the Biblical equivalent of the Nobel winning work of Warren and Marshall on stomach ulcers. This is work that not only challenges the existing paradigm but actually washes away the foundations. The house has collapsed. Something must replace it, a new paradigm. It is to that new paradigm that we must now turn our attention.

FOUNDATIONS ON ROCK: A NEW PARADIGM

Almost everything that has been written about the theology of ministry generally and the theology of the ministry of deacons throughout the twentieth century and up to our own time is wrong. This may seem an audacious claim to many readers but none the less it is true. This claim needs some qualification. That qualification is this: if the theology of ministry generally and of diaconate in particular is built upon the semantic profile of the *diacon* group of words that prevailed before John N. Collins published *Diakonia*, the theology of ministry as it developed during this period is a house built on sand. It is built upon the sand of a mistaken identity or the mis-identification of the *diacon* group of words as words that denote loving service or charity or concern for another expressed in works of mercy and justice.

We have seen in the previous chapter that a servant myth developed as the dominant paradigm for our understanding of ministry and diaconal ministry in particular. It developed because of a mutation in the genetic code of the *diacon* group of words and then filtered into theological dictionaries of the Bible and from there into translations and from there into theological discourse which relied upon these sources. Without realising the mistake, theologians writing about Christology, ecclesiology and ministry, who relied upon the wrong semantic profile of the words just kept building upon this mutated tradition. They could have happily continued to do so until John N. Collins published his major work; *Diakonia: Reinterpreting the Ancient Sources.*[1]

Paradigm shift

In his landmark work, *The Structure of Scientific Revolutions*, Thomas Kuhn demonstrated that science does not proceed solely in an orderly fashion with one scientist building on the facts of another and building up an ever-growing body of knowledge down to the present age.[2] Kuhn noted that real scientific progress does not occur through the slow accumulation of facts and knowledge, rather the history of science is about breakthroughs where an existing paradigm is shattered. A paradigm is a whole set of doctrines about science, including known facts, theoretical models and methodology which provide the foundations upon which "normal science" is built.

Normal science is what we perceive as that accumulative process. We imagine one builds on another. Normal science is actually staying within the doctrinal and dogmatic confines established by a school or way of doing science. What counts as a scientific question and what counts as evidence or

---

[1] John N. Collins; (1990) Diaconia: *Reinterpreting the Ancient Sources.* Oxford University Press: London, UK
[2] Thomas Kuhn (1962) The Structure of Scientific Revolutions. University of Chicago Press: Chicago, Ill.

outliers is determined by the normal science paradigm. Real breakthroughs in science are actually prevented largely by the dominant paradigm because it will not accept certain theories or observations which are ruled as outliers or having no statistical significance. The dominant paradigm serves as a kind of block to accepting innovation and new truth. When a breakthrough is finally accepted and the old paradigm gives way, we experience what Kuhn called a paradigm shift. Many of us are familiar with the term.

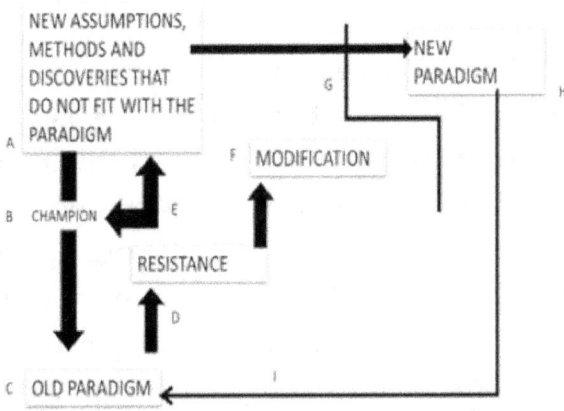

The old paradigm comes under pressure when someone comes along with a new set of observations which they are able to be accounted for only with a new theory or new explanation that is outside the dominant paradigm as we see in this diagram. Like Warren and Marshall with stomach ulcers, George Le Maître's with his singularity theory of the universe (the 'big bang') and John N. Collins with the *diakon* group of words, new discoveries are made that present a challenge to the normal science or the normal theology of ministry and diaconate. This new discovery (A) does not fit with the old paradigm. The new discovery, and sometimes the champion of the new insight, represent a challenge to the existing paradigm. The new discovery places pressure (B) on the dominant systems, methods and conclusions (C).

There are attempts by those working within the existing paradigm to resist the new insights (D). Some of this resistance is directed toward the champion of the new insights and some directed at the new insight itself (E). Sometimes the opposition to the new insights and new paradigm stem from factors that are not related to science itself, as with opposition to Fr George Le Maître's theory of the singularity event of the origin of the universe, which was dismissed and derisively referred to as 'George's Big Bang Theory'. Much of the history of the physics of cosmology in the twentieth century is concerned with physicists trying to prove George was wrong. It was only resisted because, logically, anything which did not exist and now exists has a cause. If the universe did not once exist and came into being it has a cause. That cause is what Christians call God.(At the start of the twentieth century the scientific consensus had adopt the Greek pre-Christian idea that the universe had always existed. It had abandoned the Christian ideas that the universe was created and evolving and that time was created along with it.) Research careers, research centres and funding or grants received depend upon the old paradigm remaining. Even when the science is not working any longer or producing the results claimed, commitments to it remain. We have recently seen this with IVF research and its continuing lack of success and well documented poor health and development outcomes for children conceived this way, that commitments remain to it in spite of its reported failures.[3]

After a time, some still working in the existing paradigm may try to save it by modifying the existing theory (F) while staying within the paradigm. This happened when Einstein developed his theories of relativity which seemed to challenge Newton's physics. This happened in the science of optics as contradictory evidence and theories of light had to be resolved when some could demonstrate light behaved as a wave and others as a particle. A similar attempt was made to modify relativity when quantum physics emerged. Some attempt to find ways to modify the old paradigm, to update it with some elements from the new insights, but more or less preserving the old paradigm. I detect this in some responses by theologians to John N. Collins' work. I have already mentioned in earlier chapters how some have attempted such a modification by adopting a kenotic theology of the diaconate and not limiting diaconate purely to a social service or caritative (charity) ministry, but allow for a slightly wider scope of diaconal ministry.

As more scholars begin to notice the new insights and find that working within it is effective and powerful as an explanatory tool, then a break occurs (G) and the new insights become the new paradigm (H), replacing the old (I). This is when paradigm shift occurs. For Fr George Le Maître that final break and that final replacement of the old, 'Steady State Universe' and the adoption of the 'Big Bang' as the paradigm for the origin of the universe and time took place in

---

[3] Elise Harris; Expert says IVF overused; more studies needed on infertility. *Crux* May 28, 2019

1965. That is a long time after his doctoral work in 1927 and its publication in 1931. For Warren and Marshall, the paradigm shift came within a decade of having published the research.

For John N. Collins, that paradigm shift has not yet come even though it was recognised by a number of scholars as being of this paradigmatic shifting magnitude. We saw earlier that Jerome Murphy O'Connor recognised this and so did Timothy Radcliffe in their respective reviews of *Diakonia*. We know that Anni Hentschel has re-traced the steps of Collins and replicated his results. In the world of science, independent verification via replication is a gold standard of the validity of results. Hentschel's work has been immensely significant not only for validating the original work but also the critique of the servant of charity and service dominant paradigm. John Collins' work is at a different stage from that of Le Maître and Warren and Marshall.

Kuhn notes that the three responses to challenges to the paradigm are resistance, modification and acceptance. The first two are aspects of the same attempt to preserve the existing paradigm. Only the last allows the old paradigm to pass away in favour of the new. For John N. Collins, it would seem that the majority of those writing on diaconate and

Deacon = charity, social service worker	Deacon = ecclesial minister who embodies kenotic leadership. More than charity focus.	Deacon = one commissioned by the church for the ministry of the bishop.
Rejection of Scriptural research on *diakonia*.	A move toward the research on *diakonia*.	Adopt the research on *diakonia*.

theology of ministry (ecclesiology too) are predominantly in the resistance response and a few are in the modification response. Almost none have taken up the insights and logical conclusions of his work to pass through the paradigm shift and to adopt his work as the new paradigm.

The three positions in response to Collin's are summarised in the table above. Those who reject the new semantic profile of the *diacon* group of words may do so for a number of reasons. They wish to maintain the primary or sole focus of diaconal ministry as that of servant of charity. In Germany and the Nordic countries, there are powerful reasons for doing so. There are *Diakonic* Institutes and research programs within universities dedicate to this paradigm. There is an immense network of State funded *diakonic* works or social service works. There are commitments to an ecclesiology of a so-called 'diaconal church' also founded on this notion of service and charity. Others have developed their academic careers and research profile on the theology of ministry predicated on the notions that ministry means service to another and that Christians specifically chose these words for ministry because of their lowly connotations.

There are lots of reasons for resistance but also an absence of arguments to justify the resistance and the rejection of the new semantic profile. Simply saying no to it is not an argument. There is only one way to refute the work of Collins and Hentschel and that is to re-trace the same study of the *diacon* words in the sources they have examined and demonstrate that both are mistaken in their conclusions. I am not aware of such studies and I have seen no mention of such studies in the references of those who champion the old paradigm.

The second response – modification – is not sustainable in the long run. We have seen in previous chapters that the shift to the kenotic theology of diaconate is another attempt to forestall full engagement with the new semantic profile. The two texts we examined previously, John 13 and Philippians 2:4-11, each rely on inserting *diacon* words into the text and they are not found in any Greek manuscripts. Those who wish to rely on these texts do so because of an *a priori* commitment to the servant paradigm. Without imagining that the *diacon* words are in these texts, they cannot be used to support the servant paradigm. This is the same problem faced with a theology of ministry generally when it relies on some variation of the servant and service myth. Modification faces the same problem as rejection, at some time the work of Collins and Hentschel must be re-traced and it must be demonstrated that they are mistaken. If this is not done, then the kenotic model is supported on foundations of sand just like the rejection response.

This brings us to the third response – paradigm shift. That is the only defensible position with regard to the new semantic profile developed by Collins. That is the position of the present author. We need to find a way to incorporate the insights of Collins and develop a theology of diaconate and of ministry generally that takes account of it. For Roman Catholics the building of a theology of ministry and that of deacons need not rely solely upon the semantic profile developed by Collins but it cannot proceed without it.

In this chapter, we will explore the implication of the semantic profile but draw on the theology of Vatican II on ministry to develop a more complete theory. In doing so, we need to draw on four key elements: the new semantic profile, the revision of the *cursus honorum*, the theology of episcopate, and the ecclesiology and spirituality of communion/*koinonia*. If we develop our theology of deacon in this way, we will be building on a foundation of rock.

A new semantic profile

Before we look at the semantic profile Collins developed for the *diacon* word group, we must keep in the forefront of our mind five deeply significant facts. First, we explored in the previous chapter that the old semantic profile of the *diacon* word group was not developed from a scholarly study of the meaning of the words or from the use of those words in ancient literature. It is important for us to keep in the forefront of our mind that there was no scholarly basis to the attribution to the *diacon* word group of concepts like humble or lowly service to another or with any sense of charitable activity. We need to remember that the identification of the *diacon* words with lowly and humble service and charity or charitable concern for another is a mistaken identification.

Secondly, we must remember that there is not any foundation to the claim that the early Christians believed that the *diacon* word group carried such meanings and that this is why they deliberately chose such words for ministry and ministers. We need to keep in mind that this second claim is derived from the false premise that the meaning of the *diacon* words indicates humble, lowly service. Therefore, it is a false conclusion. This is not to suggest that ministers are not called to a degree of humility and loving concern for others; all Christians are called to that. We need to keep in mind that they are not called to humility and loving concern based on any of the *diacon* words, which give us our words for ministry and ministers.

The third deeply significant fact is that John N. Collins was the first to complete a scholarly study of the Biblical and non-Biblical use of the *diacon* words from which he developed the first true semantic profile of the words. If the reader should struggle with the word 'true' in this claim, then she is still left with the first scholarly semantic profile of the word group.

The fourth deeply significant fact is that so far only one scholar, Anni Hentschel, has re-traced Collins' work on the *diacon* word group and she has independently reached the same conclusions. Our fifth and final deeply significant fact is that Collins' work has found acceptance in one of the tools of Biblical scholars use in which there was embedded the distorted and false semantic profile of the *diacon* word group, BDAG 2000 edition. His definition replaces the previous non-scholarly semantic profile.[4]

I have already referred the reader to Collins' major work *Diakonia: Reinterpreting the Ancient Sources*, where all of his work is set out in great detail, as well as to his other journal articles and books. We do not have the space here to review the full range of his work but we will trace the outline of the semantic profile which he has developed. In the table below,

---

[4] John N. Collins (2003) *Deacons and the Church: Making Connections Between Old and New*. Gracewing: Harrisburg. p13

Collins compares the profile of the *diacon* group of words as they had developed in the non-scholarly consensus that became embedded in theological dictionaries and theological discourse on ministry and the ministry of deacons.⁵

Twentieth century non-scholarly profile of *diacon* word group	Collins profile of the word group based on research 1990 (confirmed by Hentschel)
Unbiblical	Occurring in the Greek Septuagint Bible.
A fundamentally unreligious word	The *diakon* word group have deep roots in Greek religious language and culture.
No overtones of authority, officialdom, rule, dignity and power	The words can be applied at the highest levels of civic and religious functions, expressing always the notion of mandated authority.
In no danger of being misinterpreted as an honour or a new kind of rule.	In religious contexts a connotation of the noble and even the divine characterises usage.

---

5 John N. Collins (2016) *Gateway to Renewal: Reclaiming Ministries for Women and Men.* Morning Star Publications. Northcote: Vic. P180-181. Used with kind permission of the author.

An activity which at once every Greek world recognise as being one of self-abasement.	In most contexts, every Greek would hold the person and activity designated by a *diakon* word in the highest respect and even awe.
It never lost its flavour of inferiority.	On the contrary, no imputation of inferiority ever attached to the usage.
This kind of service was unthinkable for a free Greek (citizen).	On the contrary, in certain circumstances, service as *diakonia* was unthinkable for slaves.
A completely personal service is implied.	Service designated as *diakonia* could be considered personal service only in relation to the person mandating the activity; no personal service was implied in relation to the recipient of the *diakonia*.

Jesus gave the meaning of service a radical new meaning; at the very heart of his eschatological message lies his commandment to love one's neighbour.	Values expressed by *diakon* words in Christian writings were no different from those expressed in Hellenistic and classical Greek; *diakon* words never expressed or connoted love of any kind.
In contrast to all the concepts of office in existence at the time, Jesus chose and emphasised this new concept of service.	In the gospels and throughout the rest of the New Testament, the *diakon* words expressed no nuance different from the non-Christian usage.
A completely new word.	Early Christian writers simply used the *diakon* words in ways to which they had been acculturated by centuries of usage.

The summary of the semantic profile provides no basis for the servant myth, the restriction of diaconal ministry primarily to that of charitable and social works or to the notion that Christians had chosen these *diacon* words specifically because of their connotation or denotation of lowly and humble service. The kinds of people who were designated as *diaconos* in non-Biblical Greek literature included the god Hermes, magistrates, ambassadors and executive officers (*huperetai*) commissioned by governors and emperors to carry messages or carry out other tasks in their name. The closest we come to any 'waiter' type functions for a *diaconos* are those high-born free men commissioned with the leading of formal dinners (*deipnon* followed by a *symposium*) which had a religious significance in the context of Greek civil society. To be chosen as *diaconos* at such an event was considered such a great honour that men and women who had that honour would have it inscribed in their funeral monument epitaphs.

In Biblical literature, those who are called *diaconos*, include Jesus, Paul, Paul's co-workers, Phoebe the leading person (*prostasis*) of the community of Cenchreae and others who are commissioned to proclaim the Word of God, to preach, to baptise, and also the prophets. We know that in the early Church *diaconos* had become a designation for an office in the Church, it is mentioned in Scriptures and in the earliest Church records. Always deacons are mentioned in relation to the one who commissioned them and whose tasks it is that they carry out – the bishop. We always find, in the Second Testament and early Christian sources, that the direction of service of the *diaconos* is not a personal service to a recipient but service on behalf of and at the delegation of the one they serve. It is always commissioned service. Importantly, it is never, in common Greek usage or in Biblical and early Church usage, associated with charitable service. To underscore this, we can recall the reference in a previous chapter to a study by Sven Brodd which shows that the *diacon* word group are never used as synonyms for the *caritative* (charity/love) word group. The reader may find it helpful to read down the right side of the table and develop a clearer sense of the profile of the *diacon* word group before reading on.

The revision of the *cursus honorum*

This following section is largely a very brief summary of the work of Gibaut, *The Cursus Honorum: A Study of the Origins and Evolution of Sequential Ordination*.[6] I highly recommend this study to anyone wishing to understand the theology of ministry in the Roman Catholic, Eastern Catholic and Orthodox Churches. There is a *cursus honorum* in each of these Churches the evolution of the sequence has not always been identical after the schism of 1054, although most of this was in place before then. We need to understand a little of how sequential ordination developed and how this sequence influenced our thinking about the theology of ministry. We also need to understand how the *cursus honorum* looked at the time of the Second Vatican Council (1962-65) and after 1972.

Catholics believe as a matter of faith that Christ established the threefold ministry of bishop, presbyter and deacon and that such ministries are of the essence of the Church and an expression of the Divine will.[7] This doctrine was clearly affirmed at the Council of Trent in the sixteenth century counter to the claims of the Protestant party which regarded ministry not of the divine essence of the Church but as an instrumental necessity, i.e. ministry was necessary for the good ordering of the Church and the proclamation of the Word and celebration of sacraments. We saw previously that

---

6   John St.H. Gibaut. (2000) *The Cursus Honorum: A Study of the Origins and Evolution of Sequential Ordination*. Peter Lang: New York, NY.
7   CCC 1536, 1538, CIC can 207§1

the Council of Trent agreed with the Protestant objection that Catholics did not really witness to their belief in the threefold order because deacons existed largely only as a liturgical grade before that of presbyter and remained deacons for a very short time. There were no permanent deacons (generally anyway). So, the Council of Trent ordered the restoration of the permanent ministry of deacon alongside that of the permanent order of presbyter and permanent order of bishop. That decision of the Council did not take effect until after the Second Vatican Council and the publication of *Sacrum Diaconatus Ordinem* by Paul VI in 1967.[8] It may seem that this decision was a simple one and that it restored the fullness of the Catholic sacrament of Holy Orders but that is not the case. In order to understand why it did not restore the fullness of the sacrament of Holy Orders, we need to go a little deeper and look at the context in which that restoration took place.

Most Catholics today would be aware that our historical sources indicate the ministry of the Church took some time to find its present shape. In his own lifetime, Jesus only established one ministry, that of apostle. When Catholic doctrine teaches that the threefold ministry was established

---

8   I argue that Catholics have not come much further than the 16th century and the Protestant objection still stands. We see this every time a lay person is appointed as a pastoral leader under can 517 when that canon and other sources interpreting it clearly state that a deacon should be appointed. We see it every time someone asks what can a deacon do that a lay person can't. We see it every time a presbyter says, "deacons don't do much in the liturgy'. We see it every time deacon are overlooked in pastoral planning in a diocese, left out of prayers for vocations, not included in clergy functions and retreats and in many other aspects of diocesan life. That is Catholics do not witness to or practice what they profess about the threefold divinely instituted order.

by divine will, this does not mean that Jesus personally established the threefold ministry and left the Church to carry that on. The doctrine of ministry developed, just as the doctrine of all the sacraments developed. The way sacraments were celebrated and the order in which they were celebrated and the meaning attached to the sacraments grew and developed over time. Catholics believe the Holy Spirit remains as teacher of the Church and guides her to deeper understanding. That deeper understanding can only come through human language, human symbols, human customs because these are the only means by which God is able to communicate to humans. Our growth in understanding is a mediated understanding.

From the record of the Second Testament (ST) and early Church documents, we can see that in the first two centuries and into the third, what was considered a ministry varied in number, scope and even in local geographical variations. There are ministries with a variety of names: apostle, teacher, prophet, prophetess, widow, porter, deacon and bishop and sometimes presbyter is listed in some churches. Not all places seemed to have had the same list of ministries. Gradually the number of these became more fixed and also some were regarded as more fundamental than others. In the ST, there is no minister who is designated with the title priest (Greek, *hierus*/Latin, *sacerdos*) apart from the Lord Jesus. That title will take a little while to appear for a Christian minister.

Not all of these were 'ordained' ministers, whatever ordination may have meant in a variety of contexts. Ordination normally involved some sense of commissioning of the minister and often by the laying on of hands, which was a practice Christians had inherited from Jewish religious tradition. All ministries were charismatic ministries in the sense that the Church understood each to be a gift of the Holy Spirit. Charism means gift. Some charismatic ministries seemed to rely on personal gifts that a particular Christian possessed while others were related to office, status or place within the communion of the Church. Often times these charismatic ministers and gifts were regulated or supervised by other church leaders, especially the *episcopos* (bishop) who had a charism of leadership. Very early in Christian history, bishop and deacon indicated an office in the Church and in some places, presbyter was an office too.

As early as the time of Ignatius of Antioch (d. 108AD), he could write about the role of the bishops and deacons in the local Church as ministers of the mysteries of Christ and of the bishop as the one around whom each local Church was gathered in unity.[9] As we shall see in chapter six, the presbyters as a part of the ministry of the Church emerged slowly. The author of 1 Clement, a letter written to the Church of Corinth around 96AD, also outlines the church order of *episcopos* (bishop), *diaconos* (deacon) and *presbyteros* (presbyters) and indicates that it was well known in all of the Churches that Christ had willed the order of the Church and that the apostles had established bishops and deacons in all of the Churches. Although historically it is improbable that they personally appointed them, the awareness that the order of the Church came from Christ and was a participation in the apostolic ministry was embedded in ecclesiology at a

---

9   Bart Ehmann (ed. and trans.) (2003) *The Apostolic Fathers Vol 1: Loeb Classical Library 24*. Harvard University Press. Cambridge: Mass, p109

very early stage and has remained the position of the Catholic and Orthodox Churches up to this day.

Gradually, the ministries began to take a more familiar shape and, by the fourth century of the Christian era, three ministers had emerged as marked out in a way different to the others. These three were *episcopos* (bishop), *diaconos* (deacon) and *presbyter* (elder). The whole Church understood itself to be an 'ordained' people, 'a chosen race, a kingdom of priests, a holy nation, a people to be a personal possession [of God], and the Body of Christ (1 Peter 2:5, 9; Romans 12:5; 1 Corinthians 12:13). 'Ordained' comes to us immediately from the Latin word *ordines* which essentially designates a place, or a place where we stand in relation to others, the same being expressed in the Greek *taxeis*.[10] Those who are baptised take on a special character, they are baptised into Christ, the Second Person of the Holy Trinity, and therefore they become part of him and part of one another (1 Corinthians 12:13) Christians become sharers in the divine life, in a deep and mysterious exchange between heaven and earth.

Catholic liturgy captures this sense in that tiny *sotto voce* prayer when the deacon pours a small amount of water into the wine in the chalice: "By the mystery of this water and wine, may we come to share in the divinity of Christ, who humbled himself to share in our humanity." Because they are 'ordained' through baptism and chrismation/confirmation, they stand in the Body of Christ, which is the Church. They are a new people, and a people made one in the unity of the Father, the Son and the Holy Spirit.[11] They are not like any

---

10   CCC 1537
11   LG 4

other people on the planet, who are not marked by this same character. Full Christian initiation – baptism, chrismation/confirmation, and participation in the Eucharist – enables them to remain standing in the Church and to celebrate the sacred mysteries. Even catechumens, who have a special place in the Church, could not remain standing in the Church for the celebration of the mysteries (sacraments) in the early Church.[12] Christ offered the one redeeming and necessary sacrifice through, with and in his body the Church.[13]

The fully initiated are 'ordained' for the task of celebrating the Mass and filled with grace to live the Christian life and give witness to the Gospel through their lives and good works as the fruit of this salvation. What we now call the laity and the clergy are all of this 'ordained' people of God, the priestly people. The document on the Church that would become *Lumen gentium* (Dogmatic Constitution of the Church) captures this sense beautifully through its own structure. The first three chapters are about the People of God – laity, deacon, presbyters and bishops – then it moves on to consider those in Holy Orders. In doing so, LG introduces the term hierarchy and examines the hierarchical structure of the Church. The term in fact should have been introduced earlier because a complete understanding of the term hierarchy includes the laity.

For some centuries now, the term hierarchy, as applied to the Church, has been used in a more narrow and technical sense to refer to the clergy and the bishops in more restrictive

---

12 This practice of dismissing catechumens has been revived in the Roman Catholic Mass and the Rite of Christian Initiation of Adults
13 SC 47

uses of the term. Brian Horne notes in his brief study of the term hierarchy, that from the late nineteenth century and continuing up until now there has been a radical shift in the way many theologians, philosophers and many ordinary folks think about hierarchy.[14] The term has become linked to concepts of power and authority over others and is frequently connected to values that express a lack of freedom, repression and lack of personal autonomy.

Hierarchy is considered by many to be *ipso facto* oppressive and is to be avoided. There is almost an allergic reaction of some within the Church, outside of the Church, and in liberal democratic societies in general to hierarchy. There is no doubt that when hierarchy is an exercise of power and authority over others, it can be corrosive and oppressive. Many examples in church and society can be used to illustrate this. This is not what hierarchy meant in our earliest Christian sources and this meaning remained current for much of Christian history. Nor should hierarchy be exercised as power and domination over others in this way in the Church.

Hierarchy is a compound Greek word, *hierus* meaning sacred and *arche* meaning origins or beginning. For our earliest Christian sources, including the ST, hierarchy meant that the ordering of the Church has sacred origins. That is structure, ordering and offices of leadership are part of the divine nature of the Church, part of the essence of its constitution. Not an epiphenomenon and not a structure imposed on the Church out of a human necessity for leadership.[15] The expression

---

14 Brian Horne, Homo Hierarchicus and Ecclesial Order. *International Journal for the Study of the Christian Church*. Vol 7/1, February 2007, 16-28
15 Brian Horne, Homo Hierarchicus and Ecclesial Order; p20

that later theology would use for this is that the sacred ministry is of the divine will for the Church. The letters to the Ephesians and Corinthians in their own way deal with the reality of God-given structure for forming and building up the Body of Christ for mission. Ephesians 4:2-11 addresses the question of order by indicating that while all Christians are called to the same mission and holiness only some Christians are called to be ministers.[16] We need a recovery of the term hierarchy and we also need to strip it of notions of power as domination if we use the term. More importantly we must strip the practice of hierarchy in the Church and society, of any hint of the exercise of power over others in a restrictive or oppressive sense.

Christianity was embraced by the Roman Empire after 380 AD. Gibaut shows that Roman society was also a hierarchical society and civic society also had orders.[17] In Roman society, some orders were fixed by birth but there were some that one could ascend to through a progressive moving up through the ranks or orders of civic society. This progress from a lower social rank to a higher one was called the *cursus honorum* (course of honours). Gradually the pattern of the Church's ministries was aligned with the parallel structure of civic society. Ecclesiastical society developed its own *cursus honorum* for the ministries of the Church and the concept of lower and higher ranks or orders. This *cursus honorum* included lay ministries as well as clerical ones. Remember, at this stage, hierarchy simply meant the ordering of the

---

16   For a detailed analysis of this question and an explanation about why only some are ministers you may wish to read John N Collin's (1992); *Are All Christians Ministers?* E.J Dwyer Publications: Newtown, NSW.
17   Gibaut (2000) *The Cursus Honorum*, pp.2-3

Church and was related to the Eucharist. The Eucharist is the pre-eminent moment when the Church gathers as herself most clearly in order that she may receive the Eucharist to become what she receives. Liturgy is arranged hierarchically because the Church is hierarchical in her essence. The whole priestly people offer the Eucharist in head and members, that is, with differentiated places within the assembly which is the Church. This is the origin of sequential ordination in the Church.

Before the *cursus honorum* was established, direct ordination to the higher orders of deacon, presbyter and bishop from laity was possible.[18] Even after it was established, up until the ninth century, there was still a fair degree of fluidity especially with the three major orders, as they came to be known, of deacon, presbyter and bishop. Up until this time, most bishops were chosen from among deacons and not presbyters. That was logical as they were ordained for the ministry of the bishop and had a view over the whole church, whereas presbyters, once they assumed priestly duties, had a small portion of the local church to care for, what we would now call a parish.

For most of this time, deacons were not ordained as presbyters before episcopal ordination. The bishop was understood to be the priest of the sacraments and because of him the presbyters and deacons could celebrate the sacraments. The bishop celebrates the Mass because *he is* a bishop and the presbyters celebrate the Mass because *there is* a bishop even though both share in the priesthood. This is an important distinction. It was not necessary for a deacon to be

---

18   Gibaut (2000) *The Cursus Honorum*, pp.3, 11-55

sequentially ordained a presbyter before episcopal ordination since it was the bishop who caused the sacraments to be celebrated. As this process of forming the *cursus honorum* into the sequence continued, presbyters simply became known as priests (*sacerdoti* in Latin, plural). Once we move into the tenth century, positions on this ecclesiastical *cursus honorum* become fixed and gradually the lay ministries would only become steps along this pathway to presbyteral ordination and only conferred on men preparing for what would become known as the priesthood.

From the eleventh century on, two developments would have a long-lasting impact on the theology of ministry until 1965 and even into our present era. First, the orders had been formed into clear steps up the ranks toward priestly ordination. Although there were always a few exceptions, these are largely outliers, like Pope Hadrian IV who was a deacon elected as Bishop of Rome (pope), and who did not receive episcopal ordination before he died.[19] In essence all of the lower steps on the *cursus honorum* were absorbed into priestly ministry. It is important to keep in mind that they were absorbed, they did not disappear completely. It was argued that the one on his way up the ecclesiastical ranks absorbed the lower one as he stepped up and with it the powers attached. Each rank had a certain set of powers attached to it and so the one ascending the ranks was accumulating more of these powers. This is not power in the modern sense but more like faculties or permission for various liturgical acts which were ultimately related to the Eucharist.

---

19   It was because of him that a new rule was added to elections of the Bishop of Rome; anyone elected who is not a bishop, must immediately be ordained a bishop by three bishops present.

A second change was under way that would have unfortunate consequences for the theology of ministry in general and of the episcopate in particular was about the nature of the episcopate and its theological status. A theological opinion took hold that as the Eucharist makes the Church then to make (consecrate) the Eucharist must be the highest power of the sacrament of Holy Orders. Since that power was received at presbyteral ordination then the highest order must be that of presbyter/priest. What then was the episcopate? What sacramental power could it add higher than this? Most theologians resolved the issue by arguing that since priesthood was the highest step, then a bishop must still be at the level of priest as to his sacramental nature and that the ordination he receives is not of the essence of the Church but of its necessity, for the transfer and ritualisation of the power of jurisdiction over the other priests and the local church.

He was a priest-bishop and called simply the major or greater priest – in Latin, the *sacerdos magnus*. It made perfect sense for a bishop when addressing priests to use the term 'we priests' because that was what he was. And in the same way, as we have recently heard in the debate about the ordination of women deacons, the same was argued about bishops – that they were not ordained in the full sense of the word (*cheirotonia* in Greek) but received a lesser ritual or consecration (*cheirothesia* in Greek). One sometimes still hears reference to episcopal consecration and not ordination today. The theology of Holy Orders, which coupled the *cursus honorum* with a theology of accumulation of powers as a man moved toward the pinnacle of priesthood, was an ascending theology of Holy Orders. The man was ascending up the steps toward some fullness of Holy Orders. This was the theology of Holy Orders extant at the time of the Second Vatican Council (1962-65) and shortly after.

The diagram sets out the *cursus honorum* for the sacrament of Holy Orders as it existed from the thirteenth century until 1972. If you examine the diagram you will notice what is missing fairly easily. There is no bishop. The highest and last step was priest, almost never referred to as presbyter.

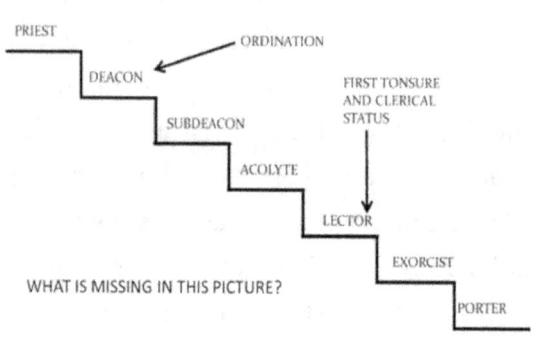

The steps of porter and exorcist were technically lay ministries but only men being formed as future priests were admitted to these ministries at various stages of their formation. A man became a cleric not through ordination but by receiving first tonsure before his admission to the ministry of lector. In those days we 'clericalised the laity' in the sense that they were not ordained but they were clerics. In countries like Australia, that tonsure had been reduced to a symbolic cutting of a few strands of hair from the crown of the head. In other counties, it was a cut and shave of a tonsure the size of the host which the people received on the crown of the head. At this point, a man was admitted to all of the rights and obligations of clerical life.

Ordination occurred at diaconate and normally in the seminary chapel with the other seminarians present and perhaps some family too. Like all of the other ceremonies leading up to presbyteral ordination, there was no requirement for a public ecclesial celebration. This was a private affair and these were changes focused on the individual who was receiving them and not the Church. The soon-to-be-priest would serve out his apprenticeship in preparation for his real ordination as a priest by being sent to a parish for six to twelve months and transition from the diaconate to priestly ordination in a public ordination ritual. In countries where full priestly tonsure was still in practice, a cut and a shave of crown of the head the size of a priest's host was made. Even at this point – of priestly ordination – there was so much focus on the ontological change of the priesthood (forgetting the ontological change of baptism) and his capacity to now make the Eucharist that the Church which the Eucharist makes was almost eclipsed. This was the ordinand's special day. There was not much awareness that this was an ecclesial event for the ecclesia.

At the direction of the Second Vatican Council, Paul VI reformed the *cursus honorum* and also implemented a partial and idiosyncratic restoration of the lay ministries of lector and acolyte and of the permanent ministry of deacon. Partial and idiosyncratic because the lay ministries and diaconate were restricted to men and bishops and local churches did not have to restore any of them. They were all optional extras. If we look at the diagram that shows the *cursus honorum* after *Ministeria quaedam,* we can see immediately one very significant addition, the bishop, who is still a *sacerdos*/priest bishop, but at least now is part of the sacrament of Holy Orders.

Some steps have been reduced in the new *cursus honorum*. We also now have two versions of deacon, lector and acolyte. There are now deacons who remain as a permanent sign of the Catholic faith regarding the threefold order and other deacons who transition through diaconate to priesthood. We have two versions of lector and acolyte. Lay men who intend to remain lay men who serve for normally a limited time of appointment as acolyte and lector (though some of these have become permanent) and transitional lectors and acolytes comprised of men on their way to diaconal and presbyteral/priestly ordination. Sadly, the formation of lay men for these ministries rarely happens beyond a cursory overview of what needs to be done and rarely are the rites of installation celebrated for them. Rarer still are they appointed by their bishop for this stable lay ministry.[20] The rites for installation as lector and acolyte are always celebrated for men preparing as deacons or priests. It is clear that the gaps we have identified here are the result of orientation of the *cursus honorum* toward priesthood. It is also a failure to acknowledge that lay people are both male and female

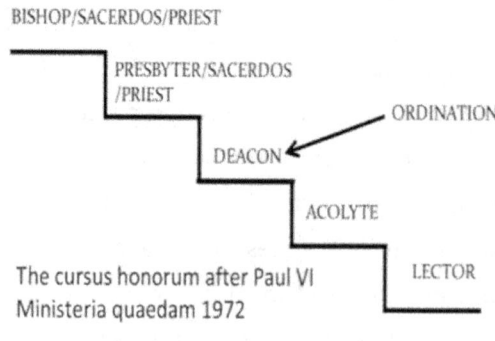

The cursus honorum after Paul VI Ministeria quaedam 1972

---

20   CIC can 230§1

and to respect that these lay ministries are lay and not steps toward something else.

There is, in fact, no theological justification for sequential ordination or transitioning candidates for the diaconate and presbyterate through the lay ministries and we must ask ourselves how much flexibility we have to engage with a new way of thinking and a new practice.[21] We should ordain men and women directly to the diaconate for which they have been prepared and ordain men for the presbyterate for which they have been prepared. We should not have men transition through the diaconate to presbyterate – a diaconate for which they are not actually formed as their formation is directed at the presbyterate, as it should be. In this way, both the presbyterate and diaconate would achieve their proper status and end.

Further, we would not have this lingering confusion about transitional deacons. Lay women and men should be formed, appointed by their bishop and installed with the appropriate rite as lectors and acolytes. In this way we show we truly value these lay liturgical ministries and demonstrate that we do not regard them as 'Father's helper' in the liturgy. The fact of sequential ordination emerged for non-theological reasons and was essentially an adaptation to the nature of the civic life of the Roman Empire and was not the practice of the early Church. The ascending nature of the theology of Holy Orders which resulted from this practice is actually counter to the ecclesiology of communion and, I argue, has been challenged by a theology of Holy Orders which is founded on the Church as a communion. We will explore this below.

---

21   Gibaut (2000) *The Cursus Honorum*. Pp. 331-334

The bishops did not make it into the *cursus honorum* in 1972 because someone thought perhaps an oversight had caused them to be omitted previously. As you may remember from the start of this book, the three most important issues that the bishops wanted to address at the Second Vatican Council in rank order were: the theology of episcopate, greater use of the vernacular in the liturgy and the restoration of the permanent ministry of deacons. In fact, the theology of the episcopate was left over from the agenda of the suspended First Vatican Council in 1870.

We can be grateful that they did not have time to consider the question then, just as we can be grateful that Trent did not ultimately restore the permanent diaconate. The late nineteenth and the twentieth centuries brought to the Church new and previously unseen resources and new methods in Biblical, patristic and liturgical studies, each of which would have a profound effect on the deliberations of Vatican II. It is to these deliberations that we now turn. What did Vatican II have to say about the episcopate?

Theology of Episcopate

As we have seen above, when the men who were called bishops assembled for the Second Vatican Council, they were known as 'greater priests'. They were priests who had undergone a public ritual which signified their taking possession of a diocese (if they were diocesan bishops) and accepting the mandate from the Bishop of Rome to govern the local Church. The power to govern the diocese (local Church) was renewed by a decree from the Holy See (diocese of Rome and the Pope) every five years. Prior to the First Vatican Council there were an increasing number of papal interventions into the life of dioceses and national and regional Churches and often times the papal intervention overruled a local decision.

Much of this papal activity was actually directed at protecting the Church from being nationalised as it had been after the French Revolution and becoming an arm of the State. After the First Vatican Council, when the infallibility of the Church was proclaimed and it was taught that the Bishop of Rome, acting as the sign of unity in the Church could under some strict conditions proclaim that a teaching was guaranteed by the infallibility of the Church, some new questions arose about the bishops.[22] Were the bishops really necessary at all? Were they merely agents of the Bishop of Rome and he some global CEO managing a vast international Church? In modern management parlance, were they all his 'direct reports' looking after a branch office of the Catholic Church? Certainly, the German Chancellor at the time of Vatican I, Bismarck, thought so.

Evidence that Vatican I did not teach that a bishop's authority was derived from the Pope may be found in the letter of the German episcopate sent to Chancellor Bismarck shortly after the First Vatican Council, a letter, which, subsequently, received endorsement by Pius IX.[23] This clearly

---

22 This teaching is sometimes erroneously referred to as papal infallibility. The First Vatican Council distinguished between the infallibility of the Church and an exercise of the teaching office of the Bishop of Rome to proclaim that teaching was guaranteed by the infallibility of the Church which ultimately derives from a gift of the Holy Spirit. This is a complex discussion for some other time.

23 The document 'Collective Statement of the German Episcopate concerning the Circular of the German Imperial Chancellor in respect of the coming Papal election' of the year 1875 provides almost the

asserted that the Pope had not absorbed the bishops' powers, and that the latter should not be considered to be instruments or vicars of the pope.[24] In his apostolic brief of March 6, 1875, Pius IX endorsed the content of the German Episcopal letter to Bismarck on the proper authority of the diocesan bishops, thus:

> Your declaration gives the genuine Catholic doctrine, which is also that of the Holy Council and of this Holy See; it defends it with illuminating and irrefutable reasoning, and it sets out so clearly that it is plain to any honest person that there is no innovation in the definitions attacked...[25]

Pius IX taught that Vatican I affirmed the teaching of the Church that the episcopate has its source of authority in the divine institution:

> It is in virtue of the same divine institution upon which the papacy rests and the episcopate also exists. It too has its rights and duties, because of the ordinance of God himself, and the pope has neither the right nor the power to change them. Thus it is a complete misunderstanding

---

only official commentary on Pastor Aeternus and in particular on the relationship between primacy and episcopate. See Jacques Dupuis and Joseph Neuner, The Christian Faith in the Doctrinal Documents of the Catholic Church. Seventh Edition. New York: Alba House. 2001.p. 322.

24 J-M.R. Tillard;(1987) Church of Churches: The ecclesiology of communion. Collegeville: Liturgical Press. p 40, Pius IX, Tuas Libenter, December 21, 1863 DS 2879

25 Tuas Libenter , December 21, 1863 DS 2879

of the Vatican decrees to believe that because of them 'episcopal jurisdiction has been absorbed into the papal', that 'the pope has in principle taken the place of the bishop', that the bishops are now 'no more than tools of the pope, his officials without responsibility of their own... under the appointment of the Holy Spirit, they succeed in the place of the apostles, and feed and rule individually, as true shepherds, the particular flock assigned to them.[26]

This teaching of the German bishops endorsed by Pius IX kept in place the teaching of Church that Holy Orders was by divine institution but it could not adequately explain why this should be so if the priesthood was the highest sacramental power.

During the late nineteenth and into twentieth century, new studies in ancient languages, including for the first time Koine Greek, the language of the ST, and new sources of information about the early Church, like the Apostolic Constitutions, became available. There was an explosion of studies of the Bible, the ancient world, patristic and liturgical sources much of which had never been seen let alone the subject of scholarly work. Collectively, this work and the scholars involved was termed the *ressourcement* movement (return to the sources of the faith) and *Nouvelle théologie* (new theology), and the work flowed directly into the Second Vatican Council.[27]

---

26 Jacques Dupuis and Joseph Neuner, *The Christian Faith*. 2001. p. 322.
27 Jurgen Mettepenningen (2010) *Nouvelle théologie-New Theology: Inheritor of Modernism, Precursor of Vatican II*. T&T Clark: New York.

From this work came a recovery at that Council of the theology and spirituality of communion which is profoundly Trinitarian and eucharistic. This is an ancient theological tradition which dominated our doctrine of the church and sacramental theology for most of the first millennium of the Christian era and survived in a remnant form up until the present. We will look at this a little more closely below. For our present purposes, we simply need to know that it furnished the Fathers of the Second Vatican Council with the language to finally consider the sacramental nature of the episcopate.

This is what the Second Vatican Council taught about the nature of the episcopate in five key passages:

> And the Sacred Council teaches that by Episcopal consecration the fullness of the sacrament of Orders is conferred...(LG 21)

> The order of bishops, which succeeds to the college of apostles and gives this apostolic body continued existence, is also the subject of supreme and full power over the universal Church, provided we understand this body together with its head the Roman Pontiff and never without this head. (LG 22)

> By virtue of sacramental consecration and hierarchical communion with the head and members of the college, bishops are constituted as members of the episcopal body. "The order of bishops is the successor to the college of the apostles in teaching and pastoral direction,

or rather, in the episcopal order, the apostolic body continues without a break. (CD 4)

A bishop marked with the fullness of the sacrament of Orders, is "the steward of the grace of the supreme priesthood", especially in the Eucharist, which he offers or causes to be offered, and by which the Church continually lives and grows. (LG 26)

Christ, whom the Father has sanctified and sent into the world, has through his apostles, made their successors, the bishops, partakers of his consecration and his mission. They have legitimately handed on to different individuals in the Church various degrees of participation in this ministry. Thus, the divinely established ecclesiastical ministry is exercised on different levels by those who from antiquity have been called bishops, priests and deacons. (LG 28)

The Second Vatican Council settled a doctrinal dispute that had been ongoing since the eleventh century about the sacramental nature of episcopal ordination. In my view, this is perhaps the most significant doctrinal teaching of this Council. For on this teaching it is possible to develop a more complete sacramental theology, ecclesiology of the local and universal Church and the nature of authority in the Church itself. There are so many more implications that flow from this solemn teaching. In using the formula "this sacred Council teaches that", the Fathers of the Council show their intention is to make a solemn, precise and authoritative teaching. Not only do they declare episcopal ordination to be a sacrament but the fullness of the sacrament of Holy Orders. Recall that prior to the Council the consensus had been that presbyteral ordination was the fulness, although such a theological opinion had never been solemnly declared. Now a clear declaration was made against the presbyter as the top of the *cursus honorum* thesis. That is how the bishop returned to the picture we saw above.

Episcopal ordination signifies a collegial dimension of the Church. For a bishop is ordained to a college, that is why three bishops in full communion with each other and the Bishop of Rome are required for valid ordination to take place. Their presence signifies the collegial dimension, which is part of the nature of the Church as a *communio* or *koinonia*. This college, or Order of Bishops, pre-exists the ordination of a particular man as a bishop. This college, as the Council teaches, is the successor of the apostolic college and its continuation in time. The one ministry that Jesus created in his life time – that of apostle –continues in this group and this group represents the fullness of the sacrament of Holy Orders. The authority and the ministry of the bishops comes from Christ in the Holy Spirit through ordination. They receive the fulness not because they have ascended to it but because it comes down or descends on them. They have the fulness because they are bishops and they can share this fulness with helpers, who since ancient times have been called presbyters/priests and deacons.

The ministry of deacons and presbyters is a participation in the fullness which the bishop has, they did not in fact accumulate their power in stages up the *cursus honorum*, as had been the theological opinion which was dominant immediately prior to Vatican II. This is why in ancient times a lay man or a deacon could be elected bishop and ordained directly as a bishop, because it was the episcopate that had the fulness of Holy Orders all along. It was the *cursus honorum*, coupled with the theology of powers that obscured the original truth. Why did this not get developed at Trent? For the very simple reason that all of the source documents, historical and language studies I mentioned that flowed into Vatican II were simply not available. They could only use the resources they had.

The *ressourcement* movement and the *nouvelle théologie* created the possibility of this recovery. I attempt to set this out diagrammatically.

To comprehend this diagram, we need a kind of three-dimensional imagination. The Council is recovering the ancient sense of hier-arche, sacred origins. We need to imagine that the ministry of Christ, handed on to the apostles, descends in its fullness on the Church, from above as it were. The fulness descends upon the whole church, which is the Body of Christ, the people of God, the *koinonia* that comes from the unity of the Father, Son and Holy Spirit, as a pure gift (charism). Shifting our perspective from above, we see now that the bishop stands in the midst of the Body as its centre and sign of unity and not above it. Because the bishop has the fulness of the sacrament of Holy Orders, he is able to share from that fulness with his co-workers in the sacred ministry, the presbyter and deacon. Together, each of these three works toward the same goal, which is to build up the communion of the local church in holiness so that all may attain to salvation (LG 32). There is no need here for a *cursus honorum* if we fully embrace the Church as a communion and the mystery of the sacrament of Holy Orders in the sense developed here from the Second Vatican Council.

The Second Vatican Council only once uses the Greek word *diakonia* and when it does it uses it to describe the ministry of the bishop, "And that duty, which the Lord committed to the shepherds of His people, is a true service, which in sacred literature is significantly called "diakonia" or ministry." (LG 24) The Scriptural references supplied to support this are all examples of the *diakon* group or words translated as ministry. Acts 1:17-25 – choosing a replacement for the *ministry* of Judas; Acts 21:19 – the *ministry* of Paul among the gentiles; Romans 11:13 – Paul speaks of his *ministry;* and 1 Timothy 1:12 – Paul gives thanks that the Lord Jesus Christ has called him into this *ministry.* This usage does not develop or restrict the ministry of the bishop to charity or social service as the

same Council begins to do when it writes about deacons, though not so completely in this vein as we find in more recent servant myth sources. All instances cited also use *diakon* words in way consistent with the semantic profile developed by Collins, in the right side of the semantic profile chart above. That is, each is about receiving a commission or mandate to carry out a task on behalf of another or in their name.

When we explore the section of *Lumen gentium* which outlines the relationship of bishop, presbyter and deacon (chapter four), we can see that the Council is trying to sketch the implications of this descending theology of Holy Orders. The bishop is the *diaconos* of Christ, who stands in the midst of the community, which is why a bishop says, "Peace be with you", echoing the words of the Risen Christ in the midst of his apostles, and why in Masses at which he presides there can be seven candles on the altar, a reference to Christ standing in the seven lamps midst of the seven Churches of Asia Minor in the Book of Revelation. He ordains two others as *diaconos* – the presbyter and deacon – to carry out the tasks he has mandated them to carry out. What distinguishes these two from one another is not rank but their primary orientation within the community. To whom are they sent and what is the primary, not sole, orientation of this sending? In this next diagram, I sketch the basic orientation, as gleaned from *Lumen gentium* but also the respective directories for the ministry and life of presbyters and deacons.

The primary orientation of the presbyter is to the gathered Eucharistic assembly (*synaxis*). This is because his ministry is primarily to represent the bishop, as his *diaconos* of the Mass, and because he presides over the Eucharist of this synaxis he also presides over the community as leader, by virtue of the eucharistic presidency. Recall that *Lumen gentium* emphasised the ancient teaching of the Church that the bishop presides at the Eucharist in person or causes it to be celebrated, and this is so with all of the sacraments. The presbyter is oriented toward the portion of the People of God who constitute this *synaxis* and he builds them up through word and sacrament for sharing in the mission of the Gospel.

The primary orientation of the deacon is toward the dispersed community. This may be particular groups within a parish such as young adults, or children in schools, or couples preparing for marriage, or for the RCIA for people wanting to become Christians or preparing Christians for the Rite of Reception who are wishing to enter full communion with the Catholic Church. Or the deacon could be sent to migrants, to refugees, to university and school chaplaincies or as hospital chaplains or in ministries of evangelisation and outreach to those who have left the Church or have never known it. He might even be sent to care for the poor and marginalised, the homeless, but that is not because deacon means servant of the poor but because the Christian community has identified a need and is sending a minister to bring the grace and presence of a Church's ministry to this situation.

Of course, there is overlap in what presbyters and deacons do in the Church, as there is with what lay people and also consecrated women and men Religious do. But doing does not define ministry; it is being that is central, and faith in sacramental grace and the specific grace or ordination. All Catholics have a liturgical ministry as they all participate in the one priesthood of Christ through which the Eucharist is offered. Christ prays through, with and in his body the Church and his priestly people offer the sacrifice of the Mass but this does not cancel out the priesthood of the *sacerdoti* (bishop and presbyter). The liturgical and sacramental ministry of the deacon is integrated with all aspects of the ministry of the deacon, just as they are for the presbyter, bishop and lay person.

Liturgy, charity, justice are not all separate doings, they are each a participation in the mission of Christ, in a different manner. The key point here is that the laity and clergy are within the one circle that is the *communio* of the Church. The laity are not just those not ordained, they are with the clergy the one People of God. Some within the *communio* are called to ministry, some called to ministry are permanently oriented to the *diakonia* and are ordained and some are not, and all are called to mission by virtue of being in communion. We need to briefly turn our attention to this concept of *communio/koinonia* before we can conclude this chapter.

Ecclesiology and Spirituality of Communion/ *communio/koinonia*

The 1985 Synod of Bishops was called to celebrate the close of the Second Vatican Council in 1965 and to evaluate the progress of implementation of its reforms. The Synod identified *communio/koinonia* as the central theme of the Council and the key to unlocking the meaning of each of the documents of the Council. "The ecclesiology of communion is the central and fundamental idea of the Council's documents. *Koinonia/communion*, founded on the Sacred Scripture, have been held in great honour in the early Church and in the Oriental Churches to this day. Thus, much was done by the Second Vatican Council so that the Church as communion might be more clearly understood and concretely incorporated into life."[28] In this same section, the bishops draw our attention to the fact that *communio* is the foundation for understanding the nature of the Church and the relationship of order that exists with it, and that the order of the church is not purely an organisation matter or a matter of powers.

> "What does the complex word "communion" mean? Fundamentally, it is a matter of communion with God through Jesus Christ, in the Holy Spirit. This communion is had in the Word of God and in the sacraments. Baptism is the door and the foundation of communion in the Church. The Eucharist is the source and the culmination of the whole Christian life (cf. LG 11) The communion of the eucharistic Body of Christ signifies and produces, that is, builds up, the intimate communion of all the faithful in the Body of Christ which is the Church (1 Corinthians 10:16). For this reason, the ecclesiology of communion cannot be reduced to purely organisational questions or to problems which simply relate to powers. Still, the ecclesiology of communion is also the foundation for order in the Church, and

---

28 Synod of Bishops 1985, Final Report. C1

especially for a correct relationship between unity and pluriformity in the Church."

In his letter *Novo Millennio Ineunte,* Pope John Paul II developed the theme of *communio* and the notion that it embraces an ecclesiology and a spirituality. *Communio* goes to the very heart of human yearning and the Church is a response to that yearning. He develops the theme in a dense paragraph number forty-three:

> To make the Church *the home and the school of communion*: that is the great challenge facing us in the millennium which is now beginning, if we wish to be faithful to God's plan and respond to the world's deepest yearnings... we need *to promote a spirituality of communion,* making it the guiding principle of education wherever individuals and Christians are formed, wherever ministers of the altar, consecrated persons, and pastoral workers are trained, wherever families and communities are being built up.

In this same paragraph, he outlines how *koinonia* opens us up to others in the Church and the world with a warm and generous capacity to love and embrace them. There is no room for rancour and a sense of not having equal dignity as a Christian in the church regardless if one is ordained or not. He writes:

> A spirituality of communion indicates above all the heart's contemplation of the mystery

of the Trinity dwelling in us, and whose light we must also be able to see shining on the face of the brothers and sisters around us. A spirituality of communion also means an ability to think of our brothers and sisters in faith within the profound unity of the Mystical Body, and therefore as "those who are a part of me". This makes us able to share their joys and sufferings, to sense their desires and attend to their needs, to offer them deep and genuine friendship. A spirituality of communion implies also the ability to see what is positive in others, to welcome it and prize it as a gift from God: not only as a gift for the brother or sister who has received it directly, but also as a "gift for me". A spirituality of communion means, finally, to know how to "make room" for our brothers and sisters, bearing "each other's burdens" (*Galatians* 6:2) and resisting the selfish temptations which constantly beset us and provoke competition, careerism, distrust and jealousy.

Ministry is situated at the heart of the ecclesia and is for the ecclesia, not above it as a dominating force. It comes to us as a gift from outside of the Church, from Christ in the Holy Spirit. When it is exercised as dominance and oppression and even arrogance, then we know that the exercise of the ministry is not enriched by a spirituality and theology of *koinonia*. We can only see what *diaconia* (ministry) is if we have the sacramental imagination to see the Church as a *communio*.

Conclusion

One of the most remarkable things about the profile of the *diacon* words developed by Collins is the degree to which they relate so clearly to the recovered sense of a descending theology of Holy Orders. This profile allows us to fill in some of the gaps in our understanding and provides a more robust foundation for the descending theology of Holy Orders found in the documents of the Second Vatican Council. Collins shows us that the *diacon* words indicate a direction of service. The apostles' *diaconia* stems from the mandate and commission they have received from Christ. They serve Christ and his Gospel.

Episcopal ordination is the reception of the mandate and commission to be an active and living sign of the presence of the apostolic ministry. Bishops serve the apostolic ministry of witness to the resurrection and proclamation of the Gospel. When the Council refers to the ministry of the bishop as a *diaconia* it does not do so with the mutated meaning of these words but with the original sense now exposed for us once again by Collins. The bishop does not accumulate the episcopate, little by little, but in one moment as it were the fulness is received from the fullness that precedes his individual ordination. That is why the practice for the first millennium allowed for direct ordination. No one had to accumulated all the powers along the way, the fullness was from Christ and was a hierarchic gift in the sense we described above. That is why it was common for deacons to be ordained bishops but not as presbyters along the way and no one considered this a theological problem to be solved. John Collins did not invent or create the definition of the *diacon* word group, he recovered it. This was the ordinary way in which the words were understood for most of Christian history and this was the way they were understood in relation to Holy Orders.

A paradigm shift is long overdue with regard to the theology and the practice of the diaconate and ministry in general. That shift must be founded on the profile of the *diacon* words developed by Collins. This profile, we have now seen, creates a harmony with the recovered descending theology of Holy Orders and the theology of *communio*. If we build our theology of diaconate on these foundations, we will have a house built on rock, a very solid foundation. If we build a theology on better foundation, we can unleash the power of this ministry for the new evangelisation and energise the mission of the Church. We will take up this theme in the next chapter.

HERALDS OF THE GOSPEL: NEW MISSION AND NEW EVANGELISATION

During the Rite of Ordination of a Deacon, and after the ordination itself, the newly ordained is presented with the *Evangeliary* (Book of Gospels).[1] The bishop says to him; "Receive the Gospel of Christ, whose herald you now are. Believe what you read, teach what you believe, and practise what you teach". The *Evangeliary* is the key symbol of the ministry of the deacon and is the symbol through which his ministry may be understood. His task is primarily that of proclaiming the Gospel or, characteristically, a ministry of evangelisation. In the ordination of a *presbyter*, the key symbols are those associated with his *sacerdotal* (priestly) functions: chalice and paten. The *presbyter* presides over the Eucharist for a portion of the diocese (a parish) in the name of the bishop, who always celebrates or causes to be celebrated the Eucharist in the local church (diocese).[2] We

---

1   Paul VI (1991) *The Roman Ritual and Pontifical*. Rite of Ordination for a Deacon. Liturgical Press: Collegeville, Minn., pp.27-38
2   SC 26, 41,42

would not interpret the symbolism of chalice and paten in any other way. We should not interpret the presentation of the Book of Gospels in any other way either. Deep in the roots of this tradition of handing the Book of Gospels is embedded the original meaning of the word deacon and *diaconia*. We encountered the recovered semantic profile of the *diacon* word group in a previous chapter.

In this chapter, we shall consider the implications of our understanding of the deacon as herald of the Gospel. In what sense can we understand this in terms of the ministry of the deacon within the local church (diocese)? What are the kinds of pastoral placements that would best express what it means to be a herald of the Gospel? If the task of the deacon is primarily concerned with evangelisation – being a herald of the Gospel – how can that ministry develop in line with the needs of our own times and the demands of the new evangelisation?

The *Norms* and *Directory* make repeated reference to the contribution of deacons to the new evangelisation. It has been the contention of this book that the diaconate restored by Vatican II is a new wine and that we have not been able to receive this new wine because we have poured it into old wineskins, and the freshness of this ministry has been lost as the skins burst. So, it is with new evangelisation. We have attempted to pour the diaconate into the old wineskins of either: a now discredited semantic profile derived from the 19th century Lutheran experience which portrays the deacon as a servant and especially a servant of the poor and marginalised or a parish model based on the transitional deacon absorbed into the *cursus honorum*, as a kind of assistant to a *presbyter* and parish.

In many places, this distortion founded on the *cursus honorum* considers the deacon as a substitute for *presbyters*. In areas where *presbyters* are in short supply, deacons are by default used as "pastors" in parishes without a resident *presbyter* especially in rural and remote areas. I consider this problem in a little more detail elsewhere. Deacons cannot be effective agents of the new evangelisation in the local church until we have come to accept the new profile and recognise that we are dealing with a new wine.

A story of our times

Let me begin with a little anecdote to illustrate. In 2012, I attended a conference, *Proclaim*: on the new evangelisation. The conference was held in Sydney, Australia. The keynote speaker was Archbishop Rino Fisichella, president of the Pontifical Council for the New Evangelisation. He won't mind my telling this story because it has a really positive outcome. In one of his presentations, he spoke eloquently and passionately about the role of the bishop, the role of priests (*presbyters*), the role of members of religious institutes and the role of the laity in the new evangelisation. At the lunch break, I happened to be standing next to him in the very long and slow-moving queue. He could have skipped the line, as an eminent guest, but chose instead to suffer the long line with the rest of us. That in itself is a witness to the new evangelisation. I said to him, with a smile on my face, how much I enjoyed his presentation on the role of each of these (bishop, *presbyter*, religious, laity) in the new evangelisation and said that as a deacon I was quite relieved that I had nothing to do with this new enterprise. I expressed how glad I was that we deacons could relax and sit this one out.

Fortunately for me, I had read his personality correctly and he laughed, sharing in the joke, and then he responded. He and I then discussed all of the places in various documents where deacons are mentioned as having a particular role in the new evangelisation. We talked about how we might be able to engage his Council in some exploration of the relationship between deacons and the new evangelisation.

That conversation Archbishop Fisichella and I had that day in Sydney resulted in a conference for deacons held during the Jubilee for the Year of Mercy in Rome 2016. I delivered a paper on the theme of deacons and the new evangelisation; and deacons came from around the world in the largest gathering of deacons ever to explore this theme through a variety of presentations in venues across Rome. A number of the presentations, including the homily delivered by Pope Francis at the concluding Mass, indicated that a number of people still have some way to go toward accepting the new paradigm.

I start with this story about my encounter at the Proclaim conference because the official source documents such as the *Norms for the Formation of Deacons* and *the Directory for the Ministry and Life of Deacons*, as well as Popes John Paul II and Benedict XVI, all mention the contribution of deacons to the new evangelisation. Yet when we do our pastoral planning in dioceses, we rarely seem to mention the role of deacons (if we have deacons in our diocese at all) or harness the potential of them for the new evangelisation. In his encyclical letter *Joy of the Gospel*, devoted to the new evangelisation, Pope Francis only mentions deacons once and then only in connection with *presbyters*, laity and deacons sharing resources for preaching.[3] In his homily for the Mass in Rome, marking the close of the Jubilee for Deacons, Francis returned to the themes of the deacon servant myth inherited from the now familiar pathway we have traced, without mention of new evangelisation.

In his most recent apostolic letter *Gaudete et exsultate*, deacons receive no mention at all unless we include St Francis of Assisi who is reputed to be a deacon. As Archbishop of Buenos Aires, Jorge Bergoglio (Pope Francis) reflected his deep roots in the *cursus honorum* and the concept of the *presbyter* as the measure of all ministry in pre-Vatican II style when he argued that he did not want to have deacons in is diocese because he feared clericalising the laity. One presumes he thought *presbyters* were born clerics or else clerics and *sacerdotal/presbyteral* ministry were identified as one and the same thing in his theological understanding. He has a very *presbyter*-centric view of ordained ministry and has frequently referred to himself as a priest or parish priest when visiting communities, even though his primary identity should be that of bishop. He never refers to himself as a deacon, though he would have been one of those too. To be fair, no bishop makes such a connection.

Although the Second Vatican Council did not use the term "new evangelisation", the concept behind it – of a robust

---

3   Francis (2013) *Evangelii Gaudium*. n159 "How good it is when *presbyters*, deacons and the laity gather periodically to discover resources which can make preaching more attractive!"

and new creative proclamation of the Gospel adapted to the needs of the women and men of our times – was present throughout. Paul VI wrote about this in *Evangelii nuntiandi* shortly after the Council, even before Pope John Paul II had coined the term "the new evangelisation".[4] The ITC document on the diaconate which we looked at in chapter one suggests that something like responding to the new evangelisation, with new and fresh methods, was in part the motivation of Vatican II for the restoration of the permanent ministry of deacon in the Latin Church.

I suggest that one aspect of the new wine of the permanent ministry of deacon is that it does have a primary orientation toward the new evangelisation. Because we have not understood that and taken this into account in our diocesan pastoral planning, we attempt to put the new wine of the permanent ministry of deacon into the old wine skin of the transitional deacon with its parochial orientation and add to it the servant of charity model inherited from the nineteenth century Lutheran initiative. As we have noted, the skins burst and the gift that we are meant to receive from the Holy Spirit in this ministry – for the building up of the Church for mission and outreach – is lost.

The deacon as minister of the new evangelisation

I wish to propose that Acts 6:1-7, the institution of the Seven (sometimes called the seven deacons, a claim which is contentious), may be taken as a paradigm of the

---

4   Paul VI (1975) *Evangelii nuntiandi*, n 26, 63

new evangelisation. We have examined this text in earlier chapters, including whether or not the text actually refers to deacons, but here we wish to focus on new evangelisation. We do need to recap some of what was said in previous chapters. The sole reason for the selection of the Seven was to respond to a new pastoral situation for evangelisation. The apostles had already been engaged in evangelisation in the Temple to Aramaic speaking people. Christ established only one ministry in his life time and that was the apostolic ministry.

The Church in Acts 6:1-7 has to find a way to adapt this apostolic ministry to new circumstances. A new situation emerges in the Church amongst the Greek speakers and for the widows within the Greek speaking community in particular. This text has the three senses of the new evangelisation indicated by Pope John Paul II: "[in] its ardour, methods and expression", in order to respond to new situations so that the Gospel may be proclaimed.[5] In this sense, it may be taken as paradigmatic for the new situation in which the Church finds herself today. This new situation was already part of the background to the Second Vatican Council and as we have seen it formed part of the motivation for the restoration of the permanent exercise of the ministry of deacon.

In Acts 6, the Greek or Hellenist members of the community complain that their widows are neglected in the daily *diaconia*. Many modern translations after 1946 add to

---

5 John Paul II New Evangelisation; The Church must face other challenges and push forward to new frontiers, both in the initial mission *ad gentes* and in the new evangelization of those peoples who have already heard Christ proclaimed. *Audience with Bishops from Columbia on their "ad limina" visit on 15 June 1996*. 'The Task of the Latin American bishops', Origins 12 (March 24, 1983), 659-62

the text – after the word "daily" – the words "distribution of food or funds" to supply a meaning for *diaconia* in this verse. That is, the translators wish to present the story as one of material neglect of the widows and not one of neglect of the proclamation of the Word and formation in faith. The term "distribution of food or of funds" is not found in any Greek manuscript of Acts 6 or translations before 1946. These are pure scribal or translators' additions to the text in very recent times. These same translations do not add food or funds or suggest a material need in any other place in the New Testament where *diaconia* or its cognates are found.[6] Normally, *diaconia* is translated by them as ministry, and as ministry of the word or similar words for ministry.

What is happening in Acts 6:1-7 if it is not about food or funds? The Hellenist widows (Greek speakers) are neglected in the daily ministry or *diaconia* of the word (*diaconia tou logou*) because of their situation. What is their situation? The Apostles who are Aramaic speakers, preaching mostly in the Temple forecourt, cannot minister to the Greek speaking widows in their homes (at tables, *trapeizes*, as the Greek expresses it).[7] Social conventions meant that they would mostly remain at home and linguistic barriers required Greek speakers to minister to their needs. The Apostles ask the community to identify seven Greek speakers to carry out

---

[6] John N. Collins (2002) *Deacons and the Church: Making Connections Between Old and New*. Leomister: Gracewing. pp27-73 For a more complete study of the true semantic scope of the *diacon* group of words refer to John N. Collins (1990) *Diakonia: Reinterpreting the Ancient Sources*. Oxford: Oxford University Press.

[7] See John N. Collins (2002) *Deacons and the Church*, for elucidation of the term "to minister tables" (*diaconein trapezais*) in Acts 6:2.

this ministry (of the Word) on their behalf. That the primary concern is one of language and access to the Gospel in a language which the Greek speakers can understand is made clear from verse one.

Luke Timothy Johnson draws our attention to the use of the Greek terms *hebraios* and *helenistes* in Acts 6:1-7, which Luke only uses to designate linguistic categories and not ethnicity.[8] These words are linguistic categories, identifying those who spoke Greek or Aramaic and not those who are ethnically Greek. These are most likely Greek speaking Jews of the *Diaspora* or the Greek speaking so called 'God-fearers'. The 'God-fearers" were gentiles who associated themselves with synagogues but who did not convert to Judaism.[9] We must presume that the Seven were multilingual and able to translate the Aramaic spoken by the Apostles into *koine* Greek for the widows and others in the Greek speaking community. The distinction is between those who speak only Aramaic and those who speak Greek. That is the only thing that Acts 6 is concerned with and not food or funds.

---

8 Johnson, L.T. (1992) The Acts of the Apostles. In *Sacra Pagina Series*. Collegeville, Minnesota: The Liturgical Press, p. 105

9 Jews were permitted under Roman Law to continue their religious traditions and were exempt from civic religious duties of worship city gods and the emperor etc. but they were forbidden to convert people to Judaism. Because bathing was a public ritual, and Jews required the circumcision of males, it would be obvious if a gentile male had converted. This had serious legal consequences for him, his family and the local Jewish community. Some gentiles chose to associate with the Jewish communities and observe what Jewish law they could without a formal conversion and circumcision.

The source of the complaint cannot be food or funds as modern translators try to assert by their scribal additions.[10] This can also be deduced from the preceding story in chapter five about the terrible consequence for withholding from the common fund. It is difficult to imagine the community could have so quickly forgotten the lesson of that story and neglected the material needs of the widows. A second problem is that the words food or funds never appear in any Greek manuscript or translation in any language before 1946. Therefore, the ministry of the Seven cannot be viewed primarily as a ministry of charity.

Fitzmyer comments on this section of Acts that; "when we read of the events in which Philip and Stephen are engaged in the rest of Book of Acts, it is clear that they were not chosen for some task of distributing food or funds. We only see these two preach, catechise, baptise and, in the case of Stephen, he dies as a witness to the faith. Philip is simply known by the title; "the evangelist, one of the Seven" (Acts 21:8)"[11]. The Seven are chosen for some position of leadership among the Hellenists or Greek speakers.[12] We also see that the

---

10 Failure to distribute food or funds could hardly have been an issue after we learn what happened to Ananias and Sapphira who are struck dead for withholding from the common contributions. An event which causes great fear to come over the whole community Acts 5:1-11.
11 "Leaving the next day, we reached Caesarea and stayed at the house of Philip the evangelist, one of the Seven." Acts 21:7
12 Joseph A Fitzmyer (1998) *Commentary on Acts of the Apostles.* Anchor Bible Commentary. New York: Doubleday. Acts 6:7-8:40 and Acts 21:8 Leaving the next day, we reached Caesarea and stayed at the house of Philip the evangelist, one of the Seven. Notice that he is simply known as the evangelist. I have written more extensively on Acts 6 in *The Pastoral Review* see, Deacons and the Servant Myth. Vol 2/6.

communities they visit are associated with the Hellenist (Greek speaking) regions outside of Palestine. Fitzmyer goes on to comment that the Seven have received, through the laying on of hands, a share of the mandate that the Twelve received from the Lord.

The Seven are chosen for the ministry of the Word (*diaconia tou logou*), a new evangelisation, among the Greek speakers. Pope Benedict suggests Stephen is a model for new evangelisation.[13] The nascent community recognised that if the Word of God is to spread and influence the wider world, a Greek speaking world, the Church needed to select people who could speak the word in a new situation and in a way that was comprehensible to a new audience. In Acts 6, we see a paradigm of the new evangelisation. That is why this section of Acts concludes; "The Word of God continued to spread" (Acts 6:7) and not "funds or food were better distributed".[14]

November 2006. p3-7, and Deacons: Herald of the Gospel. Vol 3/5 September 2007. p10-15 and Reader Response to Deacons Servants of Caritas. Vol 4/3, May 2008, pp. 44-46.

13   Pope Benedict Angelus address December 27, 2012; "the life and death of St. Stephen serves as a "model for all those who want to serve the new evangelization.

14   It is worth noting that scholarship on the semantic scope of the diacon group of words reveals that they never include a sense of service directed toward another or humble service and are never used as synonyms for any of the caritative words until the late 19th century, where the practice then become embedded in Biblical commentaries and theology of diaconate. See Sven Brodd (2000) Caritas and diaconia as perspectives on the Diaconate. In Borgegard, Fanuelsen and Hall (eds) The Ministry of the Deacon: Ecclesiological Reflections 2, Nordic Ecumenical Council, 2000, pp42-43 and also Collins below.

The deacon as herald of the Gospel of Mercy

In the bull of indiction for the Year of Mercy, Pope Francis writes, "The Church is commissioned to announce the mercy of God, the beating heart of the Gospel".[15] In the Latin Church after his ordination takes place and he is vested in stole and dalmatic, the deacon receives from the hand of the bishop the Book of Gospels (*Evangeliary*). The Evangeliary is the deacons' book. Only the deacon may process into the Church with the Evangeliary and place (enthrone) it on the altar. If he is not present, the Evangeliary is placed on the altar before Mass without ceremony.[16] At a Council, the Evangeliary is processed in carried by a deacon, accompanied by singing and incense and is enthroned before the assembly. At the close of Vatican II, Pope Paul VI asked the Master of Ceremonies if he could process in with the Evangeliary for the enthronement but was refused because only a deacon may perform this task. At a Mass where a deacon is present only, he may proclaim the Gospel. This task can never be delegated to a *presbyter* or bishop. Every deacon can recall that moment when the Book of Gospels was handed to him in the Rite of Ordination accompanied by the words, "Receive the Book of the Gospels, whose herald you have become. Believe what you read, teach what you believe, and practise what you teach". At that moment, he takes into his hand the beating heart of the Gospel. He becomes the herald of mercy.

As heralds of the Gospel of mercy, deacons must not only be doers of the word or rush to action. Pope Francis says

---

15 Pope Francis *Misericordiae Vultus*, n.12
16 GIRM 2010 Chapter IV Different Forms of Celebrating Mass. 171

that "at times we [Christians] are called to gaze even more attentively on mercy so that we may become a more effective sign of the Father's action in our lives".[17] Later he goes on to say, "In order to be capable of mercy, therefore, we must first of all dispose ourselves to listen to the Word of God. This means rediscovering the value of silence in order to meditate on the Word that comes to us. In this way, it will be possible to contemplate God's mercy and adopt it as our lifestyle."[18] A deacon is called, therefore, to embrace and nurture the contemplative dimension and allow himself to be conformed to the image of mercy through conversion of life.

Through contemplation and conversion, we discover a word of mercy the world needs to hear and learn to speak it in a way that the world can comprehend. This is a Gospel that we proclaim in both words and deeds. In many countries, especially those where the Gospel had once taken deep roots and shaped the culture and memory as well as the institutions of society, the Gospel of mercy is no longer heard. This situation prevails in Western Europe, U.K, North America, Australia and New Zealand. Such places risk becoming spiritual deserts incapable of achieving solidarity necessary for love of neighbour or capable of sustaining a meaningful life.

A symptom of this malaise is the growth in the number of people diagnosed with depression and the extension of the diagnosis reaching down from adulthood into childhood today.[19] The World Health Organisations lists depression as

---

17 Francis *Misericordiae Vultus*, n.3
18 Francis *Misericordiae Vultus*, n.13
19 Readers may wish to follow up some reports from WHO http://www.who.int/mental_health/management/depression/prevalence_

the greatest threat to health and declining life expectancy and or major health issue for the future.[20] Hedonism, a loss of meaning and hyper-individualism make each person an island unto themself, reversing the deep insight into communion of which John Donne wrote in his poem "No Man is an Island".[21]

If so, and if much of the world has become a spiritual desert, then deacons are called to pour the water of the Gospel of Mercy, that little drop they pour into the chalice, and bring the lives of all people into the heart of mystery of Jesus. In his 2013 Easter message, Pope Francis said; "God's mercy can make even the driest land become a garden, can restore life to dry bones (cf. Ezekiel 37:1-14)… Let us be renewed by God's mercy, let us be loved by Jesus, let us enable the power of his love to transform our lives too; and let us become agents of this mercy."[22] The ministry of the deacon is specifically that of bringing the water of the Gospel to a dry and thirsty land.

As heralds of the Gospel of Mercy, it is the specific duty of the deacon to bring this word into the new situation in which we find ourselves today. The deacon is called to a wider mission not confined primarily to parochial ministry. The parish is primarily the ministerial domain of the *presbyter*

---

global_health_estimates/en/

20 Readers may wish to read about the despair of modern life in this article by Aaron Keriaty, Dying of Despair. First Things. August 2017. https://www.firstthings.com/article/2017/08/dying-of-despair#print

21 John Donne, *No Man Is An Island*. In the poem Donne expresses the deepest level of human solidarity; "No man is an Island, entire of itself; every man is a piece of the Continent, a part of the main." *Meditation 17, Devotions upon Emergent Occasions. 1624 AD*

22 Pope Francis, *Easter Urbi et Orbi message on March 31, 2013*

because he is presider at the Eucharistic assembly. This is not normally the primary sphere of activity of the deacon. At least not in the sense that he is oriented toward the parish as a kind of associate to the *presbyter* in much the same way as a transitional deacon is oriented during his apprenticeship for the presbyterate.

As a herald of new evangelisation, the deacon must go where, perhaps, the church has not gone before or go in a way that the church has not gone before. Like the situation in Acts 6, he has to respond to those who are neglected in the daily *diaconia*, the ministry of the Gospel of Mercy. He does not enter into this ministry alone or by his own initiative. He is to be commissioned and sent by his bishop, who with the local church has discerned how to respond to a new pastoral situation in a reflection of the discernment process of Acts 6. At the diocesan level, or even at the level of parish, the community should be discerning which groups within the diocese or beyond the parish are neglected in this ministry of the Gospel of Mercy and the bishop appoints the deacon to go there on behalf of the local church. In reality, such discernment and commissioning of the deacon by the bishop to engage in a ministry of new evangelisation rarely happens.

Promotion of the new evangelisation within the diocese

Let us now turn our attention to the new evangelisation in the diocese. Only once in the documents of the Second Vatican Council is the word *diaconia* used and used correctly, in the sense of ministry. That place is *Lumen gentium* 24, where the episcopal office is simply called a *diaconia* or ministry.[23] In its teaching on deacons, the Second Vatican Council had three main intentions: first, to restore the diaconate as a permanent reality, though not in any particular form; and second, to re-establish the visible sign of what the Catholic faith teaches that the sacrament of apostolic ministry has this threefold order; and third, to re-establish the principle that both *presbyters* and deacons are sharers in the *diaconia* of the bishop.[24] There were three motivations that prompted the decision: the first is faith in the threefold order, the second is pastoral care of communities and what we now call new evangelisation, and the third, that the grace of the sacrament of diaconate be opened to the Church.[25]

In the renewed theology of Holy Orders which emerged from Vatican II, the bishop is the one in whom the fullness of the sacrament of orders is found.[26] *Presbyters* and deacons are collaborators with him, receiving a share in his ministry of word and sacrament.[27] For the *presbyters*, the primary work is to care for a portion of the diocese in a specific territory or parish.[28] It is the deacon who is ordained specifically for the ministry of the bishop as his right hand man who can share

---

[23] Paul VI (1965) *Lumen Gentium*, n23. And that duty, which the Lord committed to the shepherds of His people, is a true service, which in sacred literature is significantly called *"diaconi*a" or ministry. Cf Acts 1:17, 25; 21:19; Rom. 11:13; 1 Tim. 1:12

[24] International Theological Commission (ITC) (2003) *From the Diaconia of Christ Diaconia of the Apostles. Historico-Theological Research Document.* p57-59

[25] ITC 2003 *From the diaconia of Christ diaconia of the Apostles.* p57-58

[26] *Lumen Gentium,* n21 and *Christus dominus,* n15

[27] Lumen Gentium 28, Directory, n23

[28] Canon 515§1

with him the broader vision of the pastoral needs of the diocese.²⁹

"For the ministry of the bishop" is the key element of the statement above. It is half quoted in the documents of Vatican II when *Lumen gentium* notes that the deacon is ordained "not for the priesthood (*sacerdotium*), but for the ministry (*ministerium*)", and leaves out the "of the bishop" which is the qualifier clause in the source quote from the *Apostolic Constitutions*.³⁰ The way Vatican II uses (mis-uses) the text is to leave out the central qualification about the kind of service the deacon is to perform. It is a service for the bishop as his minister and executive officer. This half quote distorts the meaning of the text. It is like the half quote of Psalm 14, which clearly teaches, that there is no God. It shifts in meaning when put back into context: "A fool says in her/his heart, there is no God". Or perhaps like the half quote attributed to Pope Francis; "Who am I to judge?" When placed in its full context it does not have the meaning attributed to it or as has been used or mis-used by those who quote it.³¹

---

29 The deacon upon whom hands are imposed "not unto the presbyterate, but unto a ministry of service of the bishop. *Constitutiones Ecclesiae aegyptiacae*, III, 2: ed. Funk, Didascalia, II, p. 103. *Statua Eccl. Ant.* 371: Mansi 3, 954

30 LG 29

31 In the full quote, Pope Francis is asked a very specific question about a very specific issue involving a very specific *presbyter*. The pope is asked by a reporter about an Italian *presbyter* who was alleged to have had an intimate sexual relationship with one man and alleged to have frequented gay bars. The full context is available in the transcript provided by the Holy See. *Apostolic journey to Rio de Janeiro on the occasion of the xxviii World Youth Day, Press conference of pope Francis during the return flight. Papal Flight Sunday, 28 July 2013*. The context is specific and he talks of sin and conversion. It is not an exhortation not to make appropriate discernment and judgements about sin.

The deacon is not ordained for some vague service or a servant ministry or of a service to the poor or any other construction, but is ordained for the service of the bishop in his oversight of the local church. Interpreting the Council on ministry is not an easy task because *sacerdos* and its cognates are used interchangeably with *ministerium* and its cognates and even the variations of the use of *ministerium* relies upon context to fathom the particular meaning behind the term in any passage. There is no consistent use of these terms in the documents of Vatican II.

John N. Collins has demonstrated that the ordinary meaning of the deacon words indicates that the deacon is an emissary of the bishop, his executive officer.[32] In a similar vein, ancient writers described the deacons as the hands, eyes and ears discerning the pastoral needs of the local church and wider society thus allowing the bishop and local church to respond to these needs. The ancient documents do not present the deacon as responding to the needs but only making the bishop and local church aware of them. The deacon undertook this task of looking and listening at the commission of the bishop.[33] Even today, the liturgy of the Eucharist both East and West assigns to the deacon the task

---

Given Pope Francis's history of opposition to same sex marriage both as Pope and Archbishop of Buenos Aires, where he refers to same sex marriage as the work of the Devil, his statement "who am I to judge" can hardly be interpreted too broadly.

32   See Collins. J.N (2002) *Deacons and the Church*. Harrisburg, Penn: Gracewing. and also, Collins. J.N (1990) *Diakonia: Reinterpreting the Ancient Sources*. Oxford: Oxford University Press.

33   Apostolic Constitutions 2.44; but let the deacon be the bishop's ear, and eye, and mouth, and heart, and soul, that the bishop may not be distracted with many cares,

of announcing the needs of the Church and world during the liturgy (the intercessions, *ektanies* of the Eastern Liturgies, universal prayer as it is variously described) and at the end of the Mass the deacon, in the rite of dismissal, commissions the community to respond to the needs of the Church and world. Benedict XVI has drawn our attention to the mission character of the rite of dismissal by including new formulas.[34] Both, intercessions and dismissal, are done by a deacon and never a lay person or *presbyter* if a deacon is present at Mass.[35]

The reservation of the proclamation of the intercessions and the rite of dismissal to deacons is not merely some attachment to liturgical rubricism or legalism, it reveals the preservation of the deeper theological tradition and understanding of the diaconate that prevailed before the nineteenth century service/service/charity aberration. Deep in the liturgical tradition, going back to the first centuries of Christianity, these elements are reserved to deacons in the liturgy because the Church had a deeper understanding of the *diacon* group of words and the ministry of the deacon.[36]

Herald in the local church

There is ample scope for the deacon as herald of mercy for the new evangelisation in the diocese.[37] The *Norms* and

---

34 Roman Missal, 144 Rite of Dismissal, "Go and announce the Gospel of the Lord", and "Go in peace, glorifying the Lord by your life."
35 GIRM 171
36 These elements are mentioned in the Apostolic Constitutions, a third century document which itself has an earlier pedigree.
37 Directory 37 and 42 indicate that diocesan and parochial works of charity constitute the primary ministry of deacons (not secular employment) and some specific diocesan offices are listed but the scope of ministry is wider than these.

Directory suggest deacons have a primary role to play in new evangelisation and in parochial and diocesan ministries.[38] The Directory indicates some particular situations such as marriage preparation, support for married couples and families, youth ministry, chaplaincy in Catholic and other schools and universities, outreach to groups on the margins of Church, sacramental preparation, RCIA (for the unbaptised), Reception into Full Communion (for the baptised), works of charity and mercy and many other possibilities.[39] In fact, the scope of diaconal ministry is only limited by the imagination and the will of those who engage in reflection on pastoral planning in the diocese.

The recent emphasis given to support for marriage and the family in the Synod of Bishops on the family and the exhortation *Amoris Laetitia* may suggest once again that we look at the potential for new initiatives in these areas where deacons may be suitable ministers.[40] Deacons are engaged in the reality of marriage and family life in a way that most

---

38   Norms and Directory Joint introduction; with promising results, especially for the urgent missionary work of new evangelisation and promises to make an important contribution to New Evangelisation. Norms 79. It is particularly urgent today, in the face of the challenge of the new evangelization to which the Church is called at this difficult juncture of the millennium. Directory; 26. Contemporary society requires a new evangelization which demands a greater and more generous effort on the part of ordained ministers.
39   Directory nn26, 27, 31, 33, 37, 38, 39, 41, 42
40   Francis (2016) Post-synodal apostolic exhortation *Amoris Laetitia*. Liberia Editrice Vaticana. Especially Chapter six. Francis only mentions deacons once and again obliquely as he did in Joy of the Gospel.

presbyters in the Latin Church can not. That experience may be a useful bridge to couples and families.[41]

I am inclined to read the intention of the Council to suggest that what is envisaged is a fulltime ministry in a diocese and that the deacon in secular employment is intended to be the exception rather than the most common pattern. Certainly, in the economically developed nations, there exists the means to support such a ministry. There is also canonical provision for remuneration of deacons which can be easily managed in economically advanced nations as they are the same provisions for *presbyters*.[42] I suspect it is really a question of the will and of mindset preventing the development of diaconal ministry along these lines rather than anything in the practical order. A change of mindset is the breakthrough that is needed to allow the grace of the sacrament of diaconal ordination to flow for the new evangelisation in a diocese.

Too often, a deacon is left to work out the details of his own pastoral ministry. He frequently does so within the scope of a parish and by a handshake deal with the parish *presbyter*. As a minister of the Church and as the bishop's right-hand man, it is essential that his pastoral appointment is discerned by the bishop who alone is responsible for his appointment.[43] This rarely happens. In his letter *Gaudium*

---

[41] I do not subscribe to the view that just because they are married and have families that this confers expertise on married clergy or that celibate clergy do not have deep insights into family life that are relevant for ministry to marriage and families.

[42] Directory for the Ministry and Life of Deacons 1998; 16-20.

[43] Directory n8. Only a bishop may appointment a deacon to his ministry

Evangelii (in which there is unfortunately only one oblique reference to deacons), Pope Francis writes about new pastoral initiatives for evangelisation: "The important thing is to not walk alone, but to rely on each other as brothers and sisters, and especially under the leadership of the bishops, in a wise and realistic pastoral discernment."[44]

Finding new ways

An essential aspect of the new evangelisation is to find new ways. Pope Francis writes: "Pastoral ministry in a missionary key seeks to abandon the complacent attitude that says: 'We have always done it this way'. I invite everyone to be bold and creative in this task of rethinking the goals, structures, style and methods of evangelisation in their respective communities."[45]

I am convinced that the Holy Spirit, working through the Council, restored the ministry of deacon to furnish the Church with a means of doing something new; for proclaiming the Gospel of Mercy in new ways and in new places. The Spirit is prompting diocesan communities to discern who is neglected in the daily *diaconia* and to plan appropriate pastoral initiatives in response. Bishops have the key role in such discernment. Bold and creative thinking by bishops and their close collaborators is called for in the reception of the ministry of deacons as a central part of the new evangelisation within the diocese.

Let's turn our attention to some specific proposals and allow these to be a means to stimulate some thinking in a

---

44 Pope Francis, *Evangelii Gaudium*, n33
45 Pope Francis, *Evangelii Gaudium*, n33

missionary key as suggested by Pope Francis. I don't want these to be taken as prescriptive – only as one attempt to address a community neglected in the daily *diaconia* and the Gospel of Mercy. New evangelisation asks us to ponder new ways and new places in which to bring the Gospel. We could think about many ways and places for the pastoral ministry of deacons as ministers to families, couples preparing for marriage, couples divorced or separated, youth, migrants and refugees, in the factory or office or other workplaces as chaplain, in the local shopping mall, with the poor and homeless or turning the hearts and minds of the privileged few toward their poor and marginalised sisters and brothers. The scope is almost endless and, because it is, I will focus on one example. The reader may take the cue from this example and apply it to other areas of pastoral need.

One area for ministry suited to the needs of our situation and the new evangelisation is the Catholic school. In some countries, there is a large and well-developed Catholic school system; in other countries, there is also a well-developed college and university system. What is said below about primary and secondary schools could be easily adapted to the tertiary education field. In Australia, twenty percent of all school aged children are educated in a Catholic school. There are only two Catholic universities and a small number of theological faculties, often associated with seminary formation, operating in Australia.

Deacons as Chaplains in Catholic Schools

The Catholic school as a potential locus for the ministry of deacons is suggested in a number of parts of the *Directory*

(26, 28, 33, 37 and 42) either directly or by implication from the context of that section of Directory. In relation to the ministry of the word and the new evangelisation, the Catholic school as well as Catholic and secular universities, are suggested as potentially fruitful areas of ministry. The *Directory* suggests that diocesan and parochial pastoral ministries are historically and theologically the prime area for diaconal ministry. Schools and universities would be included among these diocesan and parochial ministries.

Pastoral and spiritual care of families is frequently mentioned throughout the *Directory* as a special area of diaconal ministry, in part because most deacons are family men and know intimately the joys and struggles, the hopes and questions that families experience daily. Schools provide one of the points of contact with families, especially families that are on the margins of the Church.

It has been well documented in recent years that in countries like Australia, many of the people who choose to send their children to Catholic schools are not strongly connected to the life of Eucharistic communities, even when they are in a parochial school. The parents may feel some level of connection with the Catholic tradition. They may have been brought up by their parents as Catholics and perhaps been exposed to Catholic schools but they maintain little or no connection to the Catholic Church apart from the schools which their children attend. Their children are not likely to form deeply rooted faith when they only have minimal exposure to Catholicism while at school and little reinforcement in living and growing in faith at home.

Teachers in Catholic schools frequently have little solid grounding in a living and mature Catholic faith. This may also be true of teachers of religious education (which is normally all primary school teachers) as well as teachers of other subjects. Teaching religious education may be experienced as a difficulty for some because they have such a diminished understanding of Catholic faith and life; and perhaps very little lived experience of the Catholic tradition outside of the school in which they work.

Some Catholics might bemoan the situation described above, suggesting it is a sign of a failed mission. With the eye trained to look through the perspective of new evangelisation, rather than signs of failure the situations described above are pastoral opportunities waiting to be developed. Our concern and our energy for mission should be especially focused on families, parents and teachers in this situation. Rather than casting the situation as a pastoral problem, it may be seen to be a pastoral opportunity. Parents entrust their children to the care of the Catholic school and its Catholic mission thirty hours of the week. Even if we look at this in a minimalist way, we are only seeking to connect them with one further hour – at the Sunday Mass. Of course, evangelisation means much more than getting to Mass.

The choice of a teacher to work in a Catholic school and that of the parents to send their children there represents – even if it is only minimal – a positive choice for Catholicism. State or public schools in Australia provide an excellent education and high levels of pastoral care and parents could choose these for their children but something about the Catholic school attracts them. Most Australian States and territories provide for one hour per week of religious instruction in publicly funded State schools. Instruction is given by volunteer catechists. Catholic schools today are putting a great deal of effort into staff formation and reflection on the quality of their Catholic identity to clearly indicate that Catholicism is not a mere addition to school education, and parents still choose Catholic schools. They clearly want something that Catholicism has.

We can see why the *Directory* regards Catholic schools and pastoral care of families as such a high priority for diaconal ministry. Clearly it is a pastoral opportunity needing creative and imaginative ways to evangelise and develop the mission.

An ideal pastoral placement for a deacon is as school, university (or even hospital) chaplain. The school chaplain role needs some creative re-working from previous models which focus on school liturgy, retreats and broadly defined pastoral support of children and teenagers. These things are still important, but looking at the picture above, the deacon could have a more expansive role. The deacon in a school chaplaincy role needs to have a wide scope to his pastoral ministry which includes the pastoral and spiritual care of pupils, teachers and parents.[46] He needs also to develop creative partnerships with local parish communities and in high schools with local and diocesan youth ministry services so that he can help connect families and young people with the parish and the broader Catholic life of the community. In secondary schools, the deacon would need to connect

---

46   Although I say 'he' and 'his' for deacon, it could be 'she' and 'her', if we follow through on the lines argued in Chapter 6.

with the parishes from which the majority of students are drawn and this could mean getting to know a dozen parish communities.

Parish-school-deacon partnerships would involve the deacon in harnessing the gifts of lay leaders, parish clergy and resources within the school to create multiple opportunities for connection between families on the margins of the Church and families in regular parish life and worship. As an ordained minister, he is able to bring the presence of the Church and the pastoral concern of the bishop more closely into the lives of those staff and families who participate only at the minimal level of being present in the Catholic school system. He would be a bridge builder, helping families to make deeper and lasting contact within parish life.

Appointment of deacons to school chaplaincy roles would be a sign of the priority that the local church places on providing pastoral and spiritual care to families on the margins of Church. In *Familiaris Consortio*, John Paul II emphasised that families like these ones should be a pastoral priority in every diocese.[10] The deacon can be a pastoral presence to them and bring them closer to the local parish and diocese. Our Church continues to expend time, money and energy on chaplaincy in hospitals, prisons and to seafarers, because we know how valuable it is to have the presence of ordained ministers in these situations of vulnerability or marginalisation. We need to harness a similar concern and missionary zeal for the pastoral opportunity provided in Catholic schools.

A deacon could have a ministry within the school community with a focus on pastoral and spiritual care of those in the community. Among the staff, he could offer pastoral support and spiritual guidance. He could be there for the staff in times of joy such as blessing expectant mothers and parents to be, as well as blessings for birthdays and other occasions. He could assist staff through times of grief and loss, in helping to organise prayer times, to provide spiritual counsel and other support. He could be a resource person for the staff, helping to locate theological resources. He could provide training in liturgy preparation. He could shed light on difficult or contentions religious and social issues or provide background briefings for teachers on units of work in religious education or Catholic Social Doctrine for economics, geography and social science teachers, or about science and religion and many other areas to help equip the teachers for their role.

Among the pupils, he could be a friendly presence of the Church's ministers and sometimes lead prayer times for important occasions like the start of term and graduations. He could help to resource teachers and pupils in the art of liturgy preparation and class prayer. He might introduce staff and pupils to the treasury of spiritual practices and traditions handed down in the Catholic tradition.

In this creative partnership, he would have a role in the pastoral and spiritual care of families with the assistance of the local parish community where the family live. Choosing a Catholic school has within it signs of a positive choice for Catholicism and the deacon could build upon these positive values to lead the family deeper into the life of the Catholic Church. When families experience loss and bereavement, the deacon can be there as pastor to them, and he can accompany them through the process of preparing a Catholic funeral with their local parish community and the *presbyter* who leads that community. In this case, he would work alongside the parish and family relationship and attempt to connect this school family with parish families who can help them during this time.

Working with school staff and parish, the deacon might be able to assist in the development of programs for adult faith formation for parents in the school. The local parish may have Lent discussion groups, or RCIA, or reception of Christians into full communion or be having a parish mission and the deacon working in partnership with the school, the parish and the parish *presbyter*, might find creative ways to engage school families. He might, for example, coordinate a Lent discussion group in the school, with participants from the local parish as well. This group might meet at 2pm and finish by 3pm in time for the end of the school day. The parents who join in this program might not be the kind of people who would know about Lent discussion groups or ever consider joining a parish group in the evening. The convenience of the school program might attract a few. Having a mix of school parents and parishioners in such a group might foster deeper connections between the families and the parish.

Bridges to parish communities

Already in the section above, we have seen how creative partnerships can continue to lay down bridges of connection between the school-families-parish. So, the creative reshaping of the chaplaincy role can be seen to respond to the new evangelisation by bringing the Gospel of Mercy to where the people are and meeting them there. If they are in our schools but not in the parish, meet them in the school where we know some positive value has drawn them to Catholicism.

Deacons in the new chaplaincy roles could work in close collaboration with the local parish when it develops its own pastoral plans. Pastoral planning is not only about responding to needs for pastoral assistance when these arrive, such as in the case of a death in the family, but to look creatively at what the parish is doing or could do to reach out to families on the margin. The deacon can present to the parish some useful information about the pastoral opportunity and scope for the new evangelisation that exists within the school community.

To illustrate this outreach model of planning, we could consider sacramental preparation programs. Most parishes simply advertise and call for enrolments through the parish and school newsletters that a new RCIA group is about to commence for non-baptised people or a similar group for Reception into Full Communion with the Catholic Church is about to commence for baptised Christians of other traditions who seek to enter the Catholic Church. Generally, the preparation sessions are conducted by volunteer catechists leading sessions over a few weeks in isolation from the rest of the community. Initiation in the Catholic Church is really an apprenticeship, only part of which involves 'classes' or 'instruction'. The majority of the formation of Catholic apprentices happens through immersion in the life of the Catholic Church. An outreach sacramental program might run for a year before the celebration of the rites and it may involve parents already connected to parish life mentoring other families through Sunday Mass attendance, invitations to parish social activities, accompanying them on a St Vincent de Paul home visitation or work in a soup kitchen and attending an adult faith formation event. The deacon might help form and guide the volunteer mentors, in collaboration with parish families, through the process of inviting and informing and forming adults into full communion with the Church.

There is much that a deacon might do among parish communities to foster deeper connection between staffs and families in Catholic schools and the Catholic parish. The potential depends to a great extent on the gifts of the deacon and the openness of parishes and school administrators to embrace a mission, rather than maintenance, model of Church and to see creative ways of engaging in new evangelisation.

Formation for mission

One of the factors that may limit the capacity of local bishop to utilise deacons in a variety of diocesan roles is the formation that deacons have received. Formation and appointment are deeply interrelated and formation programs themselves may create a "Catch 22" situation. If the formation was inadequate or deficient in some aspects, there may be many things a deacon is not prepared for in ministry and so he remains underutilised. If he is underutilised or unable to perform some ministries because of his formation, *presbyters* and others may consider this reflects on the deacon personally and the diaconate in general.

If his formation had not been deficient, he would have possessed greater pastoral capacity. The bishop would then be able to confidently appoint him to a variety of diocesan ministries. In more than a few dioceses, the deacon's formation program focused very heavily on liturgical and sacramental functions and not much else. After ordination, these deacons were appointed more or less as parish associates to support the local *presbyter*. Guess what most of their ministry involves? Liturgical and sacramental ministry. Then some *presbyters* and some lay people said, "All the deacon wants to do is dress up and do liturgy". The circularity and necessary frustration that could flow from this situation should be apparent.

Ultimately, it is the diocesan bishop who is responsible for the formation program. Normally, he will delegate the process of selection and formation to a Director of Deacon Formation and a team which supports the Director. The *Ratio fundamentalis* issued by the Congregation for Catholic Education (1998) provides an outline of what formation is required for deacons. In short, the formation of deacons parallels that of *presbyters* in terms of the four strands of formation: human, pastoral, spiritual and intellectual/theological. The *Norms for the Formation* is modelled on and complements that of *Pastores dabo vobis*, the norms for the formation of *presbyters*.[47] Deacon formation is not a mirror copy of *presbyteral* formation but it should be similar, especially in terms of theological and pastoral formation. The pastoral formation is aimed not at parochial leadership and presiding at Eucharist but to the ministry of word, liturgy and pastoral service primarily within a diocesan scope or for particular communities within a parish or diocese.

---

47 Norms and Directory, Joint Declaration.

The *ratio fundamentalis* for presbyteral and diaconal formation indicate that formation is also, to some extent, self-formation. Deacons need to take responsibility to see that they are adequately formed for ministry and continue their formation after ordination. Commitment to excellence in all aspects of formation in terms of allocation of diocesan resources will only enhance the confidence that a local bishop will have in his deacons and the *presbyters*, both of which are his co-workers in the Gospel. The laity have a right to have sacred ministers to pastor them and that right includes properly formed ministers, whether they be deacons or *presbyters*. A bishop is more likely to be persuaded he cannot afford to be without deacons when he is confident of their formation, because he has allocated adequate and high-quality resources to their initial and ongoing formation.

Can I afford this?

Deacons as clergy incardinated into a particular diocese are due the remuneration which is fitting for their own support and that of their families.[48] As clergy (deacons and *presbyters* and bishops) of the local church, they are not employees in the sense that a lay person working in a diocesan agency may be considered an employee and in fact anything which might create an impression that they are regarded as employees of the diocese is to be avoided.[49]

Given these two facts (remuneration and employment status), a bishop might be tempted to ask, "Can I afford this?"

---

48   Directory n16-18 and CIC 281 §1
49   PCILT *Ricorso contro le norme diocesane circa il fondo sostentamento clero*. N. 7194/2000. April 29, 2000

The answer has two parts. The first part concerns the practical aspects – yes, a diocese can afford it if it can afford to provide clergy remuneration for *presbyters*.[50] Remuneration can be paid through a variety of instruments. Dioceses can establish a common clergy fund for the support of all diocesan clergy, or they can choose to remunerate clergy through the budget of the diocesan agency in which the deacon (or *presbyter*) ministers or they can create some other means to remunerate clergy.[51] As clerics, deacons and *presbyters* can be paid in cash and non-reportable fringe benefits at less cost than a lay person, thereby saving money in the agency budget. At least this is the case according to Australian taxation regulations. Different taxation regulations apply in different countries and here I am applying what obtains in Australia. We also need to note that in some countries, all clergy are paid from income taxation revenue levied on citizens by government.

The practical part is made a little easier for a diocese when it comes to clergy remuneration. Australian taxation law allows churches to provide for clergy remuneration relatively inexpensively. *Presbyters* in most dioceses in Australia receive

---

50   Deacons are clerics. When a transitional deacon is ordained a diocese finds the money. If a diocese hopes to have presbyters it can find the money. In some poor countries this is not the situation. I met a presbyter from Uganda who had not received any central support from his diocese for a month or two but relied mostly on in kind donations from parishioners for his sustentation. So in some ways the question of affordability depends both on the economy of the diocese and the will to remunerate deacons.
51   The PCILT document above outlines that clergy remuneration can be provided for in a variety of ways; from salaries paid by the State to clergy, from a special fund the diocese creates for the purpose, from the budget of diocesan agencies to which a cleric is appointed or some other means.

their remuneration through a mix of elements; a cash stipend, a fully maintained motor vehicle brought at a fleet price significantly lower than retail, a house, all utilities paid for, a living allowance, study and other allowance, private health insurance (on top of publicly funded universal medical care available to all Australians), annual travel and air fares and other benefits.[52] The cash component is normally too low to be taxed or else taxed at the lowest rate and all else is anon-reportable fringe benefit on which no tax is paid. Taken together, it is a very healthy income which could, with a few adjustments support a deacon and his family.

A similar package, with perhaps slightly more cash, could easily be provided to deacons as inexpensively as it is to provide this for *presbyters*. *Presbyters* often only think of the cash component, sometimes called a stipend, as their total income. This is incorrect. All the elements outlined constitute the total remuneration package. *Presbyters* are normally the best remunerated people in the parish ministry team and often one of the best remunerated people in the parish population. Most dioceses already pay *presbyters* in special ministries, such as full-time hospital and prison chaplaincies using one of the means outlined above. Presumably, dioceses

---

52 This is how remuneration is constructed for *presbyters* and bishops in Australia. In addition, any presbyter or bishop over the age of 65 may apply for a State pension and because most fall below the assets test threshold they will receive a full pension (which few Australian qualify for) from the age of 65 until they die, which is addition to their clergy remuneration. Even before the pension age the average take home salary for a presbyter is equivalent of net $75,000, when cash components and all fringe benefits are totalled, excluding the house the presbyter lives in.

that have married *presbyters* have already had to prepare for a situation where a minister has a wife and family.

The second part of the answer to the question that begins this section is more important. How can we not afford to do this? This is by far the most significant answer to the question. The International Theological Commission noted that the diaconate offers a new way for the Church to think about ordained ministry outside of the dominant model of the *sacerdos* (*presbyter*) and parochial models of ministry.[53] As a Church, we urgently need to respond to the challenges of the new evangelisation and go out with fresh proposals and renewed energy to respond creatively to our present situation. In particular, the presence of deacons in many of the pastoral ministries briefly listed above provides the presence of the sacred ministry while at the same time freeing up *presbyters* from these tasks, allowing them to focus on parochial ministry.

We need to ponder the second answer and prayerfully open ourselves up to the creative energies of the Holy Spirit and then the practical element will follow. John Paul II regarded the temptation to jump ahead to the practical as a weakness in pastoral planning and something which would see plans end in dissipation. What is required is renewed contemplation of the face of Christ and deepening of a spirituality and theology of communion if we are to be faithful to God's plan and to respond to the world's deepest longings.[54]

---

53   ITC (2003) From the *diaconia* of Christ...
54   NMI 43

Conclusion

I want to suggest that the hopes of the Council, a hope shared by Popes John Paul II and Benedict XVI, that deacons would make a significant contribution to the new evangelisation, remains a hope largely unfulfilled. Here and there, pastoral initiatives in a diocese deliberately aim to the harness the grace of the diaconal ministry but mostly that is not so. Frequently, deacons are relegated to marginal duties, are made merely to act as substitutes, or discharge duties normally entrusted to non-ordained members of the faithful. The impression is created that they are lay people particularly involved in the Church. This is exactly opposite to the hopes expressed in the *Directory*.[55]

If we are to realise the vision of the Council and deacons are to become the image of Mercy for the promotion of the new evangelisation in the diocese, then now is the time to return to Acts 6 and to recognise that there are many women and men today living in spiritual and existential deserts, who are neglected in the daily *diaconia* in our dioceses. We need to find some, from among ourselves, who will minister to them: the deacons.

---

55 Directory n40. "In every case it is important, however, that deacons fully exercise their ministry, in preaching, in the liturgy and in charity to the extent that circumstances permit. They should not be relegated to marginal duties, be made merely to act as substitutes, nor discharge duties normally entrusted to non-ordained members of the faithful. Only in this way will the true identity of permanent deacons as ministers of Christ become apparent and the impression avoided that deacons are simply lay people particularly involved in the life of the Church."

The words Pope John Paul II spoke at the first Jubilee for Deacons in 2000 resonate today; "Dear deacons, perhaps some of you are tired because of the burden of your duties, because of frustration due to unsuccessful apostolic projects, because many misunderstand you. Do not lose heart! Throw yourselves into Christ's arms: he will refresh you. May this be your Jubilee: a pilgrimage of conversion to Jesus."[56]

The *Norms for the Formation of Deacons* and the *Directory for the Ministry and Life of Deacons* (1998) issued by the Congregation for Catholic Education and for Clergy, statements of Popes Paul VI, John Paul II, Benedict XVI, all indicate the central place the ministry of deacon should have in the new evangelisation. The motivations and intentions of the Second Vatican Council outlined above indicate openness to the development of the ministry of deacons in the Church, allowing the ministry to find new ways, new places and a renewed ardour with which the Gospel might be brought to those who are neglected in the daily *diaconia*. The Council was not reviving an ancient form of diaconate from any particular era but imagining something new for new times, a new wine. That something new the Fathers of the Council could not see; instead, they entrusted the unfolding to the Holy Spirit in a Living Church.

The failure to allow the ministry of deacon to flourish in the church and to become that something new, the bold and creative initiative, is a failure of reception of the Second Vatican Council or perhaps, more positively, is a task of reception yet to be completed. Our Scriptural, theological and

---

[56] Address Of John Paul II to, The Participants At The Jubilee For Permanent Deacons Saturday, 19 February 2000

pastoral coordinates are wrong with regard to this ministry and we are not able to arrive at the proper ends of diaconal formation or diaconal ministry in the Church because we are charting the wrong course. We need, as a Church, to go back and look once again at the renewal of the sacrament of Holy Orders initiated by Vatican II.

It seems to me we have not received that teaching, especially with regard to that of bishop and deacon. We need to look at the Scriptures in the light of the studies now available on the key words and texts, especially the *diacon* group of words and the semantic profile now newly exposed by John N. Collins. We need to look at our canonical and liturgical texts on Holy Orders, including sequential ordination and the remnant of the *cursus honorum* and ask if this allows the distinctiveness of each ministry to be seen and honours lay ministry. Some of these questions may need to be revisited and could have been given attention by the study commission on women and diaconate established by Pope Francis and which is now concluded. The scope of his commission was so limited – essentially retracing the steps of a previous work completed by the International Theological Commission – that it has not led us in any fruitful direction. Certainly, an unlikely outcome of his commission would have been the ordination of women deacons because it is was not really looking at that question at all. If they had looked in the right areas and started with the correct coordinates, they would have been able to progress further on both the theology of diaconate and the restoration of the diaconate of women as a full ministry in the Church. We take up this theme in chapter six.

The ministry of deacons is capable of making a contribution to the new evangelisation. What is required is a new discernment to identity those who are neglected in the daily *diaconia* coupled with the gift of pastoral imagination capable of taking bold initiatives. The bishop needs to pray for the gifts of wisdom and courage in discerning, with the local church, the many possibilities for the pastoral placements of deacons as ministers of the Gospel of Mercy. Only in this way will deacons be able to respond to those who are neglected in our day and make a significant contribution as heralds of the new evangelisation. The diaconate is a new wine and it requires that we fashion new wineskins. If we take this path, we will be able to conclude with Acts 6:7 "And the Word of God continued to spread and the number of disciples increased rapidly".

Setting the course: Coordinates for Formation

Every December 26 in Australia, yachts set out from Sydney and sail to Hobart (1,170km or 632 Nautical Miles) in a race. The ships could not arrive where they needed to be in the time available if they did not have the coordinates for their destination and also coordinates for the stages of the journey in between. They don't just head south in the hope of the correct currents and winds. The whole journey is mapped out with coordinates for each stage to maximise the benefits of wind and currents and also with some consideration of the size of the yacht. Some very large and some very small yachts compete in the same event. The end they wish to attain is not only arriving at the destination in Hobart but wanting to arrive at a particular time so as to win. If the wrong coordinates are plotted, they cannot arrive on time or arrive at all.

In this chapter, we will examine some of the coordinates that guide formation and determine the ends which are to be achieved or arrived at. We will not consider the minute details of programs of formation for deacons or attempt an evaluation of formation programs approved by the Holy See and in use in various regions. We are painting with broad brushstrokes here. Others have produced commentaries on formation that may be consulted. Coordinates for the end we wish to achieve need to be known before we set out on a journey. This presupposes we also know the end to be achieved. I suggest that we are not clear on the destination or the end to be achieved in deacon formation and therefore cannot arrive at the end to which we aim to attain. We have set sail with the wrong coordinates.

The *Norms* (1998) make this observation about the importance of proper coordinates for formation:

> The effectiveness of the formation of permanent deacons depends to a great extent on the *theological understanding* [my emphasis] of the diaconate that underlies it. In fact, it offers the co-ordinates for establishing and guiding the formation process and, at the same time, lays down the end to be attained.[1]

In this book, we have shown how the theological understanding we have used so far for understanding the permanent ministry of deacon has been based on false co-ordinates. This theology is incapable of bringing us to the end that we wish to seek in forming men for the permanent ministry of deacon. The theological coordinates for establishing and guiding formation cannot achieve the proper end of diaconal formation. The fleet (of diaconal ministry) – to return to the analogy above – we can imagine as having coordinates set for

---

1 Norms, (1998) n3

Auckland. With such co-ordinates, the fleet is heading south from Sydney and so is vaguely in the right direction, but it will end up in another country altogether.

The same can be said for deacon formation. It is vaguely heading in the right direction because there is some awareness that deacons are not *presbyters* and not really lay people. That suspicion – that they are kind of lay people – lingers in the minds of some *presbyters*, bishops and lay people. The sense that that deacons are somehow different means that there needs to be some "clerical" and some sacramental preparation that is similar to *presbyters* and also different and some ministerial formation similar to lay pastoral ministers but also different. These are the vague "southerly" direction co-ordinates.

It is impossible for the formation to arrive at a proper end which is to be attained because, as I have argued in previous chapters, our theology up until now has some other end in view. The two most popular ends in view are to arrive at men formed as ordained social work/charity workers or as a kind of assistant to a *presbyter* in the mode of a transitional deacon. When we pursue either of these ends, we have not really considered the diaconate as a distinct ministry with its own sacramental foundation and mission in the life of the Church. Nor have we absorbed the implications of John N. Collins' work on *diakonia*, not only for ministry in general but for our understanding of deacon in particular.

Just to recap briefly the implications of Collins' work, it demolishes the understanding of diaconal ministry as charity/social work derived from the 19th century model of deacon in the Lutheran Church and challenges the model derived from the *cursus honorum* which regards all ministry in relation to the *presbyterate* as the measure of all ministry. We have previously examined other arguments regarding the *cursus honorum* and the theological understanding of ordination and priesthood prior to Vatican II and after. We learned from this examination that the Church has not really moved from the understanding of priesthood as the pinnacle of Holy Orders and of priest as the measure of all ministries, lay and ordained.

In what follows, we will consider a few issues in formation: What do we do with men who once felt or still feel a call to the *presbyterate* and who enter deacon formation programs? Should we ordain widowed deacons as *presbyters*? To what extent should the wife of a deacon be engaged in the formation process? Who pays the costs for the formation of deacons? How do we deal with the asymmetry that is sometimes experienced between requirements for formation and eventual ministry appointment? How might we address questions of geographical distance and scarcity of formation resources? Are we really forming men for the permanent ministry of deacon or transitional deacons? How can we know? Some of the responses to these questions are interconnected as we shall see once we begin to explore them.

Discernment and stability of the order of deacon

I have met permanent deacons who have told me that they really believe that God has called them to be a priest (they never say *presbyter*). Fortunately, this is not a frequent occurrence. I say fortunately because I believe that a man who has been ordained to the permanent ministry of deacon should feel certain that he is called to be a deacon and not anything else. His formators should have the same certainty about his diaconal vocation since they will recommend to the bishop that they are certain this man has a vocation to the diaconate. The bishop must share this certainty before he ordains a man a deacon. My remarks here concern the Latin Catholic Church.

I am writing from the perspective of a deacon in the Latin Catholic Church and as one who has never felt the call to *presbyteral* ministry. Although I have no personal experience with a call to *presbyteral* ministry, while discerning a diaconal vocation, I hope what I have to say will respect that experience. I hope that I also show why in the final analysis, a potential deacon who truly feels called to the *presbyterate* in the Latin Church, and still feels this way at the end of his formation, is not someone the Church should call forth to be ordained a deacon.

I want to offer six theological reflections that I hope may play some small part in a discernment process for men in this situation and which may also be helpful for those responsible for deacon formation. First, I will look at the impact the discipline of the Church of selecting celibate men for *presbyteral* ordination has on discernment processes. Secondly, we will look at the primary focus of diaconal ministry within a diocese. Thirdly, we will examine the meaning of stability and permanence of the Order of Deacon. Fourth, we will consider the potential for frustration in a ministry which has not been properly discerned. In the fifth part, we will evaluate some attempted solutions on the part of deacons to this issue. We will conclude with a consideration of the place of trust and prayer.

Two states - celibacy and marriage

In the Latin Catholic Church, vocational discernment to the diaconate and *presbyterate* is different to the experience of the Eastern Churches.[2] The law of the Latin Church is that the order of *presbyter* is conferred "only on men who have given proof that they have been called by God to the gift of chastity in absolute and perpetual celibacy".[3] Contrary to popular perceptions, the Latin Church does not have compulsory celibacy for *presbyters* or bishops. Celibacy is a gift of the Spirit and such gifts cannot be compelled by law. A man who feels called to the *presbyterate* in the Latin Church must be a man who has also experienced the call of the Holy Spirit to the celibate life. In accepting that call, a man makes a radical and free promise to live a single and chaste life for the sake of the Kingdom of God. Few men will have the gift of celibacy

---

[2] There are twenty-three Churches that constitute, what is referred to in ecumenical dialogue as, the Roman Catholic Church. What most people call the Roman Church is actually the Latin Church which follows the liturgical and spiritual traditions of the Diocese of Rome, where currently Bishop Francis presides. The Eastern Catholic Churches are full churches, and not merely Rites, that are in full communion with the bishop of Rome. Eastern Catholic Churches have their own rites, spiritual traditions, canon law, liturgical calendar and Synodal structure. Each, apart from the Maronite Catholics, has a sister Orthodox Church.

[3] John Paul II (1992) *Pastores dabo vobis*. Boston Mass: St Paul's. §29 There are a handful of married priests in the Latin Church. These are either widowers or men who had been ministers in a Christian church before they were received into full communion with the Catholic church.

and this is borne out by experience. In the history of the Latin Church, celibate clergy has always been a very small minority of the People of God.

Deacons in the Latin Church may be chosen from among married men and celibate men.[4] There are both celibate deacons and married deacons in the Latin Church. Some, though not all of the celibate deacons, are members of religious institutes and monasteries and have made a vow of celibacy prior to ordination. Others are members of the secular or diocesan clergy. A third group have celibacy thrust upon them, in a sense, and these are widowers and divorced clerics.

Canon law for the Latin Church makes some distinctions between celibate deacons and married ones. One of the distinctions is the age for ordination. A man who is called to celibacy may be ordained a deacon at the age of twenty-five and a married man may be ordained at thirty-five years.[5] Both could commence their formation after high school or college or university; they don't have to wait until they are older. The older age for ordination of the married man is a pastoral consideration. The later time for ordination gives him time to settle into the married life and perhaps pass through the early stages of establishing a family.[6] The Directory also

---

[4] Congregation for Catholic Education. (1998) *Fundamental Norms for the Formation of Permanent Deacons.* Strathfield, NSW: St Paul's Publications. §§ 36, 37, 38 (Hereafter: Norms)

[5] Norms §35, C.I.C., can. 1031, § 2. Cf Paul VI, Ap. Lett. *Sacrum diaconatus ordinem,* II, 5; III, 12: l.c., pp. 699; 700. Can. 1031, § 3 prescribes that "Bishops' Conferences may issue a regulation which requires a later age".

[6] Norms, §37

suggests different formation paths and places for young celibate deacons and married and more mature deacons.[7]

The law of the Church, both Latin and Eastern (for Catholic and Orthodox clergy), since ancient times, has been that married men may be ordained but ordained men may not marry. Under normal circumstances, a deacon or priest, who is already married before ordination, who is widowed or divorced is not permitted to remarry.[8] Sometimes a widowed deacon who has young children may be given a dispensation to remarry as a pastoral consideration to him and his young children.[9] Divorce is another matter since any possibility of remarriage in the case where the deacon has the care of young children, depends also on an annulment of the prior marriage bond.

In preparation for the Second Vatican Council, John XXIII wrote to all of the bishops of the world (about 2,500 of them at the time) as well as the heads of clerical religious

---

[7] Norms, §50-51, C.I.C., can. 236, 1,2. Cf Paul VI, Ap. Lett. *Sacrum diaconatus ordinem*, II, 6: l.c., p. 699.

[8] Norms, §38

[9] According to canon 1078 §2, a widowed permanent deacon who wishes to remarry must receive a dispensation from the impediment of holy orders. Granting this dispensation is reserved exclusively to the Holy See. It bears noting that requests for this dispensation have not been routinely granted. In 1997, the Congregation for Divine Worship and the Discipline of the Sacraments, at the behest of Pope John Paul II, set forth three conditions under which a dispensation from the impediment of holy orders for a widowed permanent deacon to remarry would be considered: "1) the great and proven usefulness of the ministry of deacon to the diocese to which he belongs; 2) the fact that he has children of such a tender age as to be in need of motherly care; 3) the fact that he has parents or parents-in-law who are elderly and in need of care" (from New Commentary on the Code of Canon Law, pgs. 358-9).

Setting the course: Coordinates for Formation

institutes and faculties of theology around the world inviting consideration of potential topics for the Council. Many different kinds of suggestions came back for proposed topics. Three were head and shoulders above the rest: the theology of the episcopate, greater use of the vernacular in the liturgy and restoration of the permanent diaconate.[10] At the Council, the idea about the restoration of the diaconate as a permanent order received overwhelming support from the entire assembly.[11] Only one aspect of the proposed restoration was the cause of any major divisions among the Council Fathers and that was the question of celibacy. A number of bishops opposed the opening up of the sacred ministry in the Latin Church to both married and celibate men.[12] Some bishops feared allowing married men to be deacons would weaken the tradition of celibacy for *presbyters* in the Latin Church.

Celibacy for clergy has deep roots in the discipline of the Church (East and West), stretching into at least the sixth century. Among the Eastern Catholic Churches, there is a discipline of celibacy but this is mostly confined to monastic clergy. The vast majority of deacons and *presbyters* among the diocesan clergy in the Eastern Catholic as well as Orthodox Churches are married men. A bishop in the Eastern Traditions (both Catholic and Orthodox) is always chosen from among celibate men and therefore is normally chosen from among

---

10 Alberigo, G (1995) *History of Vatican II Volume 1: Announcing and Preparing Vatican Council II-Toward a New Era in Catholicism.* Maryknoll: Orbis. p109
11 Ditewig, W. (2007) *The Emerging Diaconate: Servant Leaders in a Servant Church.* Mahwah, New York: Paulist Press. p102-119 In this section Ditewig takes the reader through the fascinating voting on diaconate at Vatican II
12 Ditewig, W. (2007) *The Emerging Diaconate*, p117

monastic and not diocesan clergy. In 1962-65, the Latin Catholic Church was not ready for a debate on the discipline of celibacy, if indeed it is even now. However, it would have been a good time to confront that issue because discernment of a *presbyteral* or diaconal vocation would not have been linked to celibacy in the way that it is now for Latin Catholics. In my view, it would be wonderful if the orders of deacon and *presbyter* could truly flourish in both the married and celibate states among the diocesan clergy.

On the other side of the celibacy equation, celibate deacons among the diocesan clergy often encounter incredulity and a lack of affirmation of their vocation. They often find bishops who wish to steer them away from a diaconal vocation toward a *presbyteral* vocation during the initial period of discernment and formation. After ordination, some report that their bishop often raises the topic of *presbyteral* ordination and lets them know it can happen whenever they are ready. *Presbyters* and fellow deacons often express their incredulity that a man would choose to remain a deacon when he could be a *presbyter* and "go the whole way". Lay people are similarly perplexed. Celibate deacons among the diocesan clergy are often made to feel that they have to justify to others their call to celibacy and constantly justify their remaining within the order of deacon. The reaction to celibate deacons suggests that some among our bishops, *presbyters*, deacons and laity, do not truly comprehend that celibacy is a gift of the Holy Spirit given to some and not a canonical requirement or imposition on those who sense a vocation to the *presbyterate* or religious life.

It seems to me that the challenge and questioning that such deacons experience is a sign that some bishops, *presbyters*, deacons and lay people do not comprehend that the faith of the Catholic Church is that the sacred ministry comprises three expressions: deacon, *presbyter* and bishop. When I have encountered celibate diocesan deacons and they share these experiences, I like to remind them that they help the ministry of deacon shine more clearly. The celibate diocesan deacon is such a clear sign of the permanence and distinctiveness of the ministry of deacon within the Sacrament of Order, precisely because they could have gone "all the way" as it was considered to be prior to Vatican II and reached the top step of the *cursus honorum* of priesthood. The questioning and challenging of them is also a sign that we have not embraced the theology of orders from Vatican II and are still in our pre-Vatican II mode of thinking about ministry.

This is the first problem that confronts a married man in the Latin Catholic Church. If he ever felt, or feels now, a call to *presbyteral* ministry, there is no way for him to fulfil that call within the present discipline of the Church. Perhaps what he once felt was actually a call to ministry but not to celibacy, but in his earlier life there was no way to channel this into the diaconate. In many Latin dioceses, even now, the ministry of deacons has not been restored and so the possibility of ordained ministry without celibacy remains closed for some men. One may wonder if the call to priesthood is also a sign that this man too has not embraced the new way of thinking about the sacrament of Holy Orders that was initiated at Vatican II. Like many others in the Church, he may be thinking priesthood is the pinnacle and final step on the path of the *cursus honorum*.

A distinct ministry and focus

Whether a man is married or single, if he is discerning a call to the diaconate, he should recognise that it is a distinct and complete ministry. Diaconate is not halfway toward becoming a *presbyter* but an end in itself. The fact that the Church continues to ordain future *presbyters* as deacons may create a perception that it is merely a step along the way toward the *presbyterate*. There may be created an impression that the permanent deacon has been unable to make the last step. We addressed some of this earlier in the book.

The theological reality is that the diaconate is a sacramental participation in the apostolic ministry of the bishop, which the deacon also shares with the *presbyters*.[13] Deacons and *presbyters* are the co-workers and collaborators with the bishop in the same ministry.[14] The deacon is ordained not for the priesthood but for the ministry (*diaconia*) of the bishop.[15] It is a pity that the text we have inherited in *Lumen gentium* truncates the quote from the source document, leaving out "of the bishop".[16] The truncated version leaves us with a semantic puzzle with regard to the meaning of the word ministry. The particular ministry of the deacon in the

---

13 Congregation for Clergy, (1998) *Directory for the Ministry and Life of Permanent Deacons*. (Directory) §1 and 8 and Joint Introduction § 1
14 Paul VI; *Lumen Gentium: Dogmatic Constitution on the Church* (LG) 20, Directory § 23 and 37
15 LG 29 and Norms (1998) §5
16 *Constitutiones Ecclesiae aegyptiacae*, III, 2: ed. Funk, Didascalia, II, p. 103. Statuta Eccl. Ant. 371: Mansi 3, 954.

Church is not to preside at the Eucharist in the name of the bishop and to lead a parish community as a *presbyter* does, but to look to the wider view of the diocese or local Church on behalf of the bishop as his close collaborator, ambassador or executive officer.[17]

Some of what constituted the deacons' collaboration with the bishop in the past is now performed by auxiliary bishops and vicars general today. The primary focus of a deacon's ministry is toward the diocese. If he has any parish ministries, it is in some sense beyond the assembly at other times and in different contexts. His focus is much more about the mission of the Church, the proclamation of the Gospel in new situations, new places and with new methods, beyond the Eucharistic assembly. He complements the ministry of *presbyters* who are his fellow collaborators with the bishop. Of course, there may be overlap between *presbyteral* ministry, and that of lay pastoral workers, and the ministry of the deacon, but that is to be expected since ministry often has fluid boundaries in many areas of pastoral life.

Parish pastoral leadership is not normally the ministry of the deacon. He can be appointed to such a ministry in cases of real necessity if there are no *presbyters* available but such appointments are always extraordinary.[18] In any case, even when a deacon is appointed, a *presbyter* is always named as the one who has the *cura animarum* of the people in the parish.

---

17 I am alluding here to the semantic profile of the word *diakonos* in New Testament Greek and also the any references to the kinds of ministry placements characteristic of a deacon found in the Directory.

18 CIC can 517, Directory 41 and *Ecclesiae de mysterio: Instruction on certain questions regarding the collaboration of the non-ordained faithful with the ministry of priests*, Art 4; 1.

It is the *presbyter* who leads the parish community because as priest he presides over the Eucharist in the name of the bishop. Presiding at the Eucharist and pastoral leadership go together because the Church is most fully herself when the baptised in the local church (diocese) are gathered in the one liturgy with the bishop, deacons, *presbyters* and laity all participating according to the part assigned to them.[19]

Some dioceses confuse the distinctive nature of the *presbyterate* and diaconate by routinely appointing deacons as pastoral leaders of a parish community or because they have the expectation that parish ministry or parish leadership is the natural place for all ordained ministers. I am not thinking here of cases where a bishop really has no other option because there is not a *presbyter* available, in which case he must appoint a deacon, and not a lay person if a deacon is available.[20] The bishop must re-assign the deacon as soon as a *presbyter* becomes available to assume the pastoral leadership of the parish. In such cases, justice demands he appoint the deacon to some other ministry in the diocese. When the routine expectation is the appointment of deacons to leadership of a parish, the model of *presbyteral* ministry is being overlayed on diaconal ministry.

When deacons and dioceses think of diaconal ministry only in terms of parish-based ministry, similar to that of a *presbyter*, the confusion only deepens for a man discerning a vocation to the diaconate if he once or now feels called to be a *presbyter*. If the end which diaconal formation seeks is essentially the same end as *presbyteral* formation – pastoral

---

19   Paul VI, *Sacrosanctum concilium*, §41
20   Directory 41 and *Ecclesiae de mysterio*, Art 4; 1.

leadership of a parish, or even primarily pastoral ministry within a parish as a *presbyters'* associate – it is easy to view diaconate as a bit less of a *presbyter*'s ministry. Those men who felt called to the *presbyterate* might feel that in becoming a deacon they can become a 'bit of a *presbyter*'.

Presbyterate is a distinct and indispensable ministry in the Church and one cannot be a 'bit of a *presbyter*'. The priesthood of the ordained priest differs in degree and essence from that of the common priesthood of all the baptised and the *presbyterate* is more than priesthood.[21] Only the one ordained *sacerdos*/priest, either a *presbyter* or bishop, can preside at the Eucharist. A deacon is ordained, but not ordained as a priest (*sacerdos*) and nor is he a *presbyter*. He can gather the people to celebrate the Liturgy of the Word or the Liturgy of the Hours and, in cases of necessity, a communion service on Sunday in the absence of a priest. He cannot gather the assembly for Eucharist.

A married man who discerns a call to the diaconate should discern if he is truly called to this ministry or if his call is masking a call to be a 'little bit of a priest' because he cannot be ordained a *presbyter/sacerdos*. The diaconate is a distinct call to a ministry in the Church which is not less than that of a *presbyter* but it is not *presbyterate* or priesthood or a substitute for them.

Permanence and stability of order

The restoration of the permanent diaconate aims, among other things, to provide a permanent witness to the faith of

---

21   LG 10

the Catholic Church that the sacred ministry, instituted by Christ for the building up of his Body, has consisted from ancient times of a threefold order of deacon, *presbyter* and bishop.[22] Therefore, the restoration of the ministry presumes a stability of order and the diaconate as an end point not merely a transition to another order.[23]

With this permanence in mind, the *Directory for the Ministry and Life of Permanent Deacons* advises that widowed deacons should not normally be permitted to be ordained to the *presbyterate*. In receiving such a request from a deacon, a bishop should insist upon careful discernment on the part of the deacon and not hastily ordain a man to the *presbyterate*.[24] Perhaps the bishop should also carefully discern his own motivation in ordaining such a deacon to the *presbyterate*. Is he tempted to do so because of a shortage of *presbyters*? Does he truly value and appreciate the permanent order of deacon? Did he believe the man who had discerned a ministry as a deacon was wrong and those who recommended him for ordination were wrong in their discernment and recommendation that he be ordained to this permanent ministry? Was the judgment of the bishop wrong when he accepted the man for the Order of Deacon?

A presumption of automatic *presbyteral* ordination for a permanent deacon after his wife dies has three significant consequences. The first is that it suggests the notion of instability in the order. Second, it suggests that real ordained

---

22 LG 28 and, International Theological Commission; (2003) *From the Diakonia of Christ to the Diakonia of the Apostles*. London: Catholic Truth Society. p59
23 Directory §5
24 Directory §5

ministry is that of the *presbyter* or bishop. Thirdly the presumption may devalue the sacrament of marriage and regard the wife as an impediment to a full flourishing of her husband's ministry. In the *Norms for Formation* and the *Directory for the Ministry and Life of Permanent Deacons* there is a great deal of emphasis on the complementarity of the sacraments of Orders and Marriage. Routine presumption of *presbyteral* ordination after the death of a wife would undercut this complementarity.

Undermining of the stability of the Order of Deacon also comes from those who propose what I have called a 'long-transitional diaconate'. Some *presbyters* have encouraged men to consider the diaconate because they speculate that the Latin Church will in the near future abandon the practice of selecting *presbyteral* candidates only from among those called to celibacy. These *presbyters* argue that when this happens, the deacon will be the first among those chosen for *presbyteral* ordination as married men. In effect, what they argue is that the deacon is merely entering into a 'long transitional diaconate' where he awaits the day for this change to happen in the Latin Church. Such a notion is problematic on many levels.

This view regards *presbyteral* and episcopal ordination as the only worthwhile and perhaps real ordinations and ministry. This takes us back to before the Second Vatican Council. It continues to foster the perception that the diaconate is less than *presbyteral* ordination or merely a step toward what is considered the pinnacle of the sacrament of Orders; priesthood/*sacerdos*. That the priesthood is the endpoint or highest form of Orders is a theology of Holy

Orders which persisted from the thirteenth to the twentieth century and dominated pre-Vatican II theological manuals.[25] The Second Vatican Council was the first council to solemnly define that episcopal ordination is a sacrament and what is more, the fullness of the Sacrament of Orders.[26] Drawing on an ecclesiology of *communio* it taught that the *presbyters* and deacons participate in the ministry (*diaconia*) of the local bishop.[27] It introduced a descending theology of Orders within an ecclesiology of communion and restored both the episcopate as a sacrament and restored the permanent ordering of the sacrament as consisting of deacons, *presbyters* and bishops.

A second problem is that even if tomorrow the Latin Church did change its discipline, *presbyters* would not be permitted to marry and deacons presently ordained with the presumption of the stability of order should not be automatically ordained as *presbyters*. The church would also need to change the law that prohibits ordained men from getting married. A *presbyter* would still be faced with the problem that he had first discerned a call to celibacy before that of a *presbyteral* vocation. If the discipline changed, it would only mean that in the future married men and celibate men would each be considered for ordination as deacons and *presbyters* as is the custom of the Eastern Catholic Churches.

---

25 Gibaut, J. (2000) *The Cursus Honorum: A Study of the Origins and Evolution of Sequential Ordination*. New York: Peter Lang Publishing. pp307-366
26 LG 21; Paul VI (1965) *Christus dominus; Decree on Pastoral Ministry of Bishops* (CD); §15
27 LG 29

Although it is the not the place to evaluate the history and value of celibacy in the Church, it is worth noting that celibacy is a gift the Holy Spirit gives to the Church through the lives of some individuals. Some will use this gift of celibacy to become radically available to proclaim the Gospel as deacons, *presbyters* and consecrated religious or lay people. Others will simply witness by their celibate life to the value of chastity in their everyday lives, neither seeking ordination nor entering religious life or consecrated lay states. Celibacy has intrinsic value and should be embraced and esteemed for its own sake. It can never be imposed on an individual but only received as a gift.

A man who is discerning a vocation as a deacon needs to listen to the Spirit speaking through the Council. If he is called to the diaconate, he needs to know that it is a call to a permanent and stable order which has intrinsic value based on the unique grace of diaconal ordination. His wife is not an impediment to *presbyteral* ordination and he is not waiting for the Latin Church to make a change in its discipline regarding the sacrament of orders.

Potential for frustration and ministerial confusion

If a married man enters the discernment process for the diaconate and is unsure if he is called to the *presbyterate* I cannot see a problem with that. It is, as I have noted above, difficult to discern a call to ordained ministry in the Latin Church because of the celibacy issue. If during his formation some thoughts linger about a vocation as a *presbyter*, he should pray about this and discuss it first with his spiritual director and then with his director of formation. If he is approaching the time for being admitted as a candidate for the diaconate and he still feels this lingering sense that he should be a *presbyter*, he should tell his director of formation and withdraw from the program for that reason. He should not put himself forward nor should his formators recommend him as a candidate for the permanent order of deacon.

If such a man goes through to diaconal ordination and he has not let go of this desire or feeling that he is really meant to be a *presbyter*, he is not only receiving the ordination as a 'second best' option but he may face frustration in his ministry. If after ordination as a deacon he strives to live out as close as he can the ministry of the *presbyter* he wishes to become, rather than the deacon he is, he may come up against many frustrations in at least three domains – psychological, spiritual and pastoral.

There is a risk that such a man will try to focus his ministry exclusively on ministry to the parish in the mould of an assistant *presbyter*. He may experience frustration when he finds that he cannot lead the worship on Sunday and that he can preach only with the presider's permission, he cannot anoint the sick and minister the sacrament of reconciliation and his sacramental and liturgical role will be important but somewhat ancillary in a parish with a full-time *presbyter*. He may find that he adopts a form of clerical dress (which he is entitled to do) not so much out of a positive sense of identifying himself as a sacred minister but as a means to create an image which connotes a sense that 'I am really a *presbyter*' or really just the same as one. What I am addressing here is the motivation for adopting clerical dress. There is nothing to prevent a deacon from adopting clerical dress, including a Roman collar or cassock. Canon law simply does not oblige him to do wear distinctive dress unless his bishop obliges him to do so.[28] He does not need to ask the bishop's permission.

The deacon who after ordination feels he is really meant to be a *presbyter* may harbour resentment and frustration that he will never be appointed as pastoral leader of a parish and never preside at the Eucharist. Resentment and frustration may do spiritual harm to the deacon and may spill over into forms of anger and a desire to dominate others rather than be a minister of grace who ministers from a heart filled with peace and joy. Others may notice his frustration and this may become a cause of relationship problems with the *presbyters* he collaborates with, his brother deacons and perhaps some lay people. Peace and joy in the ministry should be evident in the life of every minister if they are to be effective witnesses to the Gospel and ministers of grace.

A deacon needs to be happy to be a deacon. A deacon grows in holiness through being an effective deacon and by using the spiritual assistance provided to him through a rule of life which is consistent with being a sacred minister.

---

28   Directory 10 and CIC can §§ 248, 288. The canon is unambiguous, the deacon does not need to ask permission of his bishop, it is simply that he is not under a general obligation to wear clerical dress unless his bishop obliges him. In the Latin Church lay men often wear Roman collars and cassocks in seminaries, and Religious Brothers who are lay men will often wear a distinctive habit, so it would be odd if an ordained man had to ask permission from his bishop. In spite of this unambiguous canon some dioceses either prevent deacons from wearing clerical dress or require permission from the bishop but this is not correct.

It can be difficult enough for a deacon being a deacon when his ministry may not be respected or accepted by *presbyters*, bishops and laity. It may be difficult if he experiences various forms of discrimination and injustice and his rights are not respected in the local Church.[29] Adding to the injustices, intended and unintended, his own frustrations that he really should be a *presbyter* may ultimately make his ministry untenable.

Solutions

There is only one viable solution to this situation of a married man who feels called to be a *presbyter* in the Latin Church and who is discerning a diaconal vocation – don't go through to diaconal ordination. He must face up to the question during formation and leave before committing himself to undertake a ministry to which he acknowledges he is not called.

After ordination, a deacon in this situation, where he still feels called to the *presbyterate*, needs to speak openly with his spiritual director and then his bishop. He needs to discern if he is able to faithfully fulfil the office which he has undertaken. Is it something he can live with and effectively minister to the People of God? Should he consider resigning from the ministry? It is not impossible for a deacon in this situation to become an effective minister but he needs to be open and honest with himself and his Church so that he can

---

29 Sometimes this type of experience is shared on blogs and discussion forums or even in gatherings of deacons. It is not an uncommon experience for many deacons. Some of it is quite scandalous.

avoid the frustration or anger that some in this situation may experience.

A solution some have attempted is to leave the Catholic Church and join a Protestant community or an Eastern Catholic or Orthodox Church in order to become a *presbyter* or Minister of the Word. *Presbyters* too have done this when they feel they should be married. I suggest that it is not a real solution but only has the appearance of one. I know there are sensitivities here and I am not commenting on any particular deacon or *presbyter*. I am only setting out some theological reasons for considering why it is not a solution.

The first reason is that ordained ministry, in the theology of the Catholic Church, always has an ecclesial dimension, it is never purely personal. Ordained ministry is a gift the Holy Spirit gives to the Church so that the Body of Christ may be built up for mission.[30] The call or vocation is formed by the Church and received within the Church. Within the framework of the ecclesiology of communion, no minister has his ministry alone as a private and personal possession. Those who are ordained are ordained as ministers of grace for the Church. Ordination is not a personal gift or capacity, even though each minister brings to the ministry his unique capacities and gifts.

The second reason is that the ecclesiology of communion gives the sacred ministry a particular actualisation as understood within Catholic sacramental theology. Ordination orients the person within a specific Catholic understanding of Church, sacraments and ministry which belongs to the nature of Catholicism as a communion of

---

30   LG 21, and Directory 45, 46

communions of local Churches. Ordination in the Catholic Church is not a universal ordination to Christian ministry but is a gift received within a particular ecclesial communion or diocese (or Religious Institute). Therefore, a vocation received by the Church and conferred on the deacon by the Holy Spirit through the Church's act of consecration is not simply an individual choice or call that a deacon can transfer from the Catholic Church to another Church or ecclesial community. Or indeed that can be transferred automatically from one Catholic Church (diocese) to another because the bond of incardination is not simply a juridic bond but is intrinsic to the nature of the sacrament.[31]

To leave the Catholic Church for the sake of being a minister in another Christian Church or community must first be a positive choice for that ecclesial community. That is, a deacon (or *presbyter*) should first discern that God is calling him into communion with the Christian community he intends to serve and that he wants to positively embrace its theology, sacramental life, spirituality and other aspects of ecclesial life. He should truly believe he is called to the Anglican/Episcopal or Lutheran or Uniting Church or whatever community he may seek to join. To enter another church solely to follow a personal dream to be a priest/minister of the Word does not honour the community to which the deacon seeks entry. He may be simply using this community as a vehicle for his personal needs. If this is the case, will he be an effective and joy filled minister of the Gospel in that community?

---

31   Norms §8 and Directory §2

I cannot comment on the practices of other Churches with regard to ministers who leave one Church to join theirs but I can reflect on the Catholic experience. In the Catholic Church a man who has been ordained to the ministry in one Church must first discern that he is called into full communion with the Catholic Church, irrespective of his ministry or any desire to continue in ministry. If he seeks to enter into full communion with the Catholic Church, as a minister, he must undergo discernment with the local bishop or his delegate. Fresh discernment is applied so that the Catholic Church can identify and receive the gift of the Holy Spirit which is an ordained minister. It happens sometimes that the Catholic Church will not accept him as a minister. Perhaps similar processes operate in other Churches.

Finally, leaving is no solution because the corollary of a positive choice for the other Church must also be a rejection of the Catholic Church or at a minimum a rejection of some of its central beliefs and practices.[32] The deacon is leaving the fullness of communion with the Catholic Church for partial communion. He is also leaving the Church in which the Church of Christ subsists in its fullness and where all of the means of salvation may be found, even if these are not utilised very well sometimes.[33] The Catholic Church, according to

---

32 The situation is different when a Latin Catholic deacon or *presbyter* seeks to enter into an Eastern Catholic Church. They must discern that this is indeed the ecclesial community to which they are called, since only one move to another *sui generis* Church is permitted (there is no going back to the Latin Church from which one came) but if they enter that Church they are still in full communion with the Catholic Church. There will also need to be permission obtained from the two bishops involved and re-train for a new Church.

33 LG 8

Vatican II, is not merely one Church among others. If this were so then the problem of Christian unity is not a problem at all and all Christians belong to the same Church celebrating the same sacraments, believing the same faith in the same way and in communion with the Bishop of Rome and all Catholic bishops. Since we know that this is not the case, a deacon (*presbyter*) who leaves the Catholic Church is not really pursuing the same vocation elsewhere but ministers in an entirely new situation and with perhaps an entirely different concept of ministry, sacraments and church.

I shall not open the bigger can of worms involved in reflection on the meaning and implications of the following section of *Lumen gentium* 14: 'Whosoever, therefore, knowing that the Catholic Church was made necessary by Christ, would refuse... to remain in it, could not be saved'. If he had known of the necessity of the Catholic Church how can he leave? If he did not know of the necessity and unique status of the Church and he has become a Catholic minister, questions arise about his formation. I cannot go into the details of the arguments here but simply note that other, deeper questions arise.

I may have provided some theological reflection on this question but that can only get a man in this situation so far. Certainly no one should make precipitous decisions based on what is written here. What is required is trust. The man in this situation should open himself to God through prayer and entrust himself to God through a wise spiritual director and formation team. Hopefully, he will begin his initial discernment with an open mind and heart and continue that discernment through the years of his formation. If, before candidature, he feels he is still called to the *presbyterate*, hopefully he can let go and trust that God will find a way to use his gifts and capacities for the good of the Church and the Kingdom; not as a deacon and not as a *presbyter*.

Wives and formation

The *Norms* (1998) suggest involvement of the wife of a married aspirant or candidate in the discernment and formation process.[34] It is important that the wife have some understanding of what the ministry may involve and the impact of that ministry on her life and that of the family. A man cannot be ordained a deacon unless he has the written consent of his wife and the bishop must have that document prior to ordination.[35] It is essential therefore that she have some involvement in the discernment and formation process so that she can give informed consent. It is not necessary that she become an active participant in the formation program and attend the formation program with her husband. I am aware that in some dioceses in some countries (not my own) that deacon formation programs mandate or strongly encourage the attendance of wives in the full formation program of their husband. I believe such requirements are unnecessary and may be unhelpful.

I will consider the unnecessary aspect first. The *Norms* do not have such a requirement or mandate so why include it in local programs? In the formation of men as deacons or *presbyters* in the Eastern Catholic or Orthodox Churches (or ministers in Protestant communities), there is no requirement

---

34 Norms (1998) §43, 56
35 Norms (1998) §61

for wives to attend formation programs so why should the Latins adopt this approach with deacons? If a man is being formed as a medical practitioner or tradesman, we do not expect his wife to attend medical or trade school. Why should we expect a wife to attend her husband's formation as a deacon? She only requires as much formation is as necessary to give informed consent. This could be achieved by a few orientation sessions about the ministry and some meetings with wives of men previously ordained to allow some honest discussion. We will consider in the next chapter – women as deacons – in which case the same would apply to a husband. Formators should reflect on why it is that they want wives in the program and consider also the impact on family life of having two parents involved in what is actually the formation of one.

I consider the requirement of wives to participate in the formation programs of their husband unhelpful for three main reasons. The first I touched on above: the impact on family life. I could imagine that making child care arrangements and problems with juggling sports training and games, dance or music lessons and a host of other things very difficult for young families. Family life can be busy enough and we should not presume that all deacon candidates will have adult children and be retired men. We would hope to have men in their twenties through to forties as the bulk of candidates.

The second reason I find the requirement unhelpful is that is fosters a sense of a joint ministry or a "deacon couple". There is no joint ministry and there is no deacon couple in the Latin or Eastern Catholic Churches. The sacrament of Holy Orders does not spill over from the husband to the wife. Only the one being ordained has a diaconal ministry. The identity and mission of the wife is not tied to the identity and mission of the husband, she is a woman with her own place and gifts among the People of God, as much as he is and in her own right. To return to the example of medical practitioner or tradesman above: when the husband completes his medical or trade qualification, the husband and wife to not become a "medical couple" or a "trade couple".

A third reason follows from the last. Does her participation in formation mean that she is expected to participate in his ministry? A kind of ordain one and get one free system. In some Protestant communities, there has been an expectation that the wife participates in some church ministries but that is not the case with Eastern Catholic or Orthodox clergy. Many wives, like my own, have their own professional identity and career that is not identified with my work as a deacon or as theologian; nor am I part of a 'clinical psychologist couple' because my wife is a clinical psychologist. We need to rethink the requirements of wives to attend formation, where such requirements are in place. It would seem best to reduce the requirements to the minimum which will aid discernment on her part.

Costs of formation

There are four dimensions to the formation program for *presbyters* and deacons: human, spiritual, pastoral and intellectual. In Australia, typically, the first three are covered in the deacon formation program by men meeting with the formators for around seven to ten weekends each year over three or four years and following up with some reading and spiritual direction as well as some practical placements and experiences of preaching, studying the administration of sacraments and other elements of ministry. Intellectual formation is normally provided by a theological college or theology faculty within a Catholic university. Typically, the intellectual formation in Australia will be equivalent to that of *presbyteral* candidates and they are likely to study together at the same institute and complete the same bachelor or master degree in theology and related disciplines.[36]

When Catholics form future *presbyters* and Religious, typically (not always in the case of diocesan seminaries) the diocese or religious institute pays for the full costs of formation. It is not uncommon in the case of men in deacon formation programs for the men and their families to bear the full or most costs for tuition, books, and travel time to and from weekend courses or theological institutes. This may amount to thousands or tens of thousands of dollars the family must provide for his formation.

As a matter of justice, bishops and formators should consider how they fund formation for deacons and it should be equivalent for that of seminarians, including tuition fees, travel expenses and some kind of book allowance as well as the costs of annual retreats. The idea of personally funding one's own formation and then finding one's own ministry placement after ordination is not uncommon in some Protestant communities, but it has not been the practice in the Catholic Church, with the exception of the formation and appointment of deacons in many dioceses.

---

36 Australian Catholic Bishops Conference (2016) Guidelines *for the Formation and Ministry of Deacons*.

Asymmetry of formation and appointments

A deacon once said to me, only a few years after his ordination, that the formation he received, which included a bachelor degree in theology and many weekends of pastoral, human and spiritual formation, was like having a V8 engine. He said his bishop made so little use of his gifts that he described his ministry as being like a golf cart. He said you don't need a V8 engine in a golf cart. We addressed some questions about ministry placement earlier in this book. In this context, we need to consider how much time and effort go into formation and the purpose of that formation, which is to build up the church in communion for mission, and how asymmetrical that is with what bishops will appoint deacons to do. That is if they appoint them at all. The deacon was not suggesting that we dial back the formation; rather, that the bishop recognises and makes better use of the minister Christ has sent the local Church. A deacon is the minister who is the bishop's close collaborator sharing in his apostolic ministry. The deacon was hoping to use his V8 capacities in a ministry that could really align with the formation, something like a "Holden Statesmen" type ministry.[37]

We should note also that deacons frequently bring with them secular qualifications and work and family experience from which the Church could also benefit and which could enrich ministry. In Australia, the majority of deacons have a secular qualification to at least master's level and several have doctoral level qualifications (both at a higher rate than

---

37 The Holden Statesmen is a large V8 luxury car in Australia which would be like a Cadillac in the context of cars in the USA.

the general population). The majority of Australian deacons come from the professions and of these many have held senior leadership positions in health, education, business, military and other sectors. This is what they bring to formation with them. Formators and bishops need to be aware of this and know personally the education, work and professional background of each candidate and deacon and take this into account in formation programs and eventual appointments. Surveys of deacons in other parts of the world – in the USA, Canada, UK and most of Europe – would reveal a similar pattern. My limited contact with deacons from parts of Asia and Africa show that among their small numbers a similar profile is emerging.

Overcoming distance

Most of Australia's population is concentrated in six state capitals and most of this in just three of them. Theological resources such as Catholic universities and seminaries are also concentrated in just four of the capital cities. Access to the kinds of theological resources required for formation can be problematic for candidates outside of the four cities and few would be able to relocate for the formation program. Some dioceses may not have the resources or personnel to provide sufficient formation in all four domains. Australia would not be alone in facing some difficulties in providing places for formation accessible to men being formed as deacons. The USA has vast distances and some places like the UK have theological and formation resources concentrated in just a few geographic locations. There are many countries and states where distances are great and theological resources are few. Unlike seminarians, most deacons could not enter a full-time, live-in formation house.[38]

Developing online resources for formation is a possibility that has not received adequate attention. I have been doing some surveys with men in formation and also men already ordained and there is a great deal of interest in exploring possibilities for online formation both initial and ongoing. I have been developing in response to this demand, resources for formation in each of the four domains to be delivered online. My proposal is to link with local formators who will be responsible for evaluating the candidate's completion and participating in modules. The content is to be provided via online lectures delivered weekly, a reading guide for journals and books to accompany the lectures, participation in an online discussion forum for registered participants and practical exercises. Participants would develop a portfolio of responses to readings and lectures, journal reflections and checklists for practical exercise, especially in areas of pastoral ministry. These portfolios are presented to the formators for their evaluation and discussion with candidates. Units in some of the intellectual formation would also be provided.

In this model, candidates would receive certificates of completion for each unit which provide a summary of the key content covered in the module, the number of hours completed for a module and any feedback on assignments completed. In this way, local formators are in control of the formation of candidates and high-quality resources are provided to supplement what local formators are able to

---

38   The Norms recommend that celibate deacons reside in a house of formation. §50

provide. Such online formation programs could go some way to addressing a gap in resources which result from geographical barriers to participation in formation.

The age profile of candidates

It is for the Episcopal Conference of each region to establish the maximum age limits for admission into the diaconal formation program.[39] We know that celibate deacons may be ordained at the age of 25 and married men at the age of 35. We are thus able to look toward the minimum age. We also know that the *Norms* recommend, but do not mandate, that the age at which a man should be ordained should not as a rule exceed the age at which men commonly retire in that nation or region. We, therefore, have some idea of the maximum possible age of men in the formation program. The age range, therefore, could be from the late teens (after high school) or early twenties (perhaps after college or university) up until around before the age of retirement. In Australia the typical retirement age is around 65 years. Therefore, the upper limit would be a man entering the formation program at 60. In other countries, the retirement age may be older or younger.

Married men with children are unlikely to enter the formation program until their thirties because of career and family stages of development. I would strongly encourage vocations offices within dioceses to target men in their twenties and thirties for discernment weekends for possible diaconal vocation. In this way, if the bulk of men come

---

39   Norms (1998) §13

through formation and are ordained between 35 and 45 years of age, not only will the church benefit from a longer life in ministry from each man but the impression may be avoided that this is something retired men take up in their later years much as they might take up a hobby. I would certainly not exclude men in their fifties and those approaching sixty because they too have gifts to offer. I believe it is critical that diocesan vocations offices promote diaconal vocations as something for younger men so that the diocesan community witnesses a vibrant and young diaconal community at work. This is essential if we are to truly embrace the diaconate as a distinct ministry and a full sacramental sign of the faith of the church in the threefold nature of Holy Orders.

Before we move off the age profile of deacons and those in formation programs, I wish to comment on vocations teams and promotions of diaconal vocations in dioceses. In a number of dioceses, I have learned that the vocations team only promote vocations to the *presbyterate*, Religious life and sometimes other states of life but not the diaconate. This situation sometimes occurs in dioceses which have a deacon's formation program. Many deacons have had the experience of being in parishes when prayers are offered for vocations and deacons are not mentioned. It is almost as if the Church is praying for vocations and when the Lord sends diaconal ones in abundance, we ask the Lord if he might give us something else instead.

The Order of Deacons is the fastest growing order in the Church and it was, as we have noted, the third top priority of the bishops' lists of topics for Vatican II. The Holy Spirit inspired the Church to restore this ministry and the full expression of the sacramental sign of Holy Orders that Catholics believe is essential to the constitution of the Church. The whole Church needs to enter a period of discernment. We need to ponder if we are truly open to the Spirit's gifts or are we frustrating the renewal of the Church and her ministries because other agendas are at work. Can we discern the new wine of the diaconate and stop trying to pour it into old wineskins?

Forming permanent not transitional deacons

One of the potential distortions in the coordinates for the formation program of deacons is that frequently the model that is being used as the template is the transitional diaconate. Transitional deacons are formed as future *presbyters* and never formed as potential deacons. This is how it should be for seminarians preparing for the *presbyterate* and one reason why I believe they should never be ordained as deacons. You may see how this focus on a transitional model presents a problem and could distort formation. A deacon told me how during his four years of formation in his diocese, the director of the deacon formation would regularly hold up *Pastores dabo vobis,* the directory for the formation of *presbyters*, and say this is my guide, my 'bible' for formation. There is obvious overlap between the two directories for formation. The *ratio fundamentalis* for deacons was seen as the completion of the project of the Congregations for Catholic Education and for Clergy as their joint effort to outline formation and ministry of all clergy which they commenced with a consideration of *presbyters*. There are many areas of divergence too. The key area of divergence is the end in view for formation. I wonder if that particular director was aware of the end that was to be attained in deacon formation.

When the formation of the transitional deacon, who is in reality an apprentice *presbyter*, is the model, formation tends to focus naturally on the parish and the kinds of things a *presbyter* would do in a parish. This model will persist unless the bishop recognises the flaw and calls for a revision in the formation program which he has personally approved for his diocese. The *Norms* are clear on his responsibility; "The Bishop will [then] take care that, on the basis of the national *ratio* and actual experience, an appropriate rule be drafted and periodically revised."[40] In order to approve a draft or revise it, the bishop would need to understand what end is to be attained in formation of deacons. If he shares the same transitional model, which is essentially a *presbyteral* model, then we are back where we were before Vatican II and all ordained ministry is identified with the priesthood probably not understood as *presbyterate*.

Formation will focus on parochial ministry and the sacramental and liturgical aspects of that ministry may dominate the formation with a little bit of Catholic Social Teaching thrown in to bolster the program and steer it in the direction of the servant of charity and justice model. But even this will most likely have as a focus a deacon as ministering within the boundaries of a parish and probably under the direction of a local parish *presbyter* who may be called the parish priest (in Australia) or commonly in the USA the parish pastor. The little bit extra charity or social justice work seems to provide a justification for the deacon's ministry which in

---

40 Norms (1998) §16

other ways is that of a transitional deacon. The permanent deacon becomes something of an assistant to the *presbyter* in the parish much as the transitional deacon does when he completes his apprenticeship.

When the transitional deacon/apprentice *presbyter* is the model for formation, the deacon is prepared as an assistant to a *presbyter* and not assistant to the bishop. He is formed to become the *presbyter*'s right-hand man and not the bishop's right-hand man. He is not formed with the pastoral needs of the diocese or groups within the diocese in mind. His formation placements will often mirror those of the transitional deacon being prepared as a future *presbyter*. These will have little connection to diocesan wide ministries or supra-parochial ministries such as a deanery appointment serving particular communities or groups or pastoral needs across parish boundaries on behalf of the bishop. Therefore, when his formation is complete, the bishop, if he thinks of it at all, will appoint the deacon to a parish and under the direction of a *presbyter* just as if he were a transitional deacon.

Of course, every deacon, as I have mentioned before, must have a parish home where he worships and participates in the liturgy as a deacon. In this parish, he may assist the *presbyter* sometimes by presiding at baptisms, weddings and funerals and he will preach there from time to time. The deacon may share some of his gifts with his parish community in other ways too and have some ministry in the parish. This parish is his home base in which he celebrates the Eucharist with the whole community that also supports him with prayer and encouragement in his ministry. His primary ministry, at least for most deacons in the diocese, should be supra-parochial and diocesan ministries. If the pattern that dominates a diocese is that deacons are appointed, or just happen to be, in parishes as their primary ministry as an assistant to a *presbyter*, then we know the transitional deacon model is the dominant one. Then we can be certain we are pouring new wine into old wineskins and wasting the gift the Holy Spirit has given to the Church.

Conclusion

In this chapter, we have not considered formation *per se* but some of the bigger coordinates that guide the formation process and the ends that we wish to attain in the formation of permanent deacons. Reflection on these questions provides us with a means to consider what we really believe the permanent ministry of deacon to be. Is it truly a new wine that we must pour into new wineskins or is it a reflection of something else, an old wineskin in which we are trying to pour the new wine the Holy Spirit gave the Church through Vatican II? We have noted earlier in the book that the foundational theological coordinates we have used so far have not allowed us to achieve the proper ends of diaconal formation. Here we have considered how the mindset about Holy Orders has not really shifted from pre-Vatican II understandings. We see this pre-Vatican II mindset: in the way we deal with men feeling called to a *presbyteral* vocation, in response to widowed deacons and sometimes eagerness to confer on them *presbyteral* ordination and how we place permanent deacons in parishes as if they are like transitional deacons.

Questions arise also about our understanding of ordained ministry when we include wives fully in the formation of deacons. It seems that we have not adopted the *novus mentis habitus*, new habit of mind or way of thinking, that the Council asked us to embrace. Discernment of diaconal vocations becomes difficult in this situation, especially around the question of celibacy. Even our incapacity to embrace celibate diocesan deacons without challenge or questions about "going all the way" suggests we are stuck in the old mindset that dominated pre-Vatican II.

It is not only the theological coordinates that we have wrong, based on the mis-understanding of the *diakon* group of words and the charity/social work model, that makes us unable to plot the correct coordinates and attain the proper ends of formation of permanent deacons. We do need to address the semantic profile John N. Collins has recovered and to a certain extent that is a task of theologians but is also one that others need to embrace if we are to attain the end of forming men as deacons and not assistant *presbyters* in the mode of transitional deacons.

The examples we explored in this chapter also show that the older pre-Vatican II mindset is so influential and the new mindset has not been fully received. We live out of a model that is not suited to our present times and almost seems to be untouched by the theology of Holy Orders we received from Vatican II. The *cursus honorum* with the "priesthood" at the pinnacle of an ascending series of steps remains in place in our consciousness. "Priesthood" and not even *presbyterate* remains as our measure and goal of formation. We need to set fresh coordinates to arrive at our proper end in the formation of permanent deacons.

OUR SISTER PHOEBE: WOMEN DEACONS

Pope Francis recently established a commission of theologians and other scholars to examine the question of admitting women to ordination as deacons in the Latin Catholic Church. That commission has completed some kind of report and the Pope has said the time is not right and the question requires further exploration.[1] I will conclude this section with some reflections on his commission and reaction to it. He is not the first pope to raise this question in recent times. Pope Paul VI asked the International Theological Commission (ITC) to explore this question. That investigation was published nearly thirty years later under the title; *From the Diakonia of Christ to the Diakonia of the Apostles.*[2] For those who have been following this book from the beginning, you will have encountered this study in previous chapters. Benedict XVI raised the question about how more women

---

1 Pope Francis establishes commission to explore the question of ordaining women as deacons. A list of members can be found on the website of Vatican Radio 25 November, 2016. http://en.radiovaticana.va

2 International Theological Commission; (2003) From *the Diakonia of Christ to the Diakonia of the Apostles.* London: Catholic Truth Society.

could be included in governance and leadership in the Church, a question which could embrace ordination.[3] Some aspects of governance in the Church require ordination. At the Second Vatican Council at least two bishops raised the possibility of admitting women to this ministry.[4] Several bishops, including some cardinals, have in the years following the Council raised the question of opening up the diaconate to women and some of these bishops admitted women to their deacon formation programs in expectation of a positive response to their request to Rome to ordain women deacons.[5]

A number of theologians and historians and many ordinary Catholics have also asked or wondered aloud about the possibility of admitting women to this ministry. As you may know, there are at the present time no women deacons in the Catholic Church and permission has been denied to include women in deacon formation programs.[6] Obviously, the question of their ordination as deacons must

---

3 Benedict XVI addressed this topic in response to a question posed by a priest of the Diocese of Rome during one of his gatherings of the clergy of the diocese; 'However, it is right to ask whether in ministerial service - despite the fact that here Sacrament and charism are the two ways in which the Church fulfils herself - it might be possible to make more room, to give more offices of responsibility to women.' Meeting of Members of the Roman Clergy. March 2 2006. See Phyllis Zagano, The Question of Governance And Ministry for Women, *Theological Studies* 68 (2007); 348-367

4 Zagano lists bishops Leon Bonaventura de Uriate Bengoa of Peru and Guiseppe Ruotolo of Ugento, Italy. Gary Macy, William Ditewig, Phyllis Zagano (2009) Women Deacons: Past Present and Future. Melbourne: John Garret. p75

5 Zagano cites a number of examples of bishops raising this question, including Cardinal's Hume and Martini. Macy, Ditewig, Zagano (2009) *Women Deacons*, p71-75

6 CDF, CC, CDWS Notification; on not admitting women to deacon formation programs. 14 September 2001

still be an open one if the present Bishop of Rome has set up a commission to investigate. That commission has reported and there is to be no change to the male only diaconate.

In this chapter, I want to explore with you my argument that women should be ordained as deacons in the Catholic Church. I hope you will ponder the arguments with me and that you find my argument convincing. A few preliminaries are in order to orient ourselves to the argument. My argument rests on developing a line of reasoning that is based upon the intentions of the Second Vatican Council regarding the restoration of the permanent ministry of deacons.

We saw from chapter one that the Council was primarily motivated by theological considerations. The Council wanted to restore a permanent sign of the sacrament of the diaconal mode of Holy Orders so that those who minister as deacons would be strengthened by grace of the sacrament and the Church enriched by the grace of Christ which flows from and though this sacrament. That is, the Council was motivated by Catholic faith in the sacrament of Holy Orders and the nature of grace. We also noted that the Council wanted to the restore the principle of the permanent ministry of deacon and not any particular form that the diaconate had taken in a particular historical epoch.

Deacons had many different functions in the past and acted within the Church in many different ways. A deacon such as Ephraim the Syrian (5th century) was a theologian and founder of theological colleges in the regions of Syria and Turkey. Lawrence of Rome (3rd century) was part of the council of seven deacons responsible for the administration of a portion of what we would now call the diocese of Rome or Holy See. Francis of Assisi (13th century) was a charismatic preacher and founder of a religious order. Cardinal Teodolfo Martel was Secretary of State in the Holy See (19th century) and a diplomat and administrator. Restoration did not rely on reviving any of these models. The Council was open to the form that the restored ministry might take in order to meet pastoral needs and situations of the present era. The key here is that principle is relevant, not form and function.

Since it is the principle, and not the form or the configuration of functions of the ministry of deacon that the Council wished to restore, we need only establish two things. We must establish that once in the undivided and orthodox Church, there were women who were called by the title deacon and who exercised a ministry which the Church recognised as diaconal. Secondly, we must demonstrate that a rite of ordination was celebrated for women in which the intention of the church was to ordain and consecrate women to ecclesiastical ministry and the sacrament of Holy Order, howsoever understood at that time. If we can establish these two things then we can say that the Tradition supports such a ministry and we can and should include women in the ministry of deacon today. By orthodox Church I do not mean the Eastern Orthodox Churches, although the term includes those, I mean those Churches which have maintained an orthodox and common tradition regarding ministry and sacraments as opposed to the beliefs sometimes held by heterodox or schismatic groups. Or, more simply, can we find within the Roman Catholic and Eastern Orthodox and Eastern Catholic traditions evidence of women as deacons?

It is entirely moot to consider the question of women deacons from what their functions may have been or how large or small or significant their functions may have been. All that we need to do is establish if there were women in such a ministry. Working from the principle and not form, we can include women in what the Church understands as diaconal ministry today, if we have an affirmative response to the two questions above. After all, the bishops at the Council did not ask what male deacons did and what their functions were in any historical period in their debates about restoration. The ITC suggest that the reason the Council offered such a vague sketch of the ministry of deacons was, in part, recognition of the historical variety that was evident and also to avoid describing the ministry so completely as to hamper its full flourishing for the present needs of the Church.[7]

The ITC suggests that the Council was open to further development and new emphases that this ministry might take as it begins to find its way again in the modern era. They suggest that canon law might catch up to this new form following pastoral experience of the exercise of the ministry of deacon. That is certainly a task that awaits completion. Canon law has very little to say about permanent deacons save for a few derogations from the law as it normally applies to *presbyter*s. Eminent canonists such as James Provost have named the diaconate as one area of canon law requiring more complete treatment.[8]

---

7   ITC; (2003) *From the Diakonia of Christ*. p62
8   James Provost (1983), Permanent Deacons in the 1983 Code. *Canon Law Society of America Proceedings* 46 (1984), p175

A second preliminary consideration is the link between presbyteral ordination and diaconal ordination. We will look at this question in more depth later. For now, we need to note three features of the supposed link between presbyteral and diaconal ordination. The first feature of this supposed link is that we do have an authoritative statement from John Paul II that the Church has no authority to ordain women as presbyters or bishops (both are *sacerdoti*/priests). Popes Benedict XVI and Francis have each reiterated the definitive status of this teaching and on more than one occasion. Second, there is no equivalent definitive statement that the Church lacks the authority to ordain women as deacons. In fact, there are no statements in recent times, definitive or otherwise, for or against, on the question or ordaining women as deacons. So, we must assume that some freedom exists regarding this question.

A third preliminary consideration, and related closely to the second, is a concern expressed by some that admitting women to the permanent ministry of deacon will in reality be admitting women to a very long transitional diaconate. This concern is not without warrant. During the nineteen seventies and eighties, as women we campaigning for presbyteral ordination in the Anglican Communion, many women opted to be ordained as deacons when that option became available to them in some provinces of the Anglican world. They did so, not with the intention of actually being or remaining deacons, but as a stepping stone and a pressure point for their continuing journey toward presbyteral and eventually episcopal ordination.

Of course, many Anglican women felt a genuine call to diaconal ministry and remain committed to that calling. Even in the Roman Catholic Church, I have heard presbyters encourage men to enter the permanent ministry of deacon because they argue that the Church will change its mind on celibacy and these will be the first cohort of married presbyters who have not come via a previous ministry in another Christian tradition. There is so much wrong with this argument and this advice that I have addressed it detail in the chapter on formation. Some aspects of the Anglican experience and the view expressed by some Catholic presbyters do give warrant to the concerns about an extremely long transitional diaconate as a precursor or even "Trojan Horse" into presbyteral and episcopal ordination. We will have to address these concerns and demonstrate that those who either fear this situation or long for it are mistaken.

Our final preliminary consideration will be the need to avoid anachronism and particularly a one-sided anachronism in evaluating evidence from the past. When we look to the past for evidence of the presence of women deacons and ordination of such women, we must not apply as our standard, current doctrine and theology of orders or current theology of sacraments and ministry in general. We need to consider first what orders meant to those contemporary with the sources and their understanding of sacrament and ministry. We know that the understanding of the sacraments in general, and of Holy Orders in particular, changed considerably over time. Sometimes these changed in surprising ways and in ways which may seem incomprehensible to us.

In the first three centuries of the Church, we find no solid evidence that presbyters presided at the Eucharist or that the assistance they rendered to the bishop was considered a ministry of the Church in the way that bishops and deacons were considered ministers. It was the bishop who was the normal presider at Eucharist and over the local Church. Presbyters were generally not called priests for a large part of the first millennium and the term eventually eclipses presbyter in the ninth century. We know that up until the ninth century, most bishops were chosen from among deacons and not presbyters and, for centuries, they were never ordained presbyters before being ordained a bishop. So, we need to take care to read and interpret ancient sources as the ancients themselves would have done, as far as that is possible, and while being aware of our interpretational bias. Ratzinger has alerted us to the false notion of completely objective observation of history and its source.

All observation of the past is interpretation and involves our hermeneutical bias.[9] In particular, we should not apply one standard to our ancient evidence for male deacons and then another standard to female deacons. If we were to find ordination rites for women deacons or documents that indicated some functions, these should be considered as equivalent to those for male deacons if they bear the same basic outline and are found in the same or similar authoritative sources. We could hardly use the same document in support of the existence of a male diaconate in the ancient world and then ignore that evidence for female deacons.

---

9 Phyllis Zagano, The Question of Governance And Ministry For Women. *Theological Studies* 68 (2007); 348-367

Now that we have outlined the preliminary considerations, which we are to explore in depth below, we are ready to proceed to a consideration of my argument. Before we do that, just consider a couple of interesting facts. No appeal was made to Acts 6:1-7, the commissioning of the Seven, during the debates on Vatican II as a reason to re-establish the permanent ministry of deacon. This was because there is ambiguity about this text in relation to deacons, as we have noted elsewhere. The primary source of that ambiguity stems from the absence of the noun *diaconos*, from which we get our word deacon. The author of Luke-Acts does not refer to the Seven as deacons but only as those who have been assigned to carry out a *diaconia* (ministry). It is Irenaeus, about a hundred years later, who provides our first source that calls them deacons. There are some scholars today who argue that they are not deacons and some who say they are. Yet in spite of the absence of the *diaconos* word, the ordination liturgy for deacons today makes reference to Acts 6, theologians write about them as deacons and homilists preach about them as deacons.

It is curious and something of a puzzle to me that so many theologians, and homilists are so quick to dismiss the possibility that "our sister Phoebe", mentioned in Romans 16 as the deacon (*diaconos*), is actually understood to be a deacon in some sense of that word. She provides the only instance of a singular designation of anyone in the ST with what could be considered the title deacon. For whatever else the title deacon may have meant in Paul's time, and it probably did not mean exactly what we mean by that title today, it is clearly used as a title and is meant to tell us something about this woman. Many credible sources from the ancient world testify to the fact that they had no problem in accepting the most straightforward reading of the designation, "the deacon Phoebe". In the East, we have evidence of support for this reading from Origen, John Chrysostom, and Theodoret of Cyrrhus and in the West Pelagius and Ambrosiaster. Why are theologians, homilists and some bishops so coy about this today?

Evidence from ancient sources

Deacon is a title used to describe some people in the ST who were understood to exercise some office of leadership in the Church. It is no interest to us at this point what they did because function and form are not criteria for the restoration of permanent deacons. Paul greets the deacons in Philippians 1:1. In the Letter to Timothy (1 Timothy 3:8-11), we find instructions about the kinds of qualities a deacon should possess. In Romans 16, he urges the church in Rome to welcome the deacon Phoebe. I am not going to refer to Acts 6:1-7 because the title deacon does not appear there. Scripture provides us with our first sources for a ministry of deacon and a minister called a deacon. Does it provide evidence of women as deacons? The answer is affirmative.

Our first obvious reference to a woman deacon is Phoebe mentioned in Romans 16. She is simply described as the deacon (*diaconos*) Phoebe. *Diaconos* is the same word Paul uses to describe male deacons. She is not called a *diaconissa* (deaconess) which is a term coined in the fourth century to refer to women deacons and also wives of deacons. When Paul wrote, he followed the usual Greek grammatical convention which is not to add a suffix to words to feminise them but to indicate gender before the noun by using a male or female article. In English, the article "the" is neuter gender but in Greek there are masculine and feminine forms of the article "the". Paul has commissioned Phoebe, or the Church of Cenchreae has commissioned her, to make preparations for a journey he had planned to make to Rome to visit the Christian community there. She must have been a significant figure in that community because he also describes her as patron and "the first (*prostasis*) among the people of that church". In early church sources, wealthy women are frequently mentioned as patrons of the local church, providing a place for the community to gather and often using their own resources to care for the poor among them and the wider community too. Did people contemporary with Paul and in the early Church understand the reference to her as deacon as title designating her participation in the ministry of deacon? The answer is affirmative.

In his very thorough and accessible study of ancient sources on women deacons, Gary Macy notes regarding Roman 16:1-2 that some of the earliest commentators understood that Phoebe was a deacon. In their commentaries on Paul, each of the following witnesses endorse this view: Origen, John Chrysostom, Theodoret of Cyrrhus in the East and Ambrosiaster and Pelagius in the West.[10] He cites the relevant portions of their commentaries to substantiate the claim. In iconography, Phoebe is always depicted with an orarion (stole) draped over her shoulders in the style of an Eastern deacon. She is also sometimes depicted holding

---

10 Macy (2009) *Women deacons*, p9-10

a chalice, which in the East is one of the symbols a deacon receives during the ordination ritual. She is listed among the saints of the Church East and West, and always as the deacon Phoebe, although rarely venerated or referred to in the West today. Her name is included among the women mentioned in the ordination rite for women deacons. We shall come to this later. All of this provides incontrovertible evidence that she was regarded as a deacon in the undivided Church. That memory is part of the Great Tradition, which is our tradition.

The second text that is of interest to us concerning women deacons is 1 Timothy 3:1-13. In this section of the pastoral letter, the author is writing about the qualities that an *episcopos* (overseer/bishop) and deacons (*diaconoi*) should possess. Deacon (3:8) is in the masculine form and in the context certainly means male deacons. A list of qualities of the *episcopos* comes first and then a list of qualities of *diaconoi* introduced by a phrase which may be translated "likewise" or "in the same way" and then a third group is addressed in 3:11 with the phrase which may be translated "women likewise" or "women in the same way", and then follows a list which replicates, in its essential content, the one addressed to male deacons. Notice the qualities a deacon should possess and women should possess are introduced by the same phrase. This phrase helps to establish the syntactic structure of the passage and indicates that the three groups, *episcopos*, *diaconoi* and women are each the subject of the entire argument.

The author is addressing the qualities which should describe the character of an *episcopos*, male deacon and female deacons. We can see that they are not generic qualities of women because the reference to them is included in a discourse on those who have served (ministered/ *diaconsuntes*) the community, a note which concludes the section and ties all three together. To suggest that the women here are not deacons, or at least ministers in the Church, and that the author has suddenly and inexplicable inserted a general statement about women cannot be supported by the syntactic structure, verbal cues and the content of the qualities required of male deacons and the women.[11] Some who are opposed to the ordination of women deacons argue that the phrase "women likewise" only means women generally in the community. One can only argue this if one ignores the syntax of the argument and verbal cues which unify the three into a discourse about those who minister in the community. Such attempts must be rejected.

When we look into the ancient sources, we discover that some of the ancient commentators were aware of rival interpretations of this text. What we also find when we look there, is that some of our most authoritative voices from the ancient world clearly support the reading that the "women likewise" can only refer to women deacons. These include John Chrysostom, Clement of Alexandria, Theodoret of Cyrrhus, Theodore of Mopsuestia and Pelagius. Chrysostom is very clear: "Some say he [Paul] is talking about women in general, but that cannot be. Why would he insert in the middle of what he is saying something about women? But rather he is speaking about women who hold the rank of

---

11 Jennifer Stiefell (1995) Women Deacons in 1 Tim: A Linguistic and Literary Look at 'Women Likewise...' (1 Tim 3:11) *New Testament Studies*. Vol 41, pp442-457. This is a very scholarly article and presumes some knowledge of Greek. Readers without the requisite knowledge can still follow the outline of her argument.

deacon".[12] Macy indicates how consistent this interpretation remained; "even during the twelfth century Abelard... would still understand both Romans 16 and 1 Timothy 3 to refer to women deacons, quoting not only Origen, but also Jerome (fourth century), Epiphanius (fourth century), Cassiodorus (sixth century) and Claudius of Turin (ninth century) to support his reading." Macy concludes; "This [13]would imply that during those centuries, the role of women as deacons was understood to have been sanctioned by Scripture and to have apostolic foundation."[14]

Until the tragic events of 1054 when the Bishops of Rome and Constantinople (Istanbul today) excommunicated each other, there was full visible unity and communion among the Churches of the Eastern and Western Roman Empire (which included northern Greece, North Africa and all of what is Western Europe today). That communion was strained at times and a number of fault lines had been developing in the relationship between East and West for some centuries before the final schism took place. Up until this time, they had full communion and as such a common faith, a common Eucharist and a common ministry. They participated in many councils together and for some centuries recognised provincial and regional councils held in each other's territories.

Since the Second Vatican Council and the lifting of the mutual excommunications in 1965, relationships have improved. Between the East and West, now termed Orthodox and Roman Catholic, there has not been lost a common

---

12   Gary Macy (2009), Women deacons. pp 10-11
13   Macy (2009) *Women Deacons*. p11
14   Macy (2009) *Women Deacons*. p11

recognition of the validity of Holy Orders in each other's churches. All of this is relevant to the documents and other evidence that we will consider. There is far more evidence in Eastern sources regarding women deacons then there is in the West but all the evidence remains part of the common patrimony up until 1054 and after this time even in the West, Eastern sources continue to be acknowledged and used in various ways. The combined evidence for the continuing presence of ordained women deacons up until around the twelfth century is impressive. It is to some of this evidence that we will now turn.

The texts that we will consider are available in English translations and commentaries which I recommend for your further consideration. John Wijngaards has assembled a number of the key ones and provides some very useful analysis.[15] Other collections and commentaries have been made by Ute Eisen and by Kyriaki Karidoyanes FitzGerald and by Gary Macy and in a collaboration of Kevin Madigan and Carolyn Osiek.[16] There is an impressive number of sources from the East including correspondence of bishops and theologians, the record of proceedings of a number of Councils and some of the canons (laws) they passed in relation

---

15 John Wijngaards (2002) *Women Deacons in the Early Church: Historical Texts and Contemporary Debates*. Crossroad Publishing: New York

16 Ute Eisen (2000) *Women Office Holders in Early Christianity: Epigraphical and Literary Studies*. Collegeville: Liturgical Press; Kyriaki Karidoyanes FitzGerald (1999) *Women Deacons in the Orthodox Church: Called to Holiness and Ministry*. Brookline: Holy Cross Orthodox Press; Kevin Madigan and Carolyn Osiek (2005) *Ordained Women in the Early Church: A Documentary History*. Baltimore: Johns Hopkins Press; Gary Macy (2008) *The Hidden History of Women's Ordination: Female Clergy in the Medieval West*. New York: Oxford University Press.

to women deacons, funerary inscriptions, iconography, churches named in honour of women deacons and, most importantly, ordination rituals; all of which confirm the place of women deacons.

Macy surveys much of this material and among the material he cites includes correspondence between several prominent women deacons who were major theologians, patrons and advisors to bishops and who were in discussion with some of the great theological minds of the period. Among such prominent women deacons, he names four of them: Amproukla, Anastasia, Celerina and Olympias.[17] According to the Canonical Collection of Patriarch Photius of Constantinople, there were forty women deacons in that Church in the ninth century. By the eleventh century, however, women were no longer ordained in the Eastern Church, although later writers certainly knew of the custom of having female deacons.[18] The tradition of women deacons is strong and well attested in the East during the period of the undivided Church. This is part of the patrimony of the West too.

Perhaps the most illuminating sources about women deacons in the East is found in ordination rituals and also ritual books for the celebration of baptism. These sources are of particular importance because they reveal that women deacons, along with male deacons, were ordained and considered part of the clergy. Both of those terms – ordination and clergy – have changed over time but the incontrovertible fact is that women were included in these terms, however

---

17 Macy (2009) *Women Deacons*. p12
18 Macy (2009) *Women Deacons*. p13

they may have been understood at the time. Because these ordination rites are so important to our discussion, we will consider them separately a little further in the discussion.

Western sources are less plentiful but no less important than those we find in the East. As in the East, the sources are various and include papal letters, proceedings of Councils, correspondence between bishops, funerary inscriptions, theological commentary, some canons and, significantly, some ordination rituals. Both Macy and Wijngaards provide a good survey of many of these sources. References to women deacons may be found in the Council of Epaon (517), Second Council of Orange (533). Even the attempts of the Merovingian Bishops (7th – 8th centuries) to ban women deacons provides evidence of their existence. Many texts in the West link the Order of Widows with that of women deacons. The tradition of women monastic deacons is found in the East and West. Macy notes; "In the Western Church abbesses were sometimes deacons... A group of ninth and tenth century commentators on canon law presumed that abbesses were deacons, simply stating, 'A female deacon is an abbess'."[19] In the eyes of medieval people, women deacons did not die out in the West. In 12th century, Abelard, the theologian, provided a major defence of the position that abbesses were known as deacons and even Heloise refers to herself as a deacon.[20] Wijngaards, Macy and others conclude that there persisted in the West the practice of having women deacons who were understood as a counterpart of the male diaconate into the beginning of the second Christian millennium.

---

19   Macy (2009) *Women Deacons*, p28
20   Macy (2009) *Women Deacons*, p29

Authors such as Martimort and Müller (Müller relies mostly on Martimort) attempt to develop an argument that women deacons were not considered a direct counterpart to the male diaconate. They argue that they were not considered clergy and had lesser functions that those of men and therefore were not considered equivalent. Further, they argue that women were not ordained in the sense that men were and therefore did not participates in the sacrament of Holy Orders. I disagree. Martimort does not examine the sources closely enough and ignores significant elements of the prayers and rubrics (instructions for celebration) in ordination rituals for women deacons. This is a significant omission coming from one who is so expert in liturgical studies. He tends to evaluate the meaning of ordination through post Tridentine categories which do not apply to the developing theology of sacraments and Holy Orders from earlier centuries. He and Müller do not engage significantly with the canonical and conciliar sources which clearly indicate women deacons are equivalent to male deacons. There is a hidden assumption in their work that women cannot be considered suitable matter for ordination and therefore they could not have been ordained. It is just inconceivable to them because of their *a priori* assumptions.

Suitable matter is a theological term, and does not refer to any personal quality of women or men, but concerns what is the appropriate matter or legitimate matter to use in as a sacramental sign. Real wheat bread and real grape wine are the only suitable matter for the sacramental sign of the Eucharist. Rice or saké, oatmeal or honey mead, cannot be the legitimate matter for the sacramental sign of Eucharist. Their argument about women's ordination as deacons seems to put the cart before the horse and that is not the correct way to hitch up the argument. Because the fact that we have ordination rituals for women deacons in the East and West from across the first millennium tells us that women were considered an effective sign of diaconate then. The term suitable matter was not in use in sacramental theology prior to the thirteenth century. We are still left with the fact that they *were* ordained and so it is to the rites of ordination that must now turn our attention.

Ordination rites

Gary Macy indicates that "the earliest rituals in the West for the ordination of a woman deacon come from the eighth century liturgical book of Bishop Egbert of York". and he suggests, "... the impression given is that the ordination rite for a male deacon is the same as that used for a female deacon".[21] A later source, the tenth-century Romano-Germanic Pontifical contains the complete liturgy for both the ordination of a woman deacon and the ordination of a male deacon.[22] It is worth noting that both male and female

---

21 Macy (2009) *Women Deacons*, p20
22 Macy (2009) *Women Deacons*, p21 A pontifical is the liturgical book used by a bishop, who is sometimes referred to as a pontiff. Catholic's today are most familiar with its use to refer to the Bishop of Rome as the Pontiff but it is in fact a general term for all bishops. These pontifical books are very significant because they were copied for use in all the churches of a diocese and sometimes widely copied across whole regions. Latin Catholics are called Roman because they copy or follow the liturgy of the Bishop of Rome. By the end of the 13th century it was by far the most common liturgical pattern in Western Europe.

deacons in these rites receive the *orarion* (Eastern style stole) which is also referred to as the *stola* (stole); because this liturgical garment of deacons signifies the right: to proclaim the gospel, to preach, to proclaim the intercessions, to assist in baptism and distribution of communion.

The rite of ordination of women deacons is found in 12th century Roman Pontifical and other sources in the West in that century.[23] It seems significant that the ritual books in use in the City of Rome as late as the 12th century still preserve the ritual. How frequently this ritual was used by this time it is difficult to judge but the existence of abbess/deacons, as we saw above, was attested in the theological works of Abelard which is contemporary with this pontifical. In any event, we must acknowledge that ordination rituals were of such importance to the Church that they were preserved long after a distinct diaconate for women, apart from the monastic diaconate, had ceased to be a regular feature of life in the Church.

In 1695, Jean Morin of Antwerp, while researching Greek liturgical manuscripts, stumbled on ancient ordination rites of women deacons. He noted that they were amazingly similar to the ordination rites of male deacons. The oldest ordination rite for women deacons comes from the *Apostolic Constitutions* (AD 380). This document is most likely Syriac in original composition and is found also in Greek and Latin versions. These are the three principal languages, including liturgical languages of the Church, East and West at that time. Though the rite is brief, most commentators believe it has all the hallmarks of a full sacramental ordination.

---

23 Macy (2009) *Women Deacons*, p23

It is also substantially identical to the ordination of a male deacon.[24] Wijngaards offers a complete commentary on the *Apostolic Constitutions*, on the ritual for the ordination of female deacons and also sets this alongside that for male deacons.[25] I recommend interested readers to follow up on his full commentary. I am providing just a few key points from his commentary here.

According to the *Apostolic Constitutions*, ordination of both male and female deacons takes place within the sanctuary behind the iconostasis. Only clergy are permitted to enter the sanctuary space behind the iconostasis and in front of the altar. Acolytes may enter the sanctuary but not via the Royal Doors at the centre and in front of the altar, only at its side. The ritual takes place within a Eucharist at which the bishop presides. The rubrics indicate that "the woman who is to be ordained enters the sanctuary, standing near the altar through the royal doors and approaches the bishop". This place is significant because only ordination to major orders takes place within the sanctuary and during Eucharist. The ordination takes place after the prayer of offering. The rite of admission or installation of lector, acolyte and subdeacon were not considered major orders and these rites were celebrated outside the sanctuary and not during Eucharist. Setting ordination within the Eucharist highlights that this is a public, ecclesial event. The ecclesial nature of ordination is reinforced by the calling of the candidate, the presentation of the candidate and acclamation of the people as an acceptance that this woman is found worthy of the ministry of deacon by

---

24　John Wijngaards (2002) *Women Deacons in the Early Church*; p19
25　John Wijngaards (2002) *Women Deacons in the Early Church*; p30-41

the whole church. In the earliest times, the whole of the local Church would be gathered in the one place for Eucharist. In the ancient church, a bishop is similar to the parish priest of today, presiding over the Eucharist and leader of the Eucharistic community. It was clear to them that ordination was a sign of God's gift to the community of a minister, which was to be received by the church with thanksgiving.

The woman to be ordained deacon approached the bishop and bowed her head for him to lay his hands upon her. Only the bishop imposes hands as with male deacons. The prayers for calling down the Holy Spirit and ordaining are virtually identical for both male and female deacons. The difference being that male saints and deacons are recalled in the prayer for male deacons and female saints and female deacons for women. We get some sense of the flavour or the ordination prayers from these samples;

> "Divine grace, which always heals what is infirm and makes up for what is lacking, promote [name] to be a deacon in [name of church]. Let us pray that the grace of the Holy Spirit will descend on her."

> "You grant not only to men but also to women the grace and coming down from above of the Holy Spirit."

> "Please, Lord, look on this your maidservant and dedicate her to the work of your diaconate, and pour out into her the rich and abundant giving of your Holy Spirit."

Once more, the ecclesial nature of the ordination is affirmed by the inclusion of the name of the Church, in our modern terms a diocese. We need to let this sink in deeply to our modern theology and spirituality of orders and ordination. Ordination is not just something happening to an individual, who happens to be the one being ordained, it is something that is happening to a church (diocese). From the 13th century onwards, the ecclesial reality of ordination tends to be eclipsed by a theology of character and of powers of ordination conferred on the ordinand. From the 16th century to the 20th, this latter understanding becomes the only way ordination is understood. The ecclesial dimension of ordination to sacramental theology before the Second Vatican Council may be compared to the appendix in the body. It is a vestige of some former reality but has no meaningful purpose. The Second Vatican Council begins a recovery of the ecclesial dimension by its reclaiming of the ecclesiology of communion/*koinonia*. That task of recovery is far from complete.

The intercessions which follow the first laying on of hands include two for her after her ordination.

"For [name], the woman deacon, who has just been ordained, and for her salvation, let us pray to the Lord."

"That the most merciful Lord may give her a sincere and faultless diaconate, let us pray to the Lord."

Only candidates for the three major orders – bishop, priests [presbyters], and deacons – receive a double imposition of hands. During the second imposition of hands, the bishop prays aloud;

"Lord, Master, you do not reject women who dedicate themselves to you and who are willing, in a becoming way, to serve your Holy House, but admit them to the order of your ministers."

"Grant the gift of your Holy Spirit also to this your maidservant who wants to dedicate herself to you, and fulfil in her the work and the office of the ministry of the diaconate, as you have granted to Phoebe the grace of your diaconate whom you had called to the work of this ministry."

The rubrics instruct that "The bishop himself invests her with the – *to diaconicon orarion* – the deacon stole around her neck". The newly ordained deacon receives communion from the bishop within the sanctuary just as male deacons do. In the Eastern tradition one portion of the consecrated bread (the Lamb) is shared by the clergy. Common to both East and West, the bishop receives his portion first and the distributes a portion to the deacons, and they consume it at the same time. Then the bishop receives from the cup followed by the deacons. Presbyters come to receive next. The deacons assist the bishop to distribute communion to the people. At an ordination ritual, there is a prayer for the handing of the chalice to the deacon, that the deacon will be a worthy minister of the mysteries (sacraments). The prayer is said for both male and female deacons but there is one difference in the handing of the cup to women deacons.

> "When the newly ordained has taken part of the precious body and blood, the archbishop hands her the holy vessel [chalice]. She accepts it and, without distributing it to others, puts it back on the holy table [altar]."

A male deacon would begin assisting in distribution of communion at his point. Handing the chalice to the woman deacon is not an empty gesture. She is an ordinary minister of communion and she will exercise that ordinary ministry by taking communion from the liturgy to places where groups of women or single women live. The *Apostolic Constitutions* and other documents indicate that one of her roles as deacon is to take communion in these circumstances so that potential scandal of men entering the houses of women alone is avoided. We also know from these same sources that she preached and instructed in the context of a ministry to women in similar circumstances.

To emphasise that she is part of the clergy, the *Apostolic Constitutions* provides another reminder that;

> "At the time of the partaking of the sacred mysteries, she shares in the divine body and blood with the deacons."

She is clearly regarded as the equal to the male deacon. One cannot argue on the basis of small liturgical differences in the ritual or some differences in the way she carries out her functions that her ordination was any less an ordination to the major order of deacon. If one attempts to make this case, and because the male and female rituals are identical, then one would have to also argue that the ordination of the men was not sacramental and not an entry into major orders. We know from the history of the Church that we understand and accept that the ordination of male deacons was and is considered a valid sacrament and so the conclusion is obvious with regard to women deacons.

Martimort and Müller and those who side with them, who argue that women did not receive a real ordination (*cheirotonia*) equivalent to male deacons or that they received only a blessing (chirothesia), are in a minority. Their position cannot be defended when matched against a close study of the historical sources. Their position cannot stand while using the same sources to defend the sacramentality of the ordination of male deacons. This is the problem I mentioned in the preliminary items of anachronistic readings and being selective in application of that reading. Wijngaards exposes the *a priori* assumption which seems to be the cause of this selective reading in Martimort's evaluation of the sources. He relies on an understanding of orders that came to dominate after the 13th century and put bluntly: "since diaconate, priesthood and service at the altar are intrinsically linked in his view, the women's diaconate *cannot* have been a sacrament."[26]

Wijngaards and Macy list an impressive number of historians, theologians and patristic scholars who have examined the sources closely and all come to the same conclusion that a real sacramental ordination happened for women deacons.[27] Cipriano Vagaggini [a liturgist] expressed

---

26 Wijngaards (2002) *Women Deacons in the Early Church;* p109 [emphasis in original]
27 Wijngaards (2002) *Women Deacons in the Early Church*; p121-126

it to be his considered opinion that the women deacons of the Greek-Byzantine era had received a full sacramental ordination. Roger Gryson, a church historian, concurred, reporting also that the women had been treated as clergy in major orders. Meanwhile, the Orthodox theologian Evangelos Theodorou had independently arrived at a similar conclusion.[28]

This conclusion is exemplified by Bishop Kallistos Ware;

"In the Byzantine rite the liturgical office for the laying on of hands for the deaconess is exactly parallel to that for the deacons; and so on the principle *lex orandi, lex credendi* – the Church's worship practice is a sure indication of its faith – it follows that the deaconess receives, as does the deacon, a genuine sacramental ordination; not just a χειρθεσια (*cheirothesia*) but a χειροτονια (*cheirotonia*).[29]

Wijngaards concludes, the vast majority of scholars who have taken the trouble to study the evidence firmly support the sacramentality of the women's diaconate in the Byzantine era.[30] The existence of pontificals including ordination rites for women deacons in the West must also be regarded in the same way.

---

28 Wijngaards (2002) *Women Deacons in the Early Church*; 9
29 Kallistos Ware (1983) "Man, Woman and the Priesthood of Christ. In Thomas Hopko; (ed.), (1983) *Women and the Priesthood*. Crestwood, New York: St Vladimir Seminary Press.; p9-37
30 Wijngaards (2002) *Women Deacons in the Early Church*; p121

A step to priesthood?

On May 22 1994, Pope John Paul II issued an Apostolic Letter, *Ordinatio sacerdotalis*; *On Reserving Priestly Ordination to Men Alone*.[31] In that letter he concludes:

> Wherefore, in order that all doubt may be removed regarding a matter of great importance, a matter which pertains to the Church's divine constitution itself, in virtue of my ministry of confirming the brethren (cf. Luke 22:32) I declare that the Church has no authority whatsoever to confer priestly ordination on women and that this judgment is to be *definitively* held by all the Church's faithful.[32]

Popes Benedict XVI and Francis have reiterated this judgment on a number of occasions and in a variety of formats. The Congregation for Doctrine (CDF) in a statement issued in 1995 about the meaning of definitive and therefore the authoritative status of this teaching has concluded that the statement represented an exercise of the infallible teaching authority of the Church.[33] An infallible teaching is one which pertains to the essential core of doctrine revealed by God, the content of which teaching cannot change. How

---

[31] John Paul II; Apostolic Letter, *Ordinatio Sacerdotalis*; To the Bishops of the Catholic Church On Reserving Priestly Ordination To Men Alone. May 22, 1994

[32] My emphasis.

[33] http://www.vatican.va/roman_curia/congregations/cfaith/documents/rc_con_cfaith_doc_19951028_dubium-ordinatio-sac_en.html

that teaching is elaborated and explained and the language used to talk about it can change but not the conclusion or teaching itself. I agree with Francis Sullivan when he determines that certainly the form of this teaching and the use of the term definitive indicates an extremely high level of teaching authority, it must be among the highest.[34] I also agree with Sullivan that the CDF statement, which is not itself infallible, fails to demonstrated with sufficient argument that *Ordination sacerdotalis* is infallible, which is the highest level of authority.[35]

An infallible teaching must clearly be demonstrated to be so.[36] The Church offers at least three criteria to determine if a teaching of the ordinary magisterium is infallible: consultation with all of the Catholic bishops, universal and constant consensus of theologians, and the common adherence of the faithful (clergy and laity).[37] The CDF does not appeal to these three criteria. It is clear that Pope John Paul II intended to close this debate and this question in the section just above his concluding definitive statement he says as much. Yet we still await an infallible statement on this in my view. There are other theologians who would agree with the judgment of the CDF that *Ordinatio sacerdotalis* is to

---

34 Francis Sullivan (1996) *Creative Fidelity: Weighing and Interpreting the Documents of the Magisterium*. E.J. Dwyer: Alexandria. p181
35 Francis Sullivan (1996) *Creative Fidelity*, p182
36 CIC can 750. We also need to distinguish been ordinary teaching office (magisterium) and extraordinary magisterium. The gift of infallibility is given to the Church by Christ in the Holy Spirit. It has rarely been exercised in an extraordinary way, when the Pope declares that the Church is making an infallible teaching. An apostolic letter fits into the category of ordinary magisterium and the CDF is proposing that is an infallible teaching of the ordinary magisterium.
37 Francis Sullivan (1996) *Creative Fidelity*, p183

be considered infallible with regard to priestly ordination.[38] There are some who would argue, that even though it does not address the question of deacons, it equally applies to deacons.

I am not going to review this debate but before we move back to deacons, I want to draw your attention to three aspects of the teaching on reserving *sacerdotal* ordination to men.[39] All the popes from Paul VI through to Francis reject any arguments for maintaining this tradition which claim

---

38   It should be noted that a definitive teaching, even if not infallible still requires the intellectual assent of Catholics to the teaching. Infallibility only determines what kind of assent. If it is infallible it requires an assent of faith. Definitive means that is it closely related to the deposit of the Catholic faith and so represents the sure doctrine of the Church. Catholics don't need to understand nor fully appreciate all of the arguments for the definitive teaching for them to give assent. There is nothing unusual or intellectually dishonest in this. In ordinary life we give our intellectual assent to lots of things about which we do not have personal full knowledge or competence to judge. I regularly drive over a large suspension bridge with many other drivers. I do not understand the mathematics or engineering that makes this structure work but I trust that someone does and so intellectually I assent to the truth of this every time I drive over. If I did not, I would have to go back to university and get a degree in civil engineering to be personally certain. Avery Dulles notes that there is more Scriptural and historical certainty about the inability of the Church to admit women to sacerdotal ordination than there is for some other infallible teachings. See Dulles article "Gender and Priesthood: Examining the Teaching," appeared in *Origins*. Vol. 25, No. 45, dated May 2, 1996.

39   I have not made a deep study of the issue of reserving priestly ordination to men and I have found for my own edification a very short book by Sara Butler. Her work is interesting because as a theologian she has taken both sides of the argument. In the 1970's she was a part of a study group that could find no objection to women's sacerdotal ordination but later she reversed course because of her experience of ecumenical dialogue which highlighted for her neglected aspects of Catholic theology of priesthood. Her book; *The Catholic Priesthood*

that women are inferior to men. Paul VI and Benedict XVI also explicitly reject any arguments for maintaining a male only ministerial priesthood based a view that a woman cannot be an image of Christ, in the technical theological vocabulary, in *persona Christi*. Christ became incarnate and as to his humanity is consubstantial with our humanity. The whole of what it is to be a human person, as a man or woman, is taken up into Christ and assumed by him in his human nature.

A woman can act in the person of Christ sacramentally. In cases of emergency a woman can baptise. In the Latin Catholic Church, a baptised man and a baptised woman (the groom and bride) are the ministers of the sacrament of matrimony and the deacon or presbyter acts only as the Church's witness. The third aspect is that all the popes indicate that a male only ministerial priesthood pertains to the constitution or essence of the Church. If there is to be any development in this teaching, including any challenge to it, it is only on this last point that there seems to be any possibility of exploration.[40] It seems to me that the teaching,

---

and Women: A Guide to the Teaching of the Church. Hillenbrand Books: Mundelein, Ill. 2006

40 I believe it is possible for theologians to put forward alternative arguments for the definitive teaching contained in *Ordinatio Sacerdotalis*, if it is done in a genuine spirit of enquiry. Such arguments may help clarify and further articulate the defined teaching of the Church in this matter. Thomas Aquinas employed this method of providing strong counter arguments and objections to church teaching in order to develop the stronger arguments to support it. Even heresies can help clarify doctrine. Arius helped the Church develop a more robust Christology because arguments had to be marshalled against his errors. It would be futile to attempt proposing such arguments in the hope of reversing this teaching. *Ordinatio Sacerdotalis* has a long history, tradition and Scripture to support it and it has been proposed as definitive.

as it is presently articulated, hangs upon this point: in what way is Christ represented in the essence of the Church such that a male only priesthood can truly express what God has revealed? Since we are dealing with only the *sacerdotal* aspect of presbyteral and episcopal ministry, the direction we should look for answers is the Eucharist, and specifically the nature of the Eucharistic assembly. Secondly, and related to Eucharist, we need to look toward episcopal ministry and the relationship of the bishop to the local Church. Thirdly, we need to focus on another term, *in persona Christi capitis*, in the person of Christ the head. There is something here too perhaps about the image of the Church as the bride of Christ and therefore Christ is groom (male). This image is frequent in the Scriptures and some liturgical imagery. To explore these requires a deep immersion in sacramental theology informed by an ecclesiology and spirituality of communion/*koinonia*.

I have mentioned elsewhere that canon law has very little to say about the permanent order of deacons. Most of what it does say is generally by way of variations or exceptions to the rule that normally apply to presbyters. Most of what it has to say about clerics betrays a sense that sacerdotal/priestly orders is the norm, as it was prior to Vatican II. The statements by popes regarding ordination are also clearly about priesthood and presiding at the Eucharist. Canon 1024 states that only a baptised male can receive sacred ordination. I would argue that given the pre-Vatican focus on sacerdotal ministry as the pinnacle of ordination, canon 1024 needs to be read in this way.

It is better expressed that only a validly baptised male may receive sacerdotal ordination. We know that there are canons from the past relating to women deacons and that there are ordination rites for the valid ordination of women who were previously validly baptised. Just as Benedict XVI corrected canons 1008 and 1009, it will be the task of a future pope to correct 1024 to make it clear that it refers to sacerdotal ordination (this could be a future 1024§2) and then add one on conditions for valid ordination of deacons, which would be that it only be conferred on a validly baptised woman or man (this could be a future 1024§1).

Wijngaards regards the question of sacerdotal ordination for women and diaconal ordination as inextricably linked. He believes that if we can prove one, then it must lead to the other, "for if the diaconate of women is a true diaconate, if it was a valid expression of the sacrament of Holy Orders, then women did in fact receive Holy Orders and the priesthood too is open to them."[41] I disagree. I do so based on the very same sources he uses to indicate that the Church did have a sacramentally valid diaconate of women and should do so again. For the first millennium of the Christian era, we can clearly demonstrate from the sources that the Church ordained women as deacons and that they exercised a diaconal ministry. However, we have no indication in any of the sources from orthodox communities that women were ever ordained as presbyters or bishops.

Wijngaards argues that to restrict women to the diaconate destroys the unity of the sacrament of Holy Orders.

---

41 Wijngaards (2002) *Women Deacons in the Early Church*; p8

He cites, among others, a theologian and canonist who support this view:

> Dirk Ansorge; "If women are ordained deacons, the unity of the sacrament of holy orders will demand their access to the sacramental priesthood."

> Charles Wilson; "If the Church does admit women to diaconal ordination, it seems to me that this action would give rise to the formidable challenging of performing the difficult mental gymnastics involved in asserting that women can validly be admitted to one grade of orders while at the same time reaffirming the definitive teaching of the Church that they cannot be admitted to others."

Contra Wijngaards, Ansorge and Wilson, the evidence from the sources demonstrates that throughout the first millennium, the Church had no difficulty in understanding diaconal ordination as quite distinct from sacerdotal. The facts as they are known from the sources tell us that women deacons were not ordained presbyters or bishops. The sources do tell us that most of the bishops up until the 9th century were chosen from among male deacons and most of these were not ordained presbyters before bishop. Remember we saw earlier that the bishop presides at Eucharist because he is a bishop and a presbyter because there is a bishop. As we move closer to the ninth and tenth centuries, sequential ordination from deacon to presbyter to bishop is becoming the norm. Even then we saw that it was not a pattern always observed. It is really only after the 13th century that the focus shifts so that the whole of the sacrament of Holy Orders is oriented toward and culminates in the ministerial priest (*sacerdos*). Priesthood becomes the last step in a seven-step process of Holy Orders.[42] A bishop was considered a *sacerdos* with no new sacramental power, and therefore not the top of the sequence of ordination. Everything about all ministries – all of holy orders – became preparation for service at the altar and Mass.

I suggest that those who argue that ordination of women as deacons inevitability leads to ordination as *sacerdoti* (priest) cannot do so based on the ancient sources. These sources support the opposite conclusion. Secondly, those who argue that one necessarily leads to the other tend to rely on a pre-Vatican II conception of Holy Orders as oriented toward the altar and priesthood as the fullness of the sacrament of Holy Orders. This is the opinion and mindset that dominated from the 13th century to Vatican II. I believe this mindset persists in the Church, if not officially in theological discourse, at least in the habits of mind we have ingrained in the Church when we think and speak about the sacrament of Orders. We still have an old habit of mind or mentality in our living, breathing expression of Holy Orders. We saw it in the discussion about the *cursus honorum* in previous chapters. The insights of Vatican II about episcopal ordination being the fullness of the sacrament, and a descending theology of Holy Order, ministry within an ecclesiology and spirituality of *communio/*

---

42   We examined the *cursus honorum* in more detail in chapter three.

koinonia and the renewal of diaconal ministry as a permanent order, have not yet been fully received into the Church from the Council. These need to be received to shift our mindset and create new habits of mind (*novos mentis habitus*) as urged by Vatican II about Holy Orders and the ecclesiology of communion.

Four sources – one ancient and three modern – help us to see more clearly the separation of diaconal ministry from *sacerdotal* ministry. These we need to add to the constant tradition of the Church which has made a distinction between diaconal and sacerdotal ministry as we have found in the sources we have considered. One ancient source is the partially quoted *Apostolic Constitutions* that we find referenced in LG 29 and CCC 1569; the deacon is "not ordained unto the priesthood but the ministry [of the bishop]." We can leave aside that at the time of AC, sacerdos/priesthood referred only to the bishop and not presbyter. Among the modern sources is CCC 1569 above and 1554 which affirm that only the bishop and presbyter are *sacerdoti*. A third source is the *motu proprio* of Benedict XVI, *Omnium in mentum*, which speaks of the unity of the sacrament of Holy Orders while also distinguishing more clearly the difference between sacerdotal and diaconal ministry as expressed in CIC.[43] Benedict writes;

> Art. 1. The text of can. 1008 of the Code of Canon Law is modified so that hereafter it will read:

---

43 Apostolic Letter "Motu Proprio *"Omnium in mentem*; of the Supreme Pontiff Benedict XVI, On Several Amendments to the Code of Canon Law. 26 October, 2009.

"By divine institution, some of the Christian faithful are marked with an indelible character and constituted as sacred ministers by the sacrament of holy orders. They are thus consecrated and deputed so that, each according to his own grade, they may serve the People of God by a new and specific title";

Art 2. Henceforth can. 1009 of the Code of Canon Law will have three paragraphs. In the first and the second of these, the text of the canon presently in force are to be retained, whereas the new text of the third paragraph is to be worded so that can. 1009 § 3 will read:

"Those who are constituted in the order of the episcopate or the presbyterate receive the mission and capacity to act in the person of Christ the Head, whereas deacons are empowered to serve the People of God in the ministries of the liturgy, the word and charity".

The key distinction takes us to the Eucharist and the capacity of the *sacerdos* to act in the person of Christ the head. Deacons participate in the apostolic ministry within Holy Orders but not in the ministerial priesthood. They, like all the baptised, participate in the one priesthood of Christ through the common or royal priesthood. This change reinforces the distinct nature of the diaconate as a permanent reality and not merely a step toward ministerial priesthood. Benedict's clarification of this canon makes the case easier for the ordination of women as deacons. It reinforces the ancient and constant tradition of the Church of a twofold, a sacerdotal and non-sacerdotal, mode of participation in the one sacrament of Holy Orders which means that women could participate in Holy Orders as permanent deacons, as do men. Approaching the question of the distinction between the ministerial and common priesthood from the point of view of a deacon's participation in the Mass, Thomas O'Loughlin argues for a more frequent experience of deacons in the liturgy so as to point to this very distinction and the Mass as more clearly a work of Christ in his Body the Church, not just as a work of the presider or head.[44] The more frequently we see a deacon at the altar, the more clear it becomes that Father is not just saying Mass but participating in an action of Christ with and through his Body the Church. Here in the deacon, the people see that the Mass is not only a work of the priest.

The fourth document is the ITC study, *From the Diakonia of Christ*, which we have already encountered. The ITC indicates that the renewed presence of a permanent ministry of deacons could help to shine greater light on the sacrament of Holy Orders and reveal that is has a wider scope than only *sacerdotal* ministry. Ordination can and does mean more than priesthood, which is the category that still dominates the language and way of thinking about the sacrament of Holy Orders. It is worth quoting the ITC in full on this question:

> Indirectly, Vatican II was also to initiate a clarification of the identity of the priest, who did not have to fulfil all the tasks necessary

---

[44] Thomas O'Loughlin (2006) Is a Deacon Anything More Than a Liturgical Frill? *The Pastoral Review*. Vol 12/4; 16-21

to the life of the Church. In consequence, the Church would be able to experience the riches of different degrees of Holy Orders. At the same time Vatican II enabled the Church to go beyond a narrowly sacerdotal understanding of the ordained minister. Since deacons were ordained *"non ad sacerdotium, sed ad ministerium"*, it was possible to conceive of clerical life, the sacred hierarchy and ministry in the Church beyond the category of the priesthood.[45]

So, it seems it is not necessary or indeed desirable that we think of all ordained ministry as essentially sacerdotal in orientation. We should conceive of the ministry of deacon as a distinct ministry from that or *sacerdos* as that ministry is expressed with the mode of presbyteral and episcopal ministry with the one sacrament of Holy Orders. Just as we can and do think of men as permanent deacons, not those waiting for priesthood, so too we can think of women in this same light. In fact, to fully receive the renewal of the sacrament of Holy Orders initiated by Vatican II it is essential that we do so.

A long transitional diaconate?

It should follow from the discussion above, about the admission of women to the ministry of deacon, that we should not propose the ordination of women deacons as a form of a long transitional diaconate. We are not ordaining

---

45   ITC (2003) *From the Diakonia of Christ*. p 58

women as deacons as a stop gap or halfway measure to "real" or presbyteral ordination. We would be ordaining women as permanent deacons, just as we ordain men as permanent deacons.

Men and women who feel called to the ministry of deacon need to discern that this is their calling and to have that call tested and affirmed or otherwise by the local church. Just as no man should proceed to ordination as a permanent deacon, if he believes in his heart that he is called to be a presbyter, neither should a woman who has no desire or intention to remain a permanent deacon. On his ordination day (some time before actually), the candidate should be certain that his calling is to the permanent ministry of deacon and he should not put himself forward in some hope that the Church will one day allow him to become a presbyter. Even if the Latin Church did accept married men as well as celibate men for the presbyterate in the future, that would be for lay men of the future to discern and not those already ordained deacons. At the time of ordination, a deacon is stating before God and the community that this is truly the ministry to which God has called him. This fact is further argument, of course, for direct ordination and elimination of the transitional diaconate.

I have dealt with the concept of the "long transitional diaconate" in the chapter on formation. Although this situation did emerge in the Anglican Communion, we need to remember that Anglicans and Catholics have a very different understanding of ministry and of priesthood in particular. Catholics need to be guided by Catholic sources and those sources tell us, with a very high level of authority and certainty, that the Church has no authority to ordain women as *sacerdoti*/priests. We must rule out the possibility, the hope and or fear, of the development of a long transitional diaconate for women emerging in the Catholic Church.

A brief comment on Francis' Commission

Most of what we will consider here comes from media outlets in lieu of any official statements from the pope or a publicly available report to scrutinise. The decision of Pope Francis to establish a commission to explore questions about women and diaconate seems to have been more or less a spontaneous response to a question put to him by a Religious Sister in a meeting of the International Union of Superior Generals of women's religious institutes which he attended. He did subsequently mention that he had discussions at some time in the past with theologians who also raised this question with him. His decision raised hopeful expectations from some and fear from others that Francis was about to do something bold and reformist.

There are some who characterise or hope and wish that Pope Francis represents some kind of break with the kind of papacy they believe characterised the years in which Benedict XVI and John Paul II guided the Church. The characterisation of Benedict XVI and John Paul II by those who see Francis as something entirely new is predicated on two foundations. The first is that the narrative that John Paul II and especially Benedict XVI were some kind of reactionaries, trying to undermine the spirit of Vatican II if not also its letter. The second foundation is that Francis is fundamentally different from these last two popes in his theological orientations. Conversely there are those who seem to fear the Francis papacy for the same reasons, precisely because they also agree with these two foundations. One might be tempted to conclude, with a sense of irony and humour intended, that Pope Francis has managed to unite the so called 'traditionalist' and the so called 'progressive' wings of the Church. I think both of the foundations are caricatures and have no basis in the reality, once careful analysis is applied.

These questions are subjects of books and scholarly articles and popular media punditry and I am not going to explore the arguments around these foundations. I simply want to note them because I believe they are relevant to assessing the commission he established. I agree there are very many differences in style between Benedict XVI and Francis but they differ little in substance and fundamental convictions and are certainly closer in thought and deed than many acknowledge.

The hopes and fears of what Francis might have been doing with this new commission also tell us something about the reaction to its conclusions. Some hoped that Francis would open the door to women as deacons and some of these hoped that would open to the door to women as presbyters and eventually bishops. We saw earlier in the chapter that Francis has repeated in speeches and in writing that the door on *sacerdotal* ordination for women is closed. He accepts that *Ordinatio Sacerdotalis* is definitive. As a Catholic, he could do nothing else. It seems many people did not listen clearly to what was being said as the purpose of the commission. In an interview with the *National Catholic Report* in June of 2016, Cardinal Ladaria, who was head of the commission said, "The Holy Father did not ask us to study if women could be deacons... the Holy Father asked us to search to say in a clear way the issues... that were present in the early church on this point of the women's diaconate... the 'primary objective' of his commission is to consider what role women who served as deacons in the first centuries of Christianity were fulfilling". He also said that there are questions over whether women deacons had the same role as male deacons of the time and over whether their role was dependent on local needs.[46] As I have noted at the start of the chapter, if the role is the question, it is irrelevant to the resolution of the question because the Second Vatican Council did not ask that question of male diaconate or want to revive any historical form of the diaconate. Therefore, the commission could never make progress on the basis of the question of roles.

Francis, in his statements of May 2019 both on-board a plane on return from a journey and in the meeting of women superiors general complicates the picture about what the task of the commission actually was. He seems to suggest that the question of ordination and the intention of the Church were being considered as well as the link between the women deacons and revelation. As reported in *Crux*, "The outcome", he said, "was inconclusive with each of the members now studying "according to her/his theory". "The formulas of female deacon ordination drawn from antiquity", Francis explained, "are not the same for the ordination of a male deacon and are more similar to what today would be the abbatial blessing of an abbess".[47]

---

46 Joshua J. McElwee *National Catholic Reporter* Jun 26, 2018
47 Claire Giangravè *Crux* May 15, 2019

That is, he presents the key division among the experts as being around the sacramental nature of the ordination. As I argue in this chapter, whatever the Church intended at the time was certainly ordination of both men and women to the order of deacon. It would be interesting to be able to read the report the Pope gave to the meeting of superiors general to investigate the assumptions of each member of the commission. It is worth noting that one of the members of the commission was not aware of the existence of a report from the group.[48] Was the report a summary from its chair, Cardinal Ladaria? As we saw earlier, the study completed by Martimort on ordination rituals for women deacons had the *a priori* assumption that women were not 'suitable matter for the sacrament of ordination' and also had assumptions about the *cursus honorum* as being an essential aspect of understanding the sacrament of Orders. We know that neither of these assumptions is relevant to assessing the evidence of women's diaconal ordination in the time in question.

In his comments, Francis seems to link thinking about women as deacons with *Ordinatio Sacerdotalis* and its definitive teaching. As relayed in the *National Catholic Reporter*, "The pontiff responded that the church develops its teachings "in fidelity with revelation." He said the nature of revelation is "continual movement to clarify itself."[49] This is the resolution with which *Ordinatio Sacerdotalis* essentially decides the matter of sacerdotal ordination for women. The Church has no authority, it cannot create its own sacraments, these are derived from revelation and are part of the deposit of

---

48 Joshua J. McElwee *National Catholic Reporter*, May 10, 2019
49 Joshua J. McElwee *National Catholic Reporter*, May 10, 2019

faith. Francis seems to be making a not so oblique connection between the two questions, women as *sacerdoti* and women as deacon.

Francis, like his immediate predecessor, is a student of Vincent of Lerins and John Henry Newman. Each elaborated theories of doctrinal development which allowed for development in understanding in organic unity with the whole Tradition without adding novelties or discontinuities in fundamental revelation.[50] It is in that context that his words about development of doctrine and understanding revelation must be understood. In the *National Catholic Reporter*, he is quoted; "If I see that this, what we think now, is in connection with revelation, good," said Francis. "But if it is a strange thing that is not according to revelation... it doesn't work... In the case of the *[women's]*diaconate, we have to see what was there at the beginning of revelation," said the pope. "If there was something, let it grow, let it live. If there was not something... it doesn't work. We cannot go beyond revelation and dogmatic expressions," he said. "We are Catholics. If someone wants to make another church, they are free to do so."[51] Given the context of his interview, he must mean not the diaconate *per se* but that of women. According to Trent and Vatican II, the threefold Order is part of revelation. Pope Francis suggests that if women's diaconate is not part of revelation and someone wants to ordain them

---

50 Thomas Guarino (2013) Vincent of Lerins and the Development of Christian Doctrine. Baker Academic: Grand Rapids.; John Henry Newman (1878) An essay on the development of Christian Doctrine.
51 Joshua J. McElwee *National Catholic Reporter*, May 10, 2019 My addition of *women's* in the quote attributed to Francis. This is to emphasise the context.

then they are outside of the Catholic Church's understanding of sacraments and of Holy Orders in particular. He is bringing the question back to revelation, which brings it into line, in this view, with the question of priestly ordination. If this is the case, then he is leaving some room open but it does not look like much room, for the possibility of ordaining women as deacons.

In reporting on Pope Francis' decision to hold off on any decision on women deacons, *The Catholic Herald* introduces two other issues, the *cursus honorum* and the unity of the sacrament of Holy Orders. I do not know if the commission studied these questions. The paper states; "There was always a strong theological argument against that. If there is one diaconate, it is impossible to see how ordaining women to it would not fall afoul of the "unity of Holy Orders": the idea that the degrees of Holy Orders are fully possessed by every bishop, and articulated in the lower degrees — Deacon and Presbyter — such that anyone receiving Orders must be capable, *ceteris paribus*, of receiving each higher degree. Women cannot be priests; hence, it seems they cannot be Deacons, either."[52]

As we have seen previously, this is putting the cart before the horse. It assumes that the seven steps to *sacerdotal* ordination in the sequence as they were prior to Vatican II or the now five step course of honours to bishop that exists after Vatican II, is a determining factor in understanding an ordination in a time where no such course of honours existed. Secondly, the changes Pope Benedict XVI precisely indicate that there is unity and diversity in the sacrament of

---

52 Christopher Altieri *The Catholic Herald* 8 May, 2019

Holy Orders as now taught in CCC and CIC. As I have argued consistently, diaconal ordination for women does not lead inexorably to sacerdotal ordination of women. Arguments for sacerdotal ordination of women, if they exist, need to be founded on an understanding of priesthood and not diaconate.

What is the future for this discussion? Is Pope Francis "just kicking the can down a timeless road" as a spokesman for the Irish Association of Catholic Priests claims?[53] Phyllis Zagano, who was on the commission, said she is "totally at peace" with the pope's remarks, and his decision to give the commission's report to Sr Carmen Sammut, the president of UISG....The Holy Father is saying ... it's up to the commissioners to continue their research and speak about it,"[54] *The Catholic Herald* offers a perhaps more cynical interpretation, picking up the Pope's own words about the commission; "It is, however, a strong indication Pope Francis doesn't have a mind to do anything about it. Quite possibly, he never did. In fact, it was in response to a question about women and the Diaconate – before he even created the commission – that Pope Francis famously quipped, "There is a president in Argentina who advised presidents of other countries: 'When you want something not to be resolved, make a commission'."[55] Three very different perspectives for interpreting the Pope on this question.

---

53 Patsy McGarry *Irish Times* Mon, May 13, 2019
54 Joshua J. McElwee *National Catholic Reporter*, May 10, 2019
55 Christopher Altieri *The Catholic Herald* 8 May, 2019

Conclusion

Albert Einstein was asked once if the world were about to come end and he only had one hour remaining what would he do? The questioner hope to elicit what was the number one priority in Einstein's life. The response may not have satisfied the reporter but it is very instructive and relevant to the present question. He replied, "I would spend fifty-nine minutes analysing the problem and use the last minute to implement a solution". That is spend fifty-nine minutes discovering what is the real question, then explore that one in order to find a solution. We have not used our fifty-nine minutes well with the question of women deacons. We have not yet understood what the question is and have sought solutions to questions that are not relevant. We have not analysed the problem sufficiently.

Wijngaards reminds us that when we consider the very certain evidence that once the Church ordained women to the ministry of deacon that; "An old Church adage comes into play here: *Ex facto sequitur posse*, which means, from the fact that the Church *has* done something it follows she *can* do it. If the Church did ordain women in the past, she can do so now."[56] It seems certain and incontrovertible that the Church did sacramentally ordained women as deacons and that they exercised a real ministry equivalent to that of male deacons. This is part of the Tradition of the Church and I believe that the full restoration of the ministry of deacon into the Church requires that we open this ministry, once again, to women. I

---

[56] John Wijngaards (2002) *Women Deacons in the Early Church;* p. 9 (emphasis in the original)

am hopeful that such a possibility will emerge and that the Church will be enriched by the presence of women among the ordained ministers of the Church.

NEW WINESKINS: RECEPTION OF THE COUNCIL

Reception of the ministry of deacon is part of the work of the receiving the Second Vatican Council into the life of the Church. The reception of a Council is frequently a long and complex process. The Council of Trent (1545 AD) has taken four hundred years to be received and still some decisions of that Council, such as triennial diocesan synods, have not found expression.[1] Pope Francis recently stated that a Council takes about one hundred years to be fully received.[2] One of the decisions of the Council of Tent was to restore the permanent ministry of deacon in response to the objections of the Reformers to the Catholic and Orthodox doctrine of the threefold order of deacon, *presbyter* and bishop. That decision

---

[1] A couple of things mark elements of the non-reception of Trent. Some German dioceses kept a different liturgical usage that which emerged from Trent, sometimes and incorrectly called the Tridentine Rite (or more incorrectly the traditional Latin Mass). The other one is the subject of this book, the restoration of the permanent ministry of deacons. Trent asked for this restoration and it did not happen until Paul VI letter *Sacrum diaconatus ordinem* 1973.

[2] In an interview with Italian daily *Avvenire*, November 2016, noted that it takes about 100 years to fully receive a council. He may have been referencing John Henry Newman, who reached a similar conclusion in the 19th century.

of Trent was only received by the Church at Vatican II and not enacted until a little later by Paul VI.

We noted at the beginning of this book that the restoration of the permanent ministry of deacon into the Church was ranked number three on the list of topics bishops requested that the Second Vatican Council consider. The vote on the restoration by the Council was almost unanimous, with only a handful of dissenting votes. The initiative for restoration grew strongly in those regions of the Church where there were large numbers of *presbyters* and not a shortage. In fact, it was the need to address the shortage of deacons, not presbyters, that provided a significant motivation for the restoration of this ministry. The movement to restore grew among the bishops of Western Europe and was later taken up by the Council. That the restoration of the ministry is a fruit of the Council is beyond dispute. It is not credible to argue that liturgical reform, renewal of religious life or other reforms that flow from the Council should be received and enacted but not restoration of the ministry of deacon.

We have seen that the drive to restore the diaconate in the lead up to Vatican II was in part guided by a sense of what we now call the new evangelisation. Already the signs of erosion of the strong Christian foundations of Europe and the inroads of secularisation were evident in the Europe emerging from World War II. Theologians and bishops were calling for new ways to engage with the mission of the Gospel and to reach those who seemed to be neglected in the daily *diaconia* (of the Word). This was an urgent call for a new evangelical presence of the Church and the presence of the ordained ministry in ways in which parish structures and *presbyters* could not be present.

We examined how the call for a new response emerged from a number of places including the reflections of priests and theologians in concentration camps in Germany during World War II and found further elaboration among post war theologians (albeit distorted by the mutation in our understanding of the *diacon* words). Reflection on the Catholic Action movement in France and Italy also moved in the direction of restoration of this ministry in the post war years. The diaconate was to be a fresh new way to meet the needs of neglected groups and bring the Church into dialogue with people on the margins of Church and with new methods and ardour, as John Paul II would develop, as new evangelisation.

We have seen from the reflections of the ITC that the Council did not intend to restore any historical model of the diaconate but had in mind something that would grow and develop in line with Scripture and Tradition and the pastoral needs of Church and society. What the Council had in mind was a new wine and this new wine required new wineskins if the gift which the Holy Spirit had given to the Church was not to be lost. As I have argued in this book, the Church is pouring the new wine into old wineskins and the gift *is* being lost. It is not too late to find a new beginning for the process of reception of this ministry and hence the Council and make new wineskins.

This final chapter is perhaps more of an epilogue, in that I revisit some of the themes from earlier and suggest a few areas to explore that may help us move toward full reception of the ministry of deacons, and hence the Second Vatican Council, into the life of the Church. If you have read the chapter on women and diaconate, then you will know that I believe that the full reception means including women in the ministry of deacon. How do we create the new wineskins for this new wine and continue the reception the Council and the ministry of deacon? The following sections invite exploration and reflection on some aspects of reception of Vatican II that, I believe, may help us move toward full reception of this ministry as a new wine. I firmly believe, as does the Catholic Church, that Christ presides and the Holy Spirit is the guide and teacher of the Church at a Council. Outright rejection of the ministry of deacon or failure to receive it as something new is in a sense a failure of "those who have ears to listen to what the Spirit is saying to the Churches" (Revelation 2:7). This final chapter invites some prayerful listening to the Holy Spirit.

An experience of reception

Reception of a council has a whole body of very subtle theological literature and a variety of arguments about the hermeneutics that guide interpretation and hence its reception. The essential concept for our purpose that we need to understand is that a council proposes some teachings or reforms and sometimes very practical measures, but none of this actually has much effect until these teachings, reforms and practical measures are given expression in the life of the Church. This is what we mean by reception. All members of the Church participate in some way in the process of reception and it can be a long and convoluted process with many surprises and unexpected developments. I want to illustrate this idea of reception by examining in a thumb nail sketch a shared experience concerning the Mass in the Latin or Roman Rite. I think we can learn something from this experience for our reflection on the diaconate and its reception or non-reception into the life of the Church.

The 1985 Synod of Bishops was convened to look at the reception of the Council twenty years on from its closing. The final report is short and instructive.[3] The bishops speak about some of the wonderful gifts of renewal the Church has received from the Council and also some shadows and mis-understandings in the process of reception. We should not be surprised or shocked that there may have been some mis-readings of the Council and some mistakes in the implementation of some of the decisions of the Council. Let's look at one very public example to illustrate how the ordinary Catholics – as opposed to theologians pondering the notion of reception – actually experienced reception of the Council.

Any of us who lived through the liturgical reforms beginning in the 1970s lived through some interesting times. We experienced interesting musical selections and some banal liturgies in the years immediately after the Council. There were some very good things happening too. We may acknowledge that some experiments did not work and these may have caused confusion or hurt to those who knew so well the older liturgy and who were nurtured in faith by it. I think sometimes that those who look back at this period of the late sixties and into the eighties and see nothing but ruin

---

3   Extraordinary Synod of Bishops (1985) *Message to the People of God and Final Report*. J. Muirhead, trans. St Pauls Publications: Strathfield.

and poorly executed liturgies and judge this to be a direct result of Vatican II or as some deliberate attempt on the part of liturgists to destroy the beauty of the liturgy, as being too harsh in their criticism. Those who take this view sometimes opt for a kind of nostalgic restoration of what they incorrectly refer to as the traditional Latin Mass, as an antidote to what they see as failure.[4]

We should be more generous in our judgment and recognise that so much reform was going on and there were few resources to help clergy or laity to adequately understand the reforms. Added to that, congregational singing was to become a feature of the liturgy at a time when the musical repertoire to support such a move was sparse and, at least in Australia, our culture was shifting away from communal singing. In the sixties, Australia still had programs on T.V. in which people at home could sing along with the bouncing ball on the screen, children would sing songs on school bus trips and there could be school picnic days in which children, teachers and parents would all join in communal sing-alongs as part of the entertainment. By the seventies much of that singing culture had disappeared.

A temporary English language translation was made of the Mass shortly after the Council concluded. Those experts who created it and those bishops who authorised it all knew

---

[4] To claim the extra-ordinary form of the Latin Rite Mass as the traditional Latin Mass is a mistake because the Mass of Paul VI, or the Ordinary form which is celebrated in every Latin Rite Catholic Church on every Sunday is the traditional Latin Mass too. The Ordinary Form comes to us from the tradition and reflects the tradition of the Church. Both liturgies, in the Ordinary Form and Extraordinary Form can be celebrated in the vernacular or Latin and both can celebrate with the presbyter, deacon and people each taking their parts.

it was to be temporary, perhaps for five or ten years. They also knew it was not a perfect translation and that it relied upon a method of translation that made the text sound much more like the language it was going into than it had come from. This is called dynamic equivalence. This way of translation explains why the *Good News Bible* (applying dynamic equivalence) is simple and readable but lacking precision compared to the *Oxford Annotated Bible* with its closer adherence to formal equivalence. In formal equivalence, the language into which the translation is going is made to conform more closely to the grammar and semantic range of the language from which it has come. That temporary text of the Mass remained in place for forty years. During this time, a team of translators was working on what was to be the final translation. That process was extended so far because new rules for translations were introduced and much work had to be re-translated before it gained approval. Among liturgists, there was some controversy about these new rules for translation and not a few resisted the new direction.

Few ordinary folk in the pews or the sanctuary knew any of this detail until suddenly (or so it seemed) a new translation was imposed on them. They did not know that this translation could have come under the authority of any of the post Vatican II popes from Paul VI onwards. The lot fell to Benedict XVI, as it were, and it is his name which is appended to this translation, but had it been delayed further it would have been Pope Francis. The fact that ordinary folk, including many clergy, were unaware of this long process in the background, and seemed surprised or shocked to encounter the new translation only highlights how complex the process of the reception of a Council is for the Church. It also points to how little adult faith formation was done to help clergy and laity understand the reforms of the Council.

Perhaps in a replay of the sixties and seventies, with the introduction or seeming imposition of the revised order of Mass in 2010, both clergy and laity felt the sudden shock that a familiar liturgy had vanished overnight. Few clergy and laity were properly prepared to understand the long history of this development and the convoluted translation processes happening in the background. They were simply not equipped for it and many reacted. I use this familiar and shared experience analogously for the process of reception of the ministry of deacon. This too has a complex history and may have seemed to clergy and laity alike as suddenly appearing in the Church.

In 1965, when the bishops overwhelmingly approved the restoration of the permanent ministry of deacon, no one had any experience of this permanent ministry. As William Ditewig observes, to any one in a seminary at the time it seemed incompressible that anyone would stop at what was merely the final stage before priestly ordination.[5] It seemed to come out of the clear blue sky to most people and was hardly noticed by many others. It seemed to make no more sense than a permanent order of porter which was also a step along the way. Almost no one knew of the decision of the Council of Trent and its motivation for restoring the ministry. Few knew of the conversation among European theologians and lay people about the ministry of deacon prior to the

---

5   Ditewig, William (2007) *The Emerging Diaconate: Servant Leaders in a Servant Church.* Paulist Press: Mahwah, N.J. p7

Council. No one had a context for it and only an experience of a transitional diaconate. Ditewig also notes that, after the Council, there was the expansion, or was it an explosion, of lay ministries at the very time bishops wanted to restore the Order of Deacon.[6] Even though it is the same Council which made both decisions – about reforming the liturgy and restoring the ministry of deacon – only one of these has been received into the life of the Church as it should and the other remains as yet not fully received. How do we account for this?

A Council about the Church

In their final report, the bishops at the 1985 synod stated that the Council was about the Church and the Church understood as a communion. We encountered the theology and spirituality of communion earlier in this book. The Synod concluded that the ecclesiology of communion is the key to interpreting all sixteen documents.[7] The ecclesiology of communion was a recovery of an ancient theological thread that weaves its way through the First Testament, where God gathers and forms a people, is developed and extended in scope and meaning in the Second Testament and is celebrated in the Christian liturgy and lived in relations among individual Christians and among Churches. Almost all of the images of the Church, which the Council draws from Scripture, are related to themes of communion, especially the term People of God. Whenever the Council applies the

---

6 Ditewig (2007) *The Emerging Diaconate*, p8
7 Extraordinary Synod of Bishops (1985) *Final report*. Part C, 1. "The ecclesiology of communion is the central and fundamental idea of the Council's documents."

ecclesiology of communion to the term 'the faithful', the word is used in its correct sense to mean the bishops, *presbyters*, deacons and laity. When it does not apply the ecclesiology of *communion*, it lapses back into applying the term 'the faithful' only to the laity. This second usage implies a clear, and also a false, division between a church that learns and a church that teaches a church that gives and a church that receives, and establishes a rigid separation between the laity and clergy.

It is significant that the Council opted for the profoundly Biblical word, *koinonia/communio*, a word deeply engrained in the earliest ecclesiology and liturgical theology and not the more recent term community. The ecclesiology of communion becomes the key to interpreting the documents not in some abstract sense of 'documents' but for understanding the newly found perspective on mission, collegiality, synodality, ministry, liturgy and the laity and much else that is found within the spirit and letter of the Council. *Communio* is central to the understanding of all aspects of the Church. There is no Christian mission without communion, collegiality expresses communion, synodality becomes lived communion, ministry aims at building up communion, liturgy is the experience of communion and the laity can only be laity because they are in communion, as those co-responsible with the clergy for the Church, as part of the *communio* of the baptised.

There was until the nineteenth century no separate sub-discipline of ecclesiology within theology because it was subsumed under liturgical and sacramental theology. This reflected the continuing, if unacknowledged, place of *communio* as the key to understanding the life of the Church. Ecclesiology emerged as a separate discipline partly in response to the Enlightenment commentary on and invention of 'religion' and its twin 'secular'.[8] *Communio* has root meanings in words such as; participation in, solidarity with, and member of, in the sense of organic union, such as arms and legs are members of a body. The roots of community go in the direction of communication and speaking with. Communion is a far deeper and richer concept than community and it demands much more of us as members of the Church.

The Church is a communion in the Body of Christ, through baptism and Eucharist. This forms the fundamental theological reality of the Church. Through participation in the life of the Second Person of the holy Trinity, the baptised are invited into the communion of the Trinity and invited to see the world and love the world as God sees and loves the world. The fulness of our being is found in communion with Being itself. The ecclesiology of communion finds expression in Scripture where Paul reflects on the Church as the Body of Christ (1 Corinthians 12:27) and links participation (communion) in the bread and wine of Eucharist as a participation (communion) in the Body of Christ (1 Corinthians 10:16) which is the Church (Colossians 1:18). At its roots, therefore, the ecclesiology of *communio* remains a Eucharistic ecclesiology.

---

8 Cavanaugh, William (2009) *The Myth of Religious Violence; Secular Ideology and the Roots of Modern Conflict.* Oxford University Press: New York, NY. In Chapter 2 he outlines how religion as a concept was re-defined and invented as a convenient concept for a certain type of secular discourse. Against this background the idea of church as a society emerges. For the development of ecclesiology see also and Himes, M (2000) The Development of Ecclesiology: Modernity to the Twentieth Century. In Phan, P; *The Gift of the Church: A textbook book on Ecclesiology.* p45-68

The centrality is expressed in the insight of Henri de Lubac that the Eucharist makes the Church.⁹ This insight paves the way for the recovery of the universal church understood as a communion of communions. Thus, the Council can teach that the one, holy, catholic and apostolic church exists in and from the communion of the local churches.¹⁰ It makes it possible for us to once again see that in a Council or a Synod, we have not only a gathering of bishops, but also a gathering of churches. Just as there is no church without a bishop, there is also no bishop without a church (a practice we honour in a strange way with our titular auxiliary bishops).¹¹ So profound is this ecclesiology of communion that we may say that there is nothing which the Church says or does which is not an experience of communion.

Ratzinger and Lonergan have both argued that the reforms which the Council set in motion will not have life or reach their conclusion without the experience of conversion in all the members of the Church. There is, they argue, a spiritual dimension to the project of reform, which should not be neglected. If *communio* is the key to interpreting the sixteen documents of the Council, then there should a corresponding conversion in our understanding of *communio*.

---

9   De Lubac, Henri (1956) *The Splendour of the Church*. Sheed and Ward: London. p92
10 LG 23
11 In large dioceses a major bishop, sometimes called an Archbishop, is assisted by auxiliary bishops. Only one – the Archbishop – is the bishop of the locality where the diocese is actually situated. The others are made bishops of diocese which exist on paper but not in reality. Often, they are found in North Africa or the middle east. Canon 6 of the Council of Nicaea said there can only be one bishop in each territory, so the auxiliaries are given a title of another diocese. Auxiliary bishops are 'visiting' bishops, helping out the local bishop.

John Paul II eloquently develop this notion in his letter *Novo Millennio Ineunte*, and argued that; "To make the Church *the home and the school of communion*: that is the great challenge facing us in the millennium which is now beginning, if we wish to be faithful to God's plan and respond to the world's deepest yearnings".[12] Not an incidental ornament to the life of the Church but central to God's plan of salvation and the yearning of the world.

John Paul II teaches that, "Before making practical plans, we need *to promote a spirituality of communion,* making it the guiding principle of education wherever individuals and Christians are formed, wherever ministers of the altar, consecrated persons, and pastoral workers are trained, wherever families and communities are being built up". I suggest that this call has largely gone unheeded and such formation is still in need of development and broad acceptance in the Church. Sometimes there is a kind of resistance to it, but mostly, I suspect, simply a lack of awareness of what it is. There are some who might propose, without justification, *communio* as somewhat in opposition to mission.

Elaborating on the meaning of *communion,* John Paul II writes, "A spirituality of communion indicates above all the heart's contemplation of the mystery of the Trinity dwelling in us, and whose light we must also be able to see shining on the face of the brothers and sisters around us. A spirituality of communion also means an ability to think of our brothers and sisters in faith within the profound unity of the Mystical Body, and therefore as "those who are a part of me". This makes us able to share their joys and sufferings, to sense their

---

12   NMI 43. Italics in the original.

desires and attend to their needs, to offer them deep and genuine friendship. A spirituality of communion implies also the ability to see what is positive in others, to welcome it and prize it as a gift from God: not only as a gift for the brother or sister who has received it directly, but also as a "gift for me". A spirituality of communion means, finally, to know how to "make room" for our brothers and sisters, bearing "each other's burdens" (*Galatians* 6:2) and resisting the selfish temptations which constantly beset us and provoke competition, careerism, distrust and jealousy. Let us have no illusions: unless we follow this spiritual path, external structures of communion will serve very little purpose. They would become mechanisms without a soul, "masks" of communion rather than its means of expression and growth".[13] Communion and mission are, therefore, intimately related.

Communion ecclesiology is also essential for liturgical reform. I have suggested in other papers that true liturgical reform is dependent on developing our awareness of this profound spirituality of *communio*, otherwise we are just fiddling with forms of worship or we are coming to worship as individuals in a 'me' and Jesus time rather than 'we' and Jesus time.[14]

I suspect that one aspect of the lack of reception of the ministry of deacon has at its root a lack of understanding of this spirituality and theology of communion. I mentioned that communion is the foundation for the renewal of the theology

---

13 NMI 50
14 Gooley, Anthony (2008) Going to Church and Being the Church. In Vivian Boland (ed.), *Don't Put Out the Burning Bush*. ATF Press: Adelaide. Pp121-134

of ministry instigated by Vatican II and that we cannot fully appreciate the renewal of the ministry of bishop, *presbyter*, deacon or lay person without this perspective. Returning to our analogy with the reform of the Mass following Vatican II, I believe that a lack of appreciation of ecclesiology of communion is hampering liturgical reform. Whenever I hear Catholics complain at a concelebrated liturgy about how many clerics or how many men are in the sanctuary and they feel it somehow 'sends the wrong signal' and 'marginalises' the laity and women in particular, I know there is still a task of reception that remains.

It is the same when *presbyters* and bishops think of themselves as 'saying' Mass or when a presbyter says to a deacon, "deacons don't do much in the liturgy do they?" In all of these cases, no one is speaking from a theology and spirituality of communion. In a theology and spirituality of communion, we understand that Christ, is offering the Mass in, through and with his Body the Church, which consists of clergy and laity. If there were a thousand clergy in the sanctuary and one lay person in the body of the Church this would still be so. If there were a single bishop or presbyter and a thousand lay people assembled, it would still be so. We have reformed the style of the liturgy but I am not convinced we have experienced the conversion of heart that is essential for reception of the reforms.

That broad and welcoming recognition of one another as brothers and sisters in communion and the profound trust and acceptance of the other in the Church as a gift for me, as John Paul II outlines in the quote above, does not seem to be very evident when it comes to deacons and their ministry.

There are some in the Church who take a strong ideological stance to reject the diaconate either as somehow in opposition to lay ministry or as somehow opposed to women or as simply more hierarchy. Without a profound conversion to the theology and spirituality of communion, it will remain this way in the Church. Without that same conversion among presbyters and bishops, many of them will continue to see themselves as above the life of the parish or the diocese and not as one who is a Christian alongside fellow Christians, first and foremost. Instead they will focus on the first part of St Augustine's reflection on his relationship to his people as bishop, and only see that 'for you I am a bishop' (presbyter) and be unable to fully live the deeper and more profound reality that 'with you I am a Christian.'[15]

A Council of Reform

The second key to interpreting Vatican II which accompanies *communio* is reform. There has been some considerable debate about hermeneutics for interpreting the Council, especially following the 1985 synod. The synod noted what it called light and shadows. The light referring to developments that had made a positive contribution to the life of the Church; among these is noted a deeper sense of liturgy among all the faithful (bishops, *presbyters*, deacons and laity), more extensive cooperation between the laity and clergy in the mission and life of the Church, specifically the

---

15 St Augustine's homily "On the Anniversary of His Ordination" (Sermon 340) "Where I'm terrified by what I am for you, I am given comfort by what I am with you. For you I am a bishop, with you, after all, I am a Christian. The first is the name of an office undertaken, the second a name of grace; that one means danger, this one salvation."

role of women and a wider knowledge of and appreciation for Scripture in the life of the Church.

Among the shadows were noted such things as a false opposition between pastoral and doctrinal interpretations of the Council, tensions between theologians and bishops which had taken the form of arguments in secular publications, a lack of liturgical formation among the clergy. The specific prompt for the opening of debate about the hermeneutics of the Council stemmed from the rather non-specific observation that some of the shadows resulted from an incorrect interpretation of the Council. Walter Kasper proposed two rules for interpreting the documents of the Council and his proposals received acceptance in the 1985 Synod; the first rule is that there must be an integral reading of the documents to comprehend their internal relationships and the second rule being to read the whole Council within the continuity of the Great Tradition of the Church and previous councils.

Reading the Council in the light of the historical context in which it occurs reveals continuity but also significant change with what had immediately preceded it or sometimes change from even earlier periods in history. Renewal and renovation are unthinkable without some measure of discontinuity, at least discontinuity with the recent or not so recent past. One need only recall that, prior to the Council, Catholics were forbidden to attend worship in Protestant Churches or even to pray with Protestants and compare that to *Lumen gentium* where Protestants are presented as being in partial communion with the Catholic Church and are regarded as communities where some of the means of salvation are still operative. In an essay Ratzinger notes that *Gaudium et spes, Dignitatis humanae* and *Nostra aetate* taken together represent a repudiation or even a counter syllabus to the *Syllabus of Errors* proposed by Pius IX.[16] The question becomes how to discern where such changes have occurred and the magnitude of such changes.

Some scholars proposed a so-called hermeneutic of continuity as a means of interpreting the Council. I think of Levering and Lamb as representative among this group, although they may not concur with my judgment.[17] In this model for interpreting the Council, the stress is placed on the elements of continuity of the Council with past teaching and discontinuity is minimised or attempts made to eliminate any suggestion of discontinuity. In my view, a hermeneutic of continuity must be rejected. Ratzinger, Kasper and Komonchak all reject such a hermeneutic of continuity on theological grounds and O'Malley rejects the proposal on historical grounds. Routhier argues in his paper on the hermeneutic of reform that "understanding the Council only as continuity means that the Council is not a moment of discernment, of a re-reading of tradition... but is envisaged as a recovery and repetition under a solemn form of the teaching of popes since the last council."[18] This is not the understanding the Church has of a Council and to argue

---

16 Joseph Ratzinger (1987), *Principles of Catholic Theology*, trans. Mary Frances McCarthy. Ignatius Press: San Francisco. Cal. p 378.
17 Levering, Matthew and Lamb, Matthew (eds) (2008) Vatican II: Renewal Within Tradition. Oxford University Press; New York, NY.
18 Gilles Routhier (2012)The Hermeneutic of Reform as a Task for Theology. *Irish Theological Quarterly*. Volume: 77 issue: 3, pp219-243

this way, one must conclude, as O'Malley suggests, "nothing happened at the Council".[19]

Kasper, Komonchak, Congar, De Lubac and Ratzinger are joined in their rejection of a hermeneutic which is at the extreme of the continuity proposal and that is a hermeneutic of rupture. That is a proposal that the Council marks a radical disjunction in time between the Church, pre-Vatican II and post-Vatican II. None of these scholars names another scholar whose work is representative of such a hermeneutic; what they seem to be rejecting is the possibility of such an interpretation. Certainly, some popular accounts in the non-scholarly literature may advocate such a hermeneutic and perhaps only the followers of Marcel Lefebvre, the Pius the X society, may be said to hold to such a position. If the report be true, Cardinal Ottaviani certainly thought Vatican II represented a rupture at the middle session of the Council, remarking to a friend; "I hope I die before the conclusion of the Council because then at least I will die a Catholic."[20] A position from which he shifted by the end of the Council.

When he became pope, Ratzinger argued for a hermeneutic of reform and thereby offered some authoritative support to this position. In a Christmas address to the Roman Curia in 2005, he outlined why he believed that a hermeneutic of reform was to be regarded as the means to arrive at an authentic interpretation of the Council.

---

19 O'Malley, John (2012) The Hermeneutics of Reform: A Historical Analysis. *Theological Studies* 73 (2012) p517-546
20 There were lots of jokes and humorous anecdotes made up about the cardinal, as he had become something of a lightning rod for many at the Council because of his intransience on so many issues. It is sometimes difficult to know which stories are true.

He also suggested what reform means when we talk about interpreting a Council.

O'Malley notes that following the 2005 speech, a number of scholars embarked on research on Ratzinger and his previous works to see whether or not his advocacy for reform represented a rupture with his previous hermeneutic. O'Malley states that, "Not surprisingly scholars have found strong affinities between the old and the new."[21] (Parenthetically, it is worth noting that two doctoral theses devoted to examining the claim of a once progressive Ratzinger and a later conservative one, have yielded similar results. The data does not support the trope which has become the standard myth in the Anglophone world.). Edward Mushi traces Ratzinger's consistent position that the Council is to be interpreted as a reform movement from his first works appearing four years after the Council and continuing through several speeches, monographs, interviews as well as correspondence between him as head of the CDF and the bishops of the Lefebvre's St Pius X Society.[22]

O'Malley argues that the description that Benedict XVI provides for reform would be difficult to improve upon: "it is precisely in this blending, at different levels, of continuity and discontinuity that the nature of reform exists".[23] Benedict builds on the insights of John Henry Newman's still significant

---

21 John O'Malley.(2008) Vatican II. Did Anything Happen? In Schultenover, D. (ed.) *Vatican II Did Anything Happen?* New York: Continuum Press. p 55-56

22 Mushi, E. Benedict XVI's hermeneutics of reform and its implications for the renewal of the Church. *Pacifica* 26 (3) 279-294,

23 O'Malley, John (2012) The Hermeneutics of Reform: A Historical Analysis

study *On the Development of Doctrine*, that allows for organic change and development within the doctrine of the Church while preserving the identity of the Church in continuity with the apostolic tradition.[24] O'Collins has pointed out in a number of places that the Council itself adopts much of Newman's language to talk of reform and development, and is especially prominent in the language of *Sacrosanctum Concilium (SC)*, the first document approved and promulgated by the Council. The language of SC offers two important counterpoints, as it were to reform and development, drawn from Newman's words; "opening a way to legitimate progress" and on the other hand "remembering and recovering forgotten or neglected teaching or practices".[25] In this way, again in Newman's words, "new forms should grow organically from already existing forms".[26] To this Ratzinger adds "combining fidelity with dynamism", "continuity and rupture" and "renewal in continuity."[27]

Komonchak proposes that the question of continuity should be considered from three perspectives: doctrine, theology and the sociological-historical perspective.[28] At the level of doctrine, he says the Council does not repudiate or change any dogma and so at the doctrinal level the continuity remains the strongest. From the second perspective, we must recognise that the theological recoveries and developments

---

24 Newman, J.H. (1878) *Essay On the Development of Doctrine*. Reprint 1998 University of Notre Dame Press
25 SC nn23-24
26 Newman, J H. (1878) Essay on development, p56
27 Benedict XVI Address to the Roman Curia, December 2005
28 Komonchak, J (2007) Benedict XVI and the Interpretation of Vatican II. *Conciliar Studies*. pp323-337

of the Council, some of which are major rupture and others minor, are the fruits of the movements that preceded the Council. The biblical, patristic, liturgical and ecumenical movements before Vatican II shaped the discourse and brought about shifts in theological expression at the Council. Among the significant shifts we should mention the resolution of the relationship between Scripture and tradition, the definition that episcopal ordination is a sacrament and indeed the fullness of the sacrament of orders, ecumenical rapprochement, religious freedom and the restoration of the permanent ministry of deacon.

At the sociological and historical level, the Council as an event had its impact on the life of the Church and had real world public consequence, not only in terms of practices but also mentalities which were shifted. One of the mentalities yet to be shifted is leaving behind the *cursus honorum* and the focus of all ministry on *presbyters* (almost always called priests). The key sociological reality, for our purposes, was the emergence of the diaconate at the same time certain lay ministers were restored (lector and acolyte) and new forms of lay ministry grew (lay pastoral worker, Director of Religious Education, Lay Pastoral Associate). Two ministerial presences emerging at the same time and at a time with increasing awareness of women in ministry in the Catholic Church outside of traditional ministries supplied by religious sisters.

When we apply both of these concepts – *communio* and reform –to our question of reception of the ministry of deacons, we begin to see why what we are trying to do with the diaconate now will simply not allow us to receive this teaching of the Council. Something needs to change for us to accomplish this full reception.

Ministry in communion

We have not received into the Church the ecclesiology and spirituality of *communio* with regard to the reform of ministry. We still operate out of the *cursus honorum*. All that has changed in the new *cursus honorum* is that the final step is priest/bishop. The step below bishop remains priests in name and orientation and we have not truly embraced the concept of *presbyter*, which is larger in scope than priest, but also includes this. Below priest is the deacon, who is not fully appreciated as part of the apostolic ministry. If he is a transitional deacon, he is an apprentice presbyter/priest. He is formed for that purpose, to be a priest. He is regarded at a sociological level as already being within the clergy of the diocese as a priest-to-be. His ministry is fully accepted by the rest of the clergy and the people and he is remunerated by his parish appointment and may receive some support from the diocese too. His status is built upon his priestly identity even if he is not yet ordained a priest.

If he is a permanent deacon, frequently neither the priests nor people know how to accept him and some choose to reject him and his ministry. It seems as if the sacramental understanding of the reality of ordination that Catholics (including bishops) hold as part of the doctrine of Holy Orders, fails when it comes to seeing a permanent deacon. In an ecclesiology of communion, it becomes so much easier to view the reality of the relationship of the clergy among themselves. The bishop's apostolic ministry, having the fullness of the sacrament of orders, flows from him to his collaborators the presbyters and deacons. As we saw earlier, the collaborators are on an equal footing but one (presbyter) is particularly oriented toward the parish and the Eucharist and the other (deacon) toward diocese and special groups or those on the margins of Church. Some lay people will also have gifts for ministry and will be appointed for a time or even installed into ministries, to support the work the mission of the Church. Rather than a theological and spiritual conversion guiding reception of the ministry of deacon it is a deeper sociological and political understanding of the Church that is hampering reception.

Laity and clergy alike are still wedded to the *cursus honorum* and regard ordained ministry as a layer on top of the Church rather than a ministry within the centre of the Church and for the up-building of the whole for mission. Viewing the Church and her ministries as primarily sociological and political realities and not theological ones obscures the theology of communion which underpins the renewal of ministry and co-responsibility of the laity with clergy for the mission of the Church. Questions of power over and questions of hierarchical structure – interpreted through political concepts of power and of social relationships – distort the theology of communion and the way ministry is thought about and put into practice.

Clergy, no less than laity, fall into the same socio-political understanding of ministry and construe their roles as power over others, a power held tightly among them. In my view, it is this socio-political view of clerical authority construed as power over others that contributes to the culture which erodes clerical accountability to the wider Church. This may be expressed in a view that presbyters never need to be appraised for the quality of their preaching, their capacity to preside at the liturgy in a worthy and dignified manner in accordance with the liturgical books or their effectiveness in ministry. At least, not a way that is analogous to that of lay workers in the Church and secular fields are made to be accountable through formal appraisal processes. This culture of socio-political power almost certainly contributed to the culture of cover-up and protection of the institution in response to allegations of sexual abuse.

There can be no renewal and reform of the clergy, as intended by Vatican II, without a profound conversion to the theology and spirituality of communion. There can be no full acceptance or reception of the ministry of deacon without the same conversion. Karl Rahner once said that the Christian of the future must be a mystic or she/he will not be a Christian at all.[29] If we cannot see and accepted the profoundly mystical dimension of the sacramental nature of the Church and the mystery by which the Holy Spirit gifts the Church with ministers for its life and well-being, then we cannot experience the spirituality and theology of communion which is the wellspring of the Church's life. We must see that each minister is not set as a power over us or is not the sole receptacle of spiritual power apart from the body of the Church but is a gift of the Holy Spirit for the life of the Church. Vatican II called us to a profound renewal of our

---

29 Karl Rahner, Christian Living Formerly and Today, *Theological Investigations*, Volume 7, translated by David Bourke. New York: Herder and Herder, 1971, p15.

Catholic faith so that we would be more faithful witnesses to the Gospel, and thereby find ways to work toward closer union among Christians and bring the world to Christ.[30] Part of that Catholic faith affirmed at Trent and received and amplified at Vatican II is that the Sacrament of Holy Orders is a divinely instituted element of the constitution of the Church and that the Order is expressed in the permanent ministry of deacon, *presbyter* and bishop. Vatican II wanted to affirm the Catholic faith in Holy Orders by restoring the permanent sign of the ministry of deacon. The ITC named affirming the Catholic faith in the reality of the threefold order as one of the central motivations of Vatican II to restore this ministry.

Catechesis and formation

Before a bishop restores the permanent ministry of deacon, the *Norms* advise the bishop to begin a catechesis for the clergy and laity of the diocese. It is sound advice. Recalling what was said earlier about most people in the Church only having knowledge of the transitional apprentice presbyter deacon, there is quite a gap to bridge in knowledge. I would suggest that several years of catechesis should be offered and a number of adult faith formation and clergy days could be held on the theme. There is at least four years before the first of any men accepted into a program may be ordained so there is no reason why this could not continue parallel with formation. There would need to be some catechesis of the bishop and the clergy even before the decision to call for the first men to express interest. The first step in catechesis

---

30   LG nn1-2

would be to start forming the diocesan bishop.

Few bishops are theologians and few have advanced degrees in Scripture and theology, so they need to keep themselves informed through a program of carefully planned reading, attending short courses and engaging in conversations with theologians and other scholars when the time presents itself. Bishops are in as much need of adult faith formation as are the rest of the Catholics in their dioceses. Theology, like all academic disciplines, requires formal training, doctoral research and time and effort to keep on top of the research literature. There are some very specialised areas of study in theology which no one theologian can remain fully appraised about. Bishops often have fewer opportunities than theologians to keep in touch with all of this and that is why they need a carefully planned adult faith formation program for themselves. A bishop may never have taken a course on the theology of ministry or may never have kept up to date with specialised areas of study like word studies about the *diacon* group.

This is where we encounter problem number one in acceptance of the ministry of deacon at the diocesan level. Where is the bishop to find the sources that will lead him to understand the theology of ministry and of diaconate in particular, which has not been corrupted with the servant myth and the misunderstanding of the *diacon* group of words? As we have seen previously almost everything written about the theology of ministry in Catholic and Protestant sources in the twentieth century has been distorted by the misunderstanding about the *diacon* group of words. Unless a bishop is reading a book like this or the work of

John N. Collins, where is he going to come into contact with theologians and Scripture scholars who are taking account of the new paradigm? How many scholars have taken up the new paradigm? How many cling to the old one against all available evidence to the contrary?

New wineskins

We have explored in this book that the Council did not wish to restore any particular historical expression of the diaconate. It was the principle of the diaconate not the form. The primary motivation for the restoration emerges from a desire to affirm the Catholic faith in the threefold sacrament of Holy Orders. Secondly, to release for the Church the grace that comes from the sacrament of diaconal ordination for the building up of the Church for mission. Finally, to respond to what we would now call the new evangelisation. It was a new wine that the Council had in mind. Vatican II did not appeal to Acts 6 for its theology of diaconate or as its foundation story. We have explored how the idea that deacons are essentially charity workers and that *diaconia* is some kind of synonym for charitable works and service, is based on a false reading of Acts 6. That has now been exposed as false since the publications of Collins' work *Diaconia* in 1990 and this study has subsequently found support from Hentschel and others.

Although the reception (non-reception) of the diaconate in the Roman Catholic Church has been heavily influenced by the largely Protestant servant of charity myth, especially in the German speaking Catholic world, there are enough countervailing elements of Catholic tradition to moderate this somewhat. The reception (non-reception) in the Roman

Catholic Church has become tangled with the *cursus honorum* and the transitional diaconate. That entanglement along with the servant myth has meant that the wrong coordinates for diaconal formation have been set and we have not arrived where we should.

New wineskins are needed for new wine. What might such skins look like, that can contain a new wine of the diaconate to achieve the three intentions of the Council in restoring this ministry? Throughout the book, we have hinted at some elements of the new wineskins and been quite clear about others. We can conclude this survey of the restoration of the permanent ministry of deacon by outlining the elements.

1. **Wrestle with the paradigm shift.** The work John N. Collins on the *diacon* words cannot be ignored. We must wrestle with the consequences it has for our understanding of deacon and diaconate. We must wrestle with the consequences for ecclesiology and leave behind concepts like diaconal church. We must wrestle with the implications for a whole body of scholarship on ministry built on the false foundations. We must embrace the paradigm shift. There are only two alternatives to embracing a paradigm shift. Re-trace the work of Collins and develop some other semantic profile (but we have already seen where that leads, as Hentschel has demonstrated). Take a less intellectually honest route and defend a house built on sand after the flood has washed away the foundations. That is, defend the old paradigm against all evidence to

the contrary.

2. **Admission of women to the ministry of deacon.** The arguments seem convincing that at one time the Church intended to ordain women to the Order of Deacon, however ordination and the sacrament of orders was understood at that time. It is the same rite for women and men that is described. We cannot use the same ordinals to affirm male ordination and to deny female ordination to the diaconate.

3. **Direct and not sequential ordination.** A man should be ordained to the presbyterate directly and not via the Order of Deacon. Nor should deacons and presbyters pass through the lay ministries of lector and acolyte. These ministries should become fully lay ministries again and for women and men. Lay people who feel called to these lay ministries should enter a period of discernment with the local parish, be formed for their ministry and be installed by their bishop for a fixed period of time.

4. **Promote the diaconate.** Promote the ministry of deacon especially for younger married and single men and women. Every diocese should have deacons. No Church is complete without the orders of laity, deacon, presbyter and bishop.

5. **Put substantial resources into deacon formation.** Today, much is expected of ministers in the Church. Deacons should be well formed in pastoral practice, liturgy, theology, Biblical studies, spirituality and the other elements required in formation according to the *Norms for the Formation of Permanent Deacons*.

6. **Be creative in pastoral planning.** The local bishop, in communion with the deacons, presbyters and lay people, should carefully discern who is neglected in the daily *diaconia* and find fresh and creative ways to appoint deacons to new ministries, to new places and to find new ways to bring the Gospel close to where people are. That place will frequently be some place other than parish. Make more, if not all, diaconal appointments full time, remunerated appointments.

7. **Observe the norms of canon law.** The rights of deacons as clergy and their obligations need to be known and observed. The theological underpinning of these rights and obligations need to be better understood and explicated in catechesis within the diocese. The universal Church needs to attend more closely to the canonical tradition regarding deacons and look to where new developments are required and propose new laws to reflect the new situation where necessary.

8. **Be immersed in the theology and spirituality of communio/koinonia.** If we are to be true to God's plan and respond to the deepest hunger of the world, we must all be formed in this spirituality and theology. The fresh contemplation of Christ will deepen our communion with the holy Trinity, with each other and lead us into the heart of the world. We cannot hope to understand the renewal of the sacrament of Holy Orders and the universal call to holiness of the Church without attending to this.

9. **Study carefully the renewal of Holy Orders emerging from Vatican II.** The meaning of Orders

can only be understood from the perspective of communion. The descending theology of Holy Orders in a communion of apostolic ministry can only find its true expression as coming from, being within, and being for, the Church which is the communion of the Body of Christ. The pre-Vatican II emphasis on priesthood, the course of honours and an overly individualistic understanding of ordination as a personal power and privilege, persists and it is having harmful effects on the Church because it is out of step with the present needs and the reforms of Vatican II.

10. **Deepen our sacramental imagination.** It seems to me that many of our objections and confusions about the diaconate reflect a lack of sacramental imagination. We seem to have adopted an overly institutionalised view of the Church and lost a sense of its mystery and sacramentality. We have an overly sociological view of the Church and of ministry as some kind of instrumental reality that the Church can change at will or simply ignore parts of the sacramental economy that do not suit us. That is why we can ask question like, "what can a deacon do that a lay person can't?" or we can say "deacons don't do much in the liturgy" or we can substitute a lay person for a deacon when a deacon must be appointed, or ask a lay person or presbyter to do the deacon's parts at a liturgy, even when the deacon is present. We are not convinced in our hearts of the sacramentality of diaconal ordination or not fired in our hearts with the sense of the sacramental mystery

of the Church and deep sense of wonder that in the Church we touch the Body of Christ. I don't deny that the Church is an institution and often an imperfect one at that – the weeds and wheat grow together. But to see the Church fully, we must be willing to see the complex reality about which *Lumen gentium* speaks:

> Christ, the one Mediator, established and continually sustains here on earth His holy Church, the community of faith, hope and charity, as an entity with visible delineation through which He communicated truth and grace to all. But, the society structured with hierarchical organs and the Mystical Body of Christ, are not to be considered as two realities, nor are the visible assembly and the spiritual community, nor the earthly Church and the Church enriched with heavenly things; rather they form one complex reality which coalesces from a divine and a human element. For this reason, by no weak analogy, it is compared to the mystery of the incarnate Word. As the assumed nature inseparably united to Him, serves the divine Word as a living organ of salvation, so, in a similar way, does the visible social structure of the Church serve the Spirit of Christ, who vivifies it, in the building up of the body.[31]

---

31 LG 8

The mystery (sacrament) of the diaconate is part of this complex mystery described above. Catholics believe the diaconate is a divine gift to the Church, along with all of the other sacraments, for the building up of the Church in grace so that it might grow in holiness. That holiness finds expression in the life of the Church and in service to the world which God loves so much. We pray for vocations in our Church and God in his wisdom sends us many men who wish to serve as deacons, answering this mysterious call. They have done so and do so with generosity in spite of the obstacles, lack of acceptance, rejection and limits placed on their ministry. The full flourishing of this gift of the Holy Spirit has been hampered by so many things. The gift is in danger of being lost if we do not place this new wine into new wineskins.

New Wineskins: Reception of the Council

www.ingramcontent.com/pod-product-compliance
Lightning Source LLC
Chambersburg PA
CBHW051935290426
44110CB00015B/1981